A CITY SO GRAND

A City So Grand

The Rise of an American Metropolis,
Boston 1850–1900

Stephen Puleo

BEACON PRESS, BOSTON

Beacon Press
Boston, Massachusetts
www.beacon.org

Beacon Press books
are published under the auspices of
the Unitarian Universalist Association of Congregations.

19 18 17   8 7 6 5 4

This book is printed on acid-free paper that meets the uncoated paper ANSI/NISO
specifications for permanence as revised in 1992.

Text design and composition by Wilsted & Taylor Publishing Services

Library of Congress Cataloging-in-Publication Data
Puleo, Stephen.
   A city so grand: the rise of an American metropolis, Boston 1850–1900 / Stephen
Puleo.
      p. cm.
   Includes bibliographical references and index.
   ISBN 978-0-8070-0149-3 (paperback : alk. paper) 1. Boston (Mass.)—History—
19th century. 2. Boston (Mass.)—Social conditions—19th century. I. Title.
   F73.5.P966 2010
   974.4'6104—dc22   2009039749

For Kate

All my tomorrows belong to you

CONTENTS

AUTHOR'S NOTE

Never underestimate the value of a good walk.

As inarguable as the advice might be from a health and fitness perspective, I discovered that it also applies to the researching and writing of narrative history.

A simple stroll I took through a relatively small portion of downtown Boston helped me draw the connections that led to this book, although, unbeknownst to me at the time, my trip occurred in reverse chronological order.

It began at the Park Street subway station, where, after disembarking from my train, I spent a few moments examining the large, grainy photos chronicling the construction of America's first subway, in 1897. These photos give me pause anytime I'm at Park Street, for their historical significance, yes, but more for the ethnic rumblings they elicit. I've written extensively about Italian immigration to Boston, and many Italian immigrants worked on the subway; at least one picture shows a group of laborers, some clearly of Italian heritage, posing for the photographer more than a century ago.

Next, I emerged from the Park Street station onto the Common, and climbed the hill toward the State House. I stopped, as I often do, at the impressive memorial dedicated to Colonel Robert Gould Shaw and the famous Fifty-fourth Massachusetts, the celebrated "colored regiment" that fought for the Union in the Civil War, suffering enormous casualties in the summer of 1863 during a courageous but unsuccessful assault on Fort Wagner in South Carolina. Shaw lost his life in the advance, and almost half the men in his regiment were either killed or badly wounded before the Fifty-fourth retreated under relentless and blistering Confederate fire. Their story, part of Boston's immense contribution to the Northern cause, is recounted in the stirring 1989 film *Glory*.

From the memorial, I made my way down Beacon Street, cut through the Public Garden, and walked onto Commonwealth Avenue in the Back Bay, perhaps Boston's most prestigious neighborhood today. But in the early 1850s, this area had been totally submerged under a filthy body of water, a "despicable eyesore" as one report labeled it. It required the country's most ambitious landfill and development project of the nineteenth century—more than thirty years of planning and construction—to transform Back Bay into one of America's most fashionable and desirable residential addresses.

When I returned home I thought more about these three locations and their common thread. All marked milestone events that had occurred in the second half of the nineteenth century, and had required vision, daring, and an almost indomitable will to succeed. All represented, in one way or another, Boston's burgeoning influence as a national and world leader.

Could these three locations and the events they represented anchor a book about Boston's growth and emergence in the second half of the nineteenth century? Were there other significant developments during this period that contributed to the transformation of the city?

After considerable research, I answered yes to both questions; without doubt, the years between 1850 and 1900 marked Boston's metamorphosis from a large and insulated town to a thriving metropolis that achieved national and international prominence in politics, medicine, education, science, social activism, literature, commerce, and transportation. Notwithstanding her indisputable and widely heralded leadership role in the Revolution, or the vast influence of her literary community in the 1830s and 1840s, no other period comes close to 1850–1900 in establishing and solidifying Boston as one of the world's most influential cities.

These were, in so many ways, her glory years.

The half century began with the abolitionist movement. Boston's contributions to the antislavery cause are almost unparalleled and laid the groundwork for its unwavering resolve to preserve the Union during the Civil War—and the eventual participation of black troops, including the Massachusetts Fifty-fourth, in the Union Army. Abolitionist Thomas Wentworth Higginson commanded the Union's first company of black troops, which paved the way for the Fifty-fourth's historic sacrifice. The ferocity of Boston's abolitionism was triggered by the strengthening of the Fugitive Slave Law in 1850 and the failure of abolitionists to prevent federal troops from returning escaped slave Thomas Sims to captivity the following year. The years preceding the Civil War saw watershed moments across the nation, but especially in Boston or involving Bostonians. What better place, then, to start the story?

The Tremont Street subway opening in 1897, America's first, was justifiably hailed as one of the country's great transportation and technological marvels, and thus provides the logical bookend to the abolitionist movement in defining Boston's half century of progress and leadership.

And the Back Bay project, an engineering and city-planning feat in its own right, mirrored Boston's own growth in stature as the second half of the century progressed.

But there was so much more.

Boston's contributions to the Union cause during the Civil War electrified the North, including its enthusiastic and immediate response to President Abraham Lincoln's call for troops; its annexation of the formerly independent towns of Roxbury, West Roxbury, Dorchester, and Charlestown dramatically increased its physical size and allowed its growing population to spread; and its absorption of thousands of Irish immigrants during the great famine forever changed the city's demographic, political, and social face. A resilient Boston rebuilt its downtown core after the Great Fire of 1872, and a proud Boston celebrated the first transmission of speech over the telephone in 1876. And prior to the subway, Boston repeatedly defined itself as a transportation powerhouse throughout this fifty-year span: with its Great Railroad Jubilee of 1851, and entrepreneur Henry Whitney's bold conversion of the city's trolley system from horse-drawn cars to electric vehicles in the early 1890s. Both are chronicled in *A City So Grand*.

The second half of the nineteenth century is, quite simply, a breathtaking period in Boston's history. While the frustrations of our modern era often make the notion of accomplishing great things appear overwhelming or even impossible, Boston distinguished itself between 1850 and 1900 by proving it could take on the most arduous of challenges with repeated, and often resounding, success.

The story of Boston's emergence as a world-class city during this fifty-year period has largely gone untold up to now. Various authors and historians have tackled, quite ably, subjects such as the abolitionist movement, or the emergence of the Irish, or the Back Bay project, or Alexander Graham Bell's invention of the telephone. Others have focused on politics or the excesses of the Gilded Age. But the full tapestry of Boston's influence during this period has remained unwoven until now. The historian who comes closest to defining the significance of the period is Harvard's Sam B. Warner Jr., in *Streetcar Suburbs*, his analytical study of Boston's physical and population growth. He wrote:

"No period in Boston's history was more dynamic than the prosperous years of the second half of the nineteenth century...In 1850 Boston was something familiar to Western history and manageable by its traditions...By 1900 it had become...something entirely new, an industrial and suburban metropolis."

This book is divided into three uneven chronological sections: 1850–1859, 1860–1875, and 1876–1900. These designations mark the natural break points in the city's growth and progress, and facilitate the flow of the narrative. The first section, while shortest in number of years, is the longest in number of pages because so much of what happens in Boston during the second half of the nineteenth century has its roots in the city's critical antebellum decade.

A brief note on source material for *A City So Grand*: a vast collection of primary sources, plus many strong secondary works—in short, layers of scholarship and research—form the heart and foundation of this book. As in my other books, all works of narrative historical nonfiction, I include an extensive bibliographic essay that details the sources and summarizes how I use them.

And a comment on the real-life characters who defined Boston during this period and whose stories are told here: while a handful of individuals are alive for the entire fifty years, no single individual's influence spans the entire half century. Some, like abolitionists Thomas Wentworth Higginson and U.S. senator Charles Sumner, cover more than two decades. Others, including inventor Alexander Graham Bell and pharmacist and photographer Thomas Dodd—who created America's first X-ray image, at Massachusetts General Hospital—are onstage for a relatively short time, yet their legacies are lasting.

Still others are lesser known, but their contributions lend a rich humanity to the city's history. Captain Robert B. Forbes of Jamaica Plain sailed the *Jamestown* from Boston to Ireland, laden with food and supplies for victims of the great famine. More than five thousand ships carried Irish emigrants away from their stricken home country during this terrible time; the *Jamestown* was one of a handful of vessels that traveled in the other direction to bring relief.

Yet, while no single person reaches across the entire fifty-year tableau, the one enduring character is the city of Boston herself: at different times between 1850 and 1900, she is, like any great leader, challenged and conflicted, brazen and resilient, humble and triumphant; on some occasions tripped up by hubris, but on most, rewarded for her vision, boldness, and perseverance.

Pulsating, vital, prideful, and irrepressible, on the doorstep of the twentieth century, the community once known as Boston Town stood as one of the world's great cities.

This book tells the story of her most fruitful, illustrious, and influential fifty years.

PART ONE

A City So Bold

1850–1859

The Boston State-House is the hub of the solar system.

—*Oliver Wendell Holmes, 1857*

CHAPTER I

Abolitionists and the Fugitive Slave Law

I think we must get rid of slavery, or we must get rid of freedom.

—*Ralph Waldo Emerson, 1856*

TUESDAY, APRIL 8, 1851. The conspirators would wait one more day, and then strike under cover of darkness.

They knew full well the risks—arrests, fines, perhaps prison—but the justness of their cause outweighed any personal consequences, and the timing of events made delay impossible. Though hastily conceived, their plan withstood scrutiny; sound in concept, its brazenness was equaled only by its simplicity.

The men stood clustered in a tight circle, their voices low, their demeanor somber, unaffected by the disbanding crowd, which still buzzed with excitement. The boisterous meeting had ended, but those who attended would long remember the thunderous speeches delivered inside the Tremont Temple this day, ten hours of addresses that represented more than rhetoric to the small band of abolitionists who now gathered in one corner of Boston's downtown meetinghouse. To them, the day's oratory cried out for justice and demanded action.

Led by the fiery Unitarian minister Thomas Wentworth Higginson, these men saw their mission in the clearest of terms: free the imprisoned runaway slave Thomas Sims and convey him to a stop along the Underground Railroad for eventual safe passage to Canada.

If they failed, Sims would be hauled back to Georgia to face punishment from his former owner and resume a pitiful existence in slavery's shackles, a life he had fled when he stowed away on a brig that left Savannah in late February.

The twenty-three-year-old Sims had already overcome daunting odds on his journey to freedom, making his current confinement all the more tragic. For two weeks during the vessel's wintry northern voyage he had escaped detection, avoiding the crew and providing for himself. Then, on March 6, with Boston's lights in sight, the brig's mate discovered the stowaway. "Sims was cursed at, struck, and brought before the captain," according to one newspaper account, and then locked in a cabin while the ship lay anchored outside Boston Harbor. But the crew had failed to take his pocketknife. That night, Sims jimmied the lock, lowered one of the ship's lifeboats into the water, and rowed toward freedom. He landed in South Boston and "took lodging in a colored seaman's boardinghouse, and while in the city, made no effort to conceal himself."

But then Sims made a grave mistake. Destitute and hoping to arrange for funds to bring his free wife and children to Boston, he wired to Savannah for money—and the telegram included his return address. Somehow, Sims's whereabouts reached one James Potter, who claimed that Sims was his property. One week later, Potter's agent, John Bacon, arrived in Boston seeking Thomas Sims as a fugitive slave. Bacon secured a warrant for Sims's arrest on the morning of April 3, and Boston police cornered the runaway slave on the street that evening. Fighting for his freedom, Sims stabbed officer Asa Butman in the thigh with his pocketknife, snapping the knife in two. Police then overpowered Sims, tossed him into a carriage, and drove him to the courthouse; witnesses heard him cry, "I'm in the hands of kidnappers!"

Now, five days later, a plan had emerged to disentangle him from those clutches.

Only a handful of men would know details of the plot, and fewer still would take part in the actual breakout. This had less to do with the need for secrecy than with the reticence of the larger abolitionist community to act boldly, a stance that had prevailed during the gathering to discuss the fugitive slave's case. In a hall that one account described as "packed almost to suffocation" with an excited and angry audience, Higginson had delivered a spellbinding speech calling for decisive action, even force, to save Sims, during which the assembly "trembled" and the community "was brought to the eve of revolution." But the speaker who followed Higginson, influential attorney Charles Mayo Ellis, protested the clergyman's combative tone, issued a plea for calm, and, Higginson despaired, "threw cold water upon all action." Instead, the group adopted resolves condemning the Fugitive Slave Law—which forced Northern states to return runaways to bondage—and the proceedings against Sims. "The law and order men prevailed," one abolitionist reported. Higginson concluded: "It was evident that if anything was done, it must be done by a very few."

He wasted no time. Immediately following Ellis's address, Higginson gathered a small group of men who were inclined to do more than pass resolutions, men who "seemed to me to show more fighting quality than the rest."

Higginson believed he had little choice but to personally engineer the captured slave's escape. For several days, his anger had mounted, over not only Sims's imprisonment but the passive response to it. Many spoke and wrote columns in opposition to the Fugitive Slave Law, but few seemed willing to actively defy the immoral statute. After Sims's capture, newspaper editor William Lloyd Garrison, Boston's most radical, outspoken, and experienced abolitionist, summoned Higginson from his pulpit in Newburyport to discuss next steps with members of the Boston Vigilance Committee. The group was formed in response to the signing of the controversial federal law as part of the Compromise of 1850; this latest version actually strengthened the original Fugitive Slave Law of 1793. The Vigilance Committee, which eventually would number more than two hundred members—including many prominent clergymen, attorneys, and writers—dedicated itself to providing money, clothing, food, legal counsel, and assistance to fugitive slaves looking for safe harbor in Boston, secret passage to Canada, or help fighting their arrests in court.

But in Garrison's office, Higginson felt stymied by the lack of assertiveness on the part of committee members. Garrison had dedicated his newspaper, the *Liberator*, to the antislavery cause for years, but it took mere moments for a disillusioned Higginson to size up the mood of the meeting. Talk—and only talk—was the order of the day. Neither Garrison, who "stood composedly by his desk preparing his next week's editorial," nor his supporters appeared willing to move beyond words. Brave pronouncements and a "dedication to the cause" filled the small room, but the group's obvious reluctance to *do* anything on Sims's behalf galled Higginson. While he admired the committee members personally, he noted that it was "impossible to conceive of a set of men…less fitted on the whole…to undertake any positive action in the direction of forcible resistance to authorities."

In his own mind, Higginson quickly divided the recalcitrant group into two camps. There were the "non-resistants" like Garrison, "almost exasperating the more hot-headed among us by the placid way in which he looked beyond the rescue of an individual to the purifying of a nation." Then there were the "political Abolitionists," who were "personally full of indignation," but "extremely anxious not to be placed for one moment outside the pale of good citizenship." The action-oriented Higginson and his few like-minded colleagues had their "attitudes constantly damped" by both groups.

Higginson's irritation intensified in the succeeding days. On Friday morning, April 4, the day after Sims's arrest, a group of abolitionists had arrived at the federal courthouse in Court Square to protest Sims's detention. Sims was confined at the courthouse because he could not legally be placed in a state jail (he had not violated a Massachusetts law) and the federal government had no prison in Boston. Nonetheless, Higginson was aghast at the transformation of the courthouse. On Thursday night while Boston slept, City Marshal Francis Tukey had ordered the building encircled with chains, and directed hundreds of Boston police and armed federal guards to surround the courthouse. "It was enough to keep the whole city in awe," Higginson recounted of one of the most extraordinary spectacles in Boston history. Only authorized people could get within ten feet of the building's entrance. Iron chains blocked the doorways, and attorneys and judges "had to crouch quite low" to get beneath the barriers and enter the building. Higginson wasn't alone in his distaste for the courthouse scenario. Garrison termed it "one of the most disgraceful scenes ever witnessed in this city," since it illustrated how completely the legal system upheld the interests of slaveholders. Harvard librarian and abolitionist sympathizer John Langdon Sibley bemoaned the fact that the state's chief justice, Lemuel Shaw, "had to crawl under the chains to get to his own Court Room." The courthouse was in fetters "bound…to the cotton presses," lamented one press report.

Later that same day, twenty-three members of the Vigilance Committee petitioned the Massachusetts House of Representatives to use the State House Yard for a public gathering that afternoon. The committee posted notices throughout the city: "PUBLIC MEETING— KIDNAPPERS IN BOSTON. Men of Boston, one of your fellow citizens was last night seized by slave hunters. He is in most deadly peril. The citizens of Boston and its neighborhoods are earnestly invited to assemble without arms in front of the State House, at four this afternoon, to consult for the public good." However, shortly after the notices went up, the legislature rejected the petition. The group convened instead on Boston Common, more than one thousand strong, and heard attorney Wendell Phillips shout that "before a slave should be carried out of Massachusetts, its railroads and steamboats should be destroyed." He also counseled the colored men of the city to arm and defend themselves. Referring to the federal troops surrounding the courthouse, Phillips declared: "This is the first time hostile soldiers have been in our streets since the red-coats marched up Long Wharf. May the Government which sends us these earn the same hatred that the masters of the red-coats won!"

Still, despite Phillips's "treasonably violent" remarks, Higginson sensed little appetite for any organized attempt to free Sims.

On Saturday Higginson visited the courthouse again and witnessed a similar sight. Huge crowds milled outside the building to get a glimpse of the principals in the proceedings or word on the outcome of the legal maneuverings. Poet Henry Wadsworth Longfellow, in the April 5, 1851, entry of his journal, wrote: "Troops under arms in Boston; the court house guarded; the Chief Justice of the Supreme Court forced to stoop under chains to enter the temple of Justice!" Higginson wrote that the courthouse chains "readily symbolized the manacled status of Massachusetts justice." Worse, the handful of lawyers who had ventured upstairs in the courthouse reported that the third-floor room in which Sims was held was guarded by at least twenty police officers.

The fortress-like conditions made it clear to Higginson that "absolutely nothing could be accomplished in the courtroom...it seemed necessary to turn all attention to an actual rescue of the prisoner from his place of confinement."

—⁓—

In the days following Higginson's visit to the courthouse, volunteer attorneys for Sims, including leading abolitionist Richard Henry Dana, tried every conceivable method to interrupt the proceedings against him. They petitioned Lemuel Shaw for a writ of habeas corpus, requesting that Sims be allowed to call witnesses in his own defense to prove he was a free colored man and not a slave. Shaw declined on the grounds that he had little jurisdiction to interfere in a federal law. Shaw also upheld the constitutionality of the Fugitive Slave Law, pointing out that the initiative was an "essential element" in the formation of the Union when it was first passed nearly sixty years earlier, "necessary to the peace, happiness, and highest prosperity of all the states." The fact that Congress toughened the law in 1850 was hardly grounds to rule it unconstitutional. "What a moment was lost when Judge Shaw declined to affirm the unconstitutionality of the Fugitive Slave Law!" exclaimed Ralph Waldo Emerson. "This filthy enactment…I will not obey it, by God." Rev. Theodore Parker, another ardent abolitionist, lost all sympathy for Shaw's forced crawl under the courthouse chains on the first day of Sims's confinement, announcing that once the chief justice upheld the Fugitive Slave Law, he "spit in the face of Massachusetts."

The twenty-seven-year-old Higginson, who once resolved "never to be intimidated against opening my eyes or my mouth," remained uninterested in the legal nuances of the Sims case, and disgusted with the inertia of his fellow abolitionists. "There is neither organization, resolution, plan nor popular sentiment [to take action to free Sims]," he wrote on Sunday, April 6. "The Negroes are cowed & the abolitionists irresolute & hopeless, with nothing better to do…than to send off circulars to clergymen!"

Higginson was possessed of a blazing moral clarity in his belief that the Fugitive Slave Law was one of the great outrages in the history of the Republic. Nearly as dismaying, the offensive legislation would be forever linked to Massachusetts, since its chief architect was Daniel Webster, who represented the state in the U.S. Senate when the bill was passed. Abolitionists vilified Webster for his insistence that the law was the only way to preserve the Union; they became incensed when President Millard Fillmore, a stalwart Unionist himself, rewarded Webster by nominating him for secretary of state.

With respect to Webster's damnable law, Higginson had counseled his congregation to "DISOBEY IT…and show our good citizenship by taking the legal consequences!" He would set the example by drawing a line of impenetrable resistance at the front door of his own home: "If Massachusetts is not free, I know at least of one house that shall be…and [if] I close my door against a hunted guiltless man, or open it to his pursuers, then may the door of God's infinite mercy be closed forever against me."

The Sims case wasn't the first time that Boston's legal and civic apparatus would join with the federal government and conspire with slaveholders to return runaway slaves to their owners. In October of 1850, shortly after Congress approved the Fugitive Slave Law, warrants were issued in Boston for William and Ellen Craft, a Negro couple who had resided in the city for two years and were popular lecturers. When slave hunters arrived in Boston from Georgia to arrest the Crafts, abolitionists hid the couple and dogged the agents' every step, making their task impossible. After a week, the slave hunters left the city and the Vigilance Committee, taking no chances, sent the Crafts on a speaking tour of England. Before the Crafts left Boston, Theodore Parker married the couple in a formal ceremony denied them in bondage. "I thank God," Parker said, "that Old England, with all her sins and shames, allows no Slave-Hunter to set foot on her soil." Parker also "dared President Fillmore to indict him for aiding his parishioners in defiance of the law," historian Henry Mayer wrote.

And then in February of 1851, just two months before the Sims case, the city had arrested and imprisoned Frederick Jenkins, a waiter in a Boston coffeehouse, and charged him with being the escaped fugitive slave Shadrach Minkins, whose Virginia master demanded his return. Nearly twenty activists, all of them black, seized Minkins from the courtroom at the conclusion of a hearing while the federal marshal was preoccupied with newspaper reporters. Minkins's rescuers carried him outside, and then helped him flee to Concord, and eventually, Canada.

Later, Parker called the daring Minkins rescue "the noblest deed done in Boston since the destruction of tea in 1773." Conversely, President Fillmore, still infuriated by Boston's aiding of the Crafts, said the city was "stained" by the illegal rescue. His administration indicted eight men for violating the Fugitive Slave Law and abetting Minkins. Divided juries resulted in no convictions, but to prevent a repeat of the Shadrach Minkins affair, Fillmore authorized the use of federal troops to quell any future agitation that might arise in Boston.

On this April night, those federal troops now joined Boston Police guarding the courthouse in which Thomas Sims was held. Higginson's final, vain plea had been a letter to his schoolmate, U.S. Marshal Charles Devens, asking the lawman to resign "rather than be the instrument of sending a man into bondage." Devens's reply was courteous, but he declined Higginson's request. Higginson thus concluded that it was up to him and his small group—"the few whose temperaments prevailed over the restrictions of non-resistance on the one hand and of politics on the other"—to right the injustice perpetrated on Sims.

Within the last few days, Higginson and those "few who really, so to speak, meant business" had considered "all sorts of fantastic and desperate projects." Finally, in the wake of the clamor at the Tremont Temple, the group had settled on the current plan, one based on the principle that the fewer number of variables yielded the greatest opportunity for success. As they bid their farewells, each man knew his responsibilities. They would take care of details tomorrow, Wednesday, and put their plan into motion after dark.

Boston had yet to return a man to slavery under this infernal new law, and Higginson vowed that Thomas Sims would not be the first. Rather, with any luck, Sims would be halfway to Canada by the time the guards discovered him gone on Thursday morning.

WEDNESDAY, APRIL 9, 1851. Higginson and his cohorts entrusted an African American clergyman, Rev. Leonard J. Grimes, with the key role in the escape plot. As pastor of the Twelfth Baptist Church for the past three years, Grimes had aided scores of self-emancipated slaves who had made the dangerous trip from South to North, seeking Boston's tolerance and opportunities. Many of these former slaves remained loyal to Grimes and joined Twelfth Baptist, which was also known unofficially as the Fugitive Slave Church. Higginson knew well that they had helped transform Twelfth Baptist from a struggling church to a burgeoning, active, and influential Negro congregation. Because of Grimes's standing within his community, he alone was allowed by the federal marshal to visit Sims and provide him with religious counsel and comfort—and access to the prisoner was critical to the plan's success.

But there was another reason the conspirators chose Grimes for this special assignment. Unlike so many of Boston's abolitionists, Grimes had experienced frontline action in the fight against slavery. Born, registered, and raised as a free Negro in Leesburg, Virginia, he became a hackney coach driver, providing transportation for politicians and businesspeople in and around the nation's capital. Yet Grimes also led a secret life. At great risk to his wife and two children, he served as a conductor in the Underground Railroad, "a role for which his job as a hackney driver gave him the perfect cover," author Deborah Lee has noted. He participated in many missions and helped dozens of slaves escape, but was finally caught after spiriting a mother and her six children to freedom. In early 1840 he was tried, convicted, and sentenced to two years in state prison in Richmond, plus a one-hundred-dollar fine, the lightest possible penalty, which the court credited to his good character.

After his release, Grimes and his family moved North, first to New Bedford, Massachusetts, where he joined a network of antislavery activists who provided assistance to fugitive slaves, and later to Boston, where the fledgling Twelfth Baptist congregation needed a minister. After a trial period, Grimes was ordained and installed as pastor, and quickly built a twenty-three-person church into an active center of social protest whose congregation soon exceeded 250 members, many of whom helped Grimes solidify Twelfth Baptist as a critical station on the Underground Railroad.

With his access to Sims and his battle-tested credentials, Grimes was the perfect choice to take the point position in the Sims rescue plot. During his visit today, he would deliver more than prayers and spiritual sustenance to Thomas Sims.

Today, he would also deliver a message.

When night fell, Sims was to remain awake, alert, and fully dressed, and in the early-morning hours, move to the window—"as if for air" in Higginson's words—and keep a close watch outside. Because his room was three stories up, and considered "safe by reason of its height from the ground," his window had not been fitted with gratings of any kind. This meant that Sims might better see the flicker of a candle outside or hear sounds coming from below.

Even more important, the unobstructed opening provided the slender prisoner with the means to wriggle onto the window ledge, and, when the time was right, jump out into the darkness, and to freedom.

—ᴟ—

While Grimes was issuing instructions to Sims, Higginson and a few others spent Wednesday quietly gathering several thick mattresses from the homes of Vigilance Committee members and surreptitiously transporting them to the office of Sims's attorney, Richard Henry Dana, across from the courthouse. They also arranged to pick up a rented carriage later in the day.

The plan called for the men to wait until full darkness, when the guards would be less alert, drag the mattresses to the courthouse, and pile them beneath Sims's window. At the designated hour, Sims would "spring out on to the mattresses," quickly make his way to the carriage, and begin his trek along the Underground Railroad. Though risky, the plan's likelihood of success was high, *if* Sims could manage the jump without injuring himself, and *if* the horses pulling the coach remained reasonably quiet. Higginson harbored some doubt about Sims's willingness to leap: "We were not sure that Sims would have the courage to do this, rather than go back to certain slavery." Still, by late afternoon, "all was arranged; the message sent, the mattresses ready, the carriage engaged as if for an ordinary purpose." As a final precaution, Higginson and a fellow Vigilance Committee member decided to stroll past the courthouse at dusk for one more look at the scene.

When they arrived, the sight they encountered turned their optimism to despair. "Behold!" a despondent Higginson cried, as he recognized in an instant that all their preparations had been for naught. He and his companion stared in shock at what was happening on the courthouse's third floor.

Masons were "working busily" fitting iron bars across Sims's window.

It was over. There would be no late-night jump by Sims. There would be no escape by carriage to the Underground Railroad. Higginson never forgot the disappointment of the moment. "The whole plan was thus frustrated," he would write years later. He chastised himself for failing to devise a backup plan, remembering the words of a military officer acquaintance: "[He] used to say, 'It is always best to take for granted that your opponent is at least as smart as you yourself are.' This, evidently, we had not done." Richard Henry Dana, watching from his office as workers affixed the iron grating to the courthouse window, commented: "Our temple of justice is a slave pen."

Had word of the rescue plot been leaked? Had a guard overheard

Grimes explaining the plan to Sims? Had Sims somehow aroused suspicion by venturing to the window too often, envisioning his three-story plunge to freedom? Higginson had no answers at the moment, nor would any be forthcoming. Afterward, he would write of the foiled rescue, "Whether we had been betrayed, or whether it was simply a bit of extraordinary precautions [taken by the federal marshal], we never knew."

THURSDAY, APRIL 10–FRIDAY, APRIL 11, 1851. Over the next two days, while abolitionist lawyers made last desperate attempts to appeal Sims's remanding back to slavery, Higginson and the Vigilance Committee gathered in secret "in meetings where everyone present had to be identified and every window closed." Could anything be done to prevent Sims's return to slavery, now that the courthouse rescue had been thwarted? Again, even with Sims's days in Boston down to a precious few, most members discussed the situation in academic, even hypothetical, tones. "Each man [had] his own plan or theory," a bewildered Higginson noted, "perhaps stopping even for anecdote or disquisition, when the occasion required the utmost promptness of decision and the most unflinching unity in action." Higginson once again lamented that "our most reliable men were non-resistants."

Finally, with the minister's prodding during a meeting in Parker's study, the group's thoughts turned to piracy. The men authorized Vigilance Committee member and sea captain Austin Bearse to procure a fast vessel and dependable crew. Once authorities placed Sims aboard the ship that would transport him back to Savannah, Bearse would pursue and overtake the vessel, rescue Sims, and sail him to safety by hugging the coastline until the boat reached Canada.

If anyone was capable of accomplishing this feat, it was Bearse. In his younger days he had served on ships that engaged in the Atlantic coastal trade, transporting goods from port to port. These duties included shipping "gangs of slaves" upriver to inland plantations after their owners had purchased them in Charleston. Bearse witnessed both men and women working "above their knees in water" on rice plantations in the brutal heat of South Carolina summers, in the charge of equally brutal overseers. Bearse, who witnessed slavery "in Spanish and French ports...in Algiers...and among the Turks," concluded that American slavery, "as I have seen it on the rice and sugar plantations...was *full as bad* as any slavery in the world—heathen or

Christian." Northerners who might take pleasure trips through the Southern states "cannot possibly know those things which can be seen of slavery by shipmasters who run up into the back plantations of countries, and who transport the slaves and produce of plantations."

In 1834 Bearse first encountered Garrison's the *Liberator*, and it changed him forever. "I read it with delight," he recounted. Bearse became involved with the seafaring component of the Underground Railroad, stowing away slaves whenever he could safely do so and transporting them to New York, Boston, or other stops along their journey to freedom. He befriended and conversed with several once they were safely away from shore, "after informing them when [they] could safely show themselves on deck."

Now, with the Vigilance Committee's blessing, Bearse and two colleagues searched the Boston docks for two boats—a rescue vessel they could procure and another that might be preparing to convey Sims back to slavery. At the end of Long Wharf, they spotted a small brig, *Acorn*, which appeared ready to fulfill the latter task. "I found the owners were having a little house built on deck, and I immediately mistrusted the house was to stow away Sims in on the return voyage," Bearse noted. His friend questioned the mate about the deckhouse. "That's the place we are to put Sims to take him back to Savannah," came the reply. Armed with this intelligence, Bearse continued to search for the appropriate vessel to overtake the *Acorn* at sea.

Meanwhile, attorneys were exhausting their final appeals on Sims's behalf. Charles Sumner, whom the Massachusetts legislature was considering as Webster's replacement in the Senate, applied to the U.S. District Court for a writ of habeas corpus on the grounds that Sims was held for three days under a criminal warrant without seeing a magistrate. Another petition asked the federal court to rule unconstitutional the Compromise of 1850. Still another asked a single justice of the U.S. Supreme Court to allow Sims to argue his case before a jury. All of these efforts were rejected. As his fate became clear, Sims exclaimed to his counsel: "I will not go back to slavery. Give me a knife, and when the Commissioner declares me a slave I will stab myself in the heart, and die before his eyes! I will not be a slave."

On Friday, April 11, when the court issued a certificate attesting that Sims was indeed the property of James Potter and identifying him as "a chattel personal to all intents, uses, and purposes whatsoever," the legal proceedings in the case were over.

With Sims's forcible return now imminent, all hope appeared lost, especially when Bearse sent word to the Vigilance Committee that he had not been able to procure a vessel capable of overtaking the *Acorn* and was doubtful he could do so in the time remaining before Sims's departure.

Higginson's hopes for a miracle dissipated. He maintained a vigil on both Thursday and Friday, and was chilled by the sight of the police drilling at dawn, preparing to escort Sims to the docks. He watched them "march and countermarch," draw their cutlasses, form up into a "horrible hollow square," which marched as a whole up and down Court Street. It was clear that Sims would walk at the center of this configuration—a single man imprisoned within a moving rectangle of heavily armed guards—to the ship that would deliver him back to the slave masters. Describing the efficiency of the troop maneuvers, a pained Higginson noted: "Massachusetts ceased to exist and we seemed to stand in Vienna."

Though it seemed inevitable, the thought of Boston police and federal soldiers returning Sims to bondage was unimaginable. "I do not believe they will dare to carry out this plan," Higginson wrote with a certainty he knew was misplaced. Would not even prominent members of Boston's business community, many of whom sought obedience to the Fugitive Slave Law to maintain good trading relations with the South, be offended by this? Armed men in Boston's streets preparing not to defend her citizens but to enslave one of them? If Sims were returned to bondage, Higginson asserted, "I do not think the blood of even Boston merchants could bear it."

Nor could Higginson bear to remain in Boston to watch the spectacle of Sims's forced march to the docks. By Friday afternoon, after reflecting on "the great want of preparation, on our part, for this revolutionary work," and having "no wish to look on at the surrender, with my hands tied," he returned to Newburyport "in deep chagrin."

SATURDAY, APRIL 12, 1851. In the early-morning dampness, Boston police and federal troops mustered by the weak light of a single gas lamp. It was just after 3:00 a.m., and some members of the Vigilance

Committee had been meeting all night in Garrison's office, expecting the worst and watching for evidence that today would be among the darkest in Boston's storied history. "The dreaded moment was at hand," historian Leonard Levy wrote. "The authorities meant to sneak Sims back into slavery while the city slept. It was not the bravest way to uphold the constitution, but it was the safest."

More than one hundred police officers, armed with double-edged Roman swords that Marshal Tukey had borrowed from the U.S. Naval Yard in Charlestown, plus another hundred volunteers armed with clubs and hooks, drilled for more than an hour, their heavy boots clomping upon the dirt-packed street. The police officers manned the inner rectangle of the hollow-square formation and the volunteers formed the outer square. Members of the Vigilance Committee spread the word that Sims's departure was at hand, and by 4:00 a.m., between 150 and 200 horrified abolitionists looked on as the drilling continued.

At about 4:15, "after the moon had gone down, in the darkest hour before daybreak," the officers and volunteers assembled and marched in formation to the east door of the courthouse. There, they were joined by one hundred more armed officers from the City Watch, which formed another double file around the hollow square. Then, the main doors of the Courthouse opened and Sims appeared. "Tears were streaming down his face, but he held his small dark frame erect," Levy described. Sims was escorted into the center of the procession. At Tukey's command of "March!" the three hundred guards "began a slow regular tramp" toward the dock.

Abolitionists and Vigilance Committee members preceded them, followed them, and flanked them as the guards continued their relentless march down State Street, encircling a despondent Sims. "His sable cheeks were bathed in tears, and although he evinced the greatest grief and sorrow, he marched with a firm and manly step, like a martyr and a hero to his fate," reported the abolitionist newspaper *Commonwealth*. The antislavery observers hissed and shouted "Shame!" and "Infamy!" but one witness noted that "no other attempt at disorder was made." As the procession arrived at the spot where Crispus Attucks, the colored patriot, was shot by the British during the Boston Massacre, a number of spectators shouted at the troops, and "pointed out to those minions of slavery the holy spot over which they were treading," physician and abolitionist Henry Ingersoll Bowditch wrote.

He added: "Gloomy and silent these wretched men passed on, sacrilegiously desecrating by their act this martyr of the Revolution."

The procession finally arrived at Long Wharf, near the site of the Boston Tea Party, where colonists had once famously protested oppression—the irony of which was also not lost on the abolitionists. The brig *Acorn*, its sails unfurled, was ready for sea. The vessel was owned by John H. Pearson, whom Wendell Phillips would one day castigate in a stinging speech, promising that abolitionists would never forget "the infamous uses he made of the *Acorn*. We will put the fact that he owned the brig so blackly on record...that his children—*yes, his children*—will, twenty years hence, gladly forego all the wealth he will leave them to blot it out." Phillips added: "The time shall come when it will be thought the unkindest thing in the world for anyone to remind the son of that man that his father's name was John H. Pearson and that he owned the *Acorn*."

Now, though, the ship stood in the glimmer of dawn just breaking across Boston Harbor, prepared to transport its human cargo to Georgia. The armed police surrounding Sims marched close to the vessel, and one section broke ranks momentarily, like a door opening, to deliver its prisoner to a contingent of guards waiting on board. As Sims reached the *Acorn*'s deck, a man standing on the wharf cried out, "Sims! Preach liberty to the slaves!" With the last words he uttered in Boston, Sims answered with a sharp rebuke to his captors: "And is this Massachusetts liberty?" He was ushered below immediately, and within two minutes, at just after 5:00 a.m., the *Acorn* was moving. As the vessel left the dock, the stunned spectators listened in solemn silence to the Reverend Daniel Foster, who asked them to kneel and pray for "the poor brother who is carried by force to the land of whips and chains."

Boston, the birthplace of the struggle for America's liberty seventy-five years earlier, had returned her first person—a free man in the North—back to slavery.

With heavy hearts the abolitionists and Vigilance Committee members left the dock, stopped in respectful silence at the spot where Crispus Attucks was killed, and then gathered in Garrison's office. There, at 5:30 a.m., they drafted a resolution asking the people of Massachusetts to "toll the [church] bells in their several towns" as word of Sims's return reached them. That day, the bells of Lynn, Plymouth, Newton, and Waltham sounded in sympathy.

As word spread of Sims's departure, so too did the reactions in and around Boston. "Shame on my country! Shame on Boston!" wrote Harvard's John Langdon Sibley in his April 12 diary entry. "What will posterity say of the conduct of the sons of the Pilgrims? What a blot on the name and fame of Daniel Webster...and of the despicable men who feared the loss of the southern trade if the negro or mulatto was not restored." A Lowell, Massachusetts, newspaper blamed a "combination of money and the Websterism of Boston" for a "victory of cotton over the conscience of the people." The *Norfolk* [Mass.] *Democrat* labeled the Sims affair the "darkest and most disgraceful crime that ever has been perpetrated" in Boston's history. Feelings in Boston ran so high that city fathers refused to rent historic Faneuil Hall to a committee of Webster supporters who wished to welcome him there days later.

The Massachusetts Senate joined in the criticism in its report on the incident ten days later, chastising Boston municipal authorities and its police force for involving themselves in Sims's capture and return, actions that were "hostile to the laws and judicial processes of this Commonwealth." The Senate expressed disappointment that "fifteen hundred of the most wealthy and respectable citizens, merchants, bankers, and others volunteered their services to aid the marshal on this occasion." Wendell Phillips concurred, leveling a searing indictment against "these peddling hucksters of State and Milk streets...they owe me full atonement for the foul dishonor they have brought on the city of my birth." Phillips condemned the business community for allowing John Pearson, the *Acorn's* owner, to "walk up State Street, and be as honored a man as he was before...that no merchant shrinks from his side."

But that same group of merchants and citizens—Boston's much larger nonabolitionist community—along with much of its establishment press, were, according to Leonard Levy, "relieved to be done with a disagreeable but necessary job." Most of the newspapers applauded the city's law enforcement apparatus for its efforts in returning Sims. "Boston is sound to its heart's core in her attachment to the Union," declared the *Boston Courier*, which commended officials for having done their duty "in the handsomest manner during the whole of this exciting and harassing business." The *Boston Herald* expected the South to now "please accord us all the credit which is due."

Some Southern newspapers granted the *Herald's* wish, but the favorable reaction was far from unanimous. While Sims's hometown paper, the *Savannah Republican*, acknowledged that Boston deserved "great credit" for complying with the Fugitive Slave Law, another Savannah paper opined: "If our people are obliged to *steal their property out of Boston in the night*, it would be more profitable to adopt a regular kidnapping system at once, without regard to law." The *Republic*, a paper out of nearby Augusta, Georgia, reprimanded Boston judicial authorities for keeping the Sims case in court "and before a commissioner for a whole week," and pointed out that "the military had to be kept on guard to prevent [Sims's] forcible rescue. The whole case looks more like a successful farce than anything else." The *Louisville Journal*, in language with which Thomas Higginson might have concurred, ridiculed the cowardice of the abolitionists, who at the crucial moment, as Sims was hustled aboard the *Acorn* for the return trip to Georgia, had lost their courage and turned to prayer rather than arms.

Elsewhere in the nation, as Leonard Levy points out, there was much rejoicing in the vindication of the Compromise of 1850. Daniel Webster wrote President Fillmore, arguing that the next step was to discredit some of the "insane" abolitionists. Fillmore replied by congratulating Boston on "a triumph of law...She has done nobly. She has wiped out the stain of the former rescue and freed herself from the reproach of *nullification*." In Washington, D.C., the *National Intelligencer* headlined its front-page lead story, "Supremacy of the Law Sustained." The *New York Express* praised Chief Justice Shaw and singled out Marshal Tukey for "so beautifully" enforcing the Fugitive Slave Law. "He ought to be a field marshal before he dies," the paper gushed.

Amid all of this reaction, word finally arrived from Georgia that on April 19, 1851, one week after he left Boston, Thomas Sims arrived in Savannah and was whipped in the public square. He was administered thirty-nine lashes across his bare back. The date was not lost on one publication, which noted that, precisely seventy-six years earlier, Massachusetts farmers and militiamen had begun America's struggle for independence against British regulars in an early-morning battle on Lexington Green. Ironically, Sims was "the first slave Massachusetts had returned since she had made that date memorable." Grief-stricken at the turn of events, former slave and prominent black abolitionist Frederick Douglass expressed his fury at Webster and his role in the passage of the Fugitive Slave Law: "Let the Heavens weep and Hell

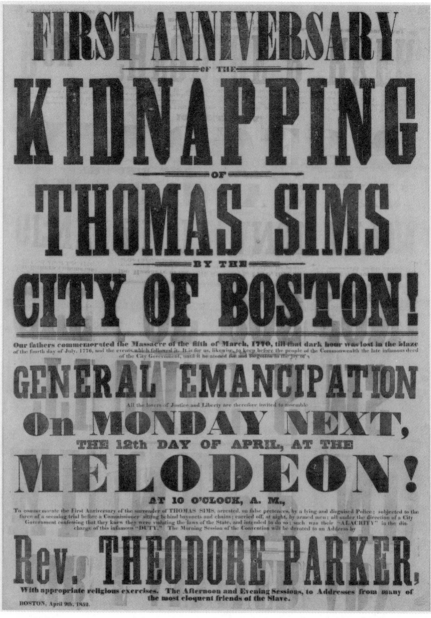

Figure 1. In April of 1852, one year after Boston complied with the Fugitive Slave Law and returned runaway slave Thomas Sims to captivity, the city's abolitionists held an emancipation rally to commemorate what they considered one of Boston's most shameful acts. (*Photo courtesy of the Boston Public Library, Print Department*)

be merry! Daniel Webster has at last obtained from Boston...a living sacrifice to appease the slave god of the American Union."

Disappointed but undaunted, the ever-hopeful and prophetic Garrison roared: "Though a victim has been dragged back to bondage, it will prove a disastrous triumph to the slave power." Sims's return would "serve to augment and extend that popular agitation which alone is needed to effect the utter overthrow of the slave system."

Abolitionists may have lost the Sims battle, but the war was just beginning. "We may be defeated," a gritty Garrison conceded after Sims's departure aboard the *Acorn*. "But our principles—never."

History is replete with examples of seemingly unconnected events coalescing to alter the course and behavior of people and nations. Although the relationships between such events are often obscured by the exigencies of the present, with time and distance, a broader picture emerges, the timeline sharpens, and the bonds that link these ostensibly discrete occurrences become clear, even undebatable.

There are few better illustrations of this historical phenomenon than the discovery of gold at Sutter's Mill in northern California in January of 1848 and Thomas Sims's arrest and return to slavery, which ultimately propelled Boston into the forefront of the North's abolitionist movement. This, in turn and in time, reinforced Boston's reputation as a crucible of political activism, a reputation she had enjoyed since the Revolution, and catapulted her to prominence as America's—and perhaps the world's—foremost center of progressive thought and social change.

The California Gold Rush, one of the seminal events in American history and second only to the Civil War in significance during the tempestuous nineteenth century, attracted tens of thousands of people from across the globe. Intrepid fortune-seekers sailed from Europe, Asia, Australia, South America, and, of course, the East Coast of the United States (the latter journey requiring a harrowing seventeen-thousand-mile ocean trek that included the treacherous waters of Cape Horn at the tip of South America). Thousands more embarked on the grueling overland journey, braving shrieking winds that knifed across the Great Plains, battling walls of snow that clogged the dangerous passes through the Rockies, enduring the relentless heat that blanketed the parched vastness of Death Valley. And after all that, these adventurers still faced the last hurdle, the towering Sierras, the final obstacle to California's hailed rivers of gold. Westward they came, from eastern cities, southern ports, midwestern farms. They traveled on foot, on horseback, on burros, or in wagons. Many—though certainly not all—survived aching hunger and thirst, sickness and injury, Indian raiding parties and white bandits who preyed on the weakest of travelers, and the despair, loneliness, fear, and second-guessing that accompanied hundreds or thousands of miles of emptiness and uncertainty.

Men and women alike risked everything, depleted their savings, quit their jobs, jeopardized their children's safety, fled from debtors, abandoned their families, endured injury and disease, and buried loved ones in shallow graves on the prairie, in the desert, or along mountainsides; all of them delirious with gold fever, which conjured up visions of indescribable riches. Gold's siren song drew so many people to California after 1848 that the region skipped the territorial stage and jumped straight to statehood; by 1850, California had become a state, the fastest journey to statehood in United States history, and its admittance to the Union reverberated across the land.

By nature and definition, then, the thousands who faced and overcame near-insurmountable odds on their trek, and populated California in two short years, possessed self-reliance, independence, courage, determination, and a deep reservoir of optimism and resilience common to successful entrepreneurs. These qualities influenced their outlook and their politics. They moved quickly and decisively. The California Constitutional Convention enacted a governing document in October of 1849, and on November 13, California voters almost unanimously ratified it (of a total vote of 12,785 qualified voters, only 811 were against the constitution, California historian Rockwell Hunt noted). California's first legislature assembled on December 15 and established the state government five days later.

John C. Frémont and William Gwin, who would become California's first two elected senators, set out for Washington in January of 1850, and in March arrived at the capital and requested, "in the name of the people of California, the admission of the State of California into the American Union."

But it was at this point that California's momentum slowed. Her approved constitution had sent ripples across the continent. Voters in the land of gold had adopted a governing document that forbade slavery in the proposed new state. Reflecting the will of the population, a March 1848 issue of the *Californian* had listed nine reasons why slavery should not be introduced in California, with the first declaring "it is wrong for it to exist anywhere." (These sentiments were not based entirely on humanitarian or moral reasons; reason number seven in the *Californian*'s list stated: "We desire only a white population in California.")

By itself, California's admittance as a free state would have been objectionable enough to the South, but the impact was exacerbated by simple mathematics. As Congress considered California's request, the American Union consisted of thirty states—fifteen slave and fifteen free—a fragile balance that had existed for decades. If and when California joined the Union as the thirty-first state, Northern abolitionists and even moderate antislavery elements would rejoice, believing, probably correctly so, that the future of slavery was doomed: that the newly acquired territories of New Mexico and Utah would follow suit, that Southern political power would be irreparably weakened, that slave owners would become further isolated, and that the peculiar institution, unlikely to spread further, would eventually wither and die. Southerners believed almost all of the same things, and they viewed with a sense of foreboding California's admittance as a free state.

The nation was at a crossroads. Whatever Congress did with California's petition could have, undeniably *would* have, profound consequences. The admittance of the far-western state threatened to shake both North and South.

How could the Union survive?

With the stakes so high, the nation looked to the Senate, and three men in particular, for answers: Henry Clay of Kentucky, John C. Calhoun of South Carolina, and the senator whose remarks and opinion would generate the greatest interest among Boston's abolitionists and merchants alike, Daniel Webster of Massachusetts. They had worked together before to achieve compromise on sectional differences, and though aging (all three would be dead within two years), each commanded the respect of his colleagues and the population at large. These three individuals, whose reputations transcended politics and defined them as statesmen, assumed familiar leadership roles in the all-important Compromise of 1850.

Debate on the measure began in March. Several components made up the compromise, including, of course, California's admittance as a free state. One other controversial element was seen as the counterweight to the California decision, the component of the legislation that would most placate the South, shush the whispers of secession, and perhaps hold the Union together.

Southern slave owners demanded it and Northern abolitionists dreaded it: a harsher and more stringent Fugitive Slave Law.

"I wish to speak today, not as a Massachusetts man, nor as a northern man, but as an American, and a member of the Senate of the United States," Daniel Webster began his soon-to-be historic March 7, 1850, speech on the Senate floor before a hushed chamber.

Clay and Calhoun had already addressed their colleagues. Clay had outlined and advocated passage of the lengthy compromise that he himself had drafted, imploring his colleagues "solemnly to pause at the edge of the precipice, before the fearful and disastrous leap is taken in the yawning abyss below, which will inevitably lead to certain and irretrievable destruction." An ailing Calhoun, his voice barely a hoarse whisper, had asked a colleague to read his reply. If he had to support Clay's compromise as a political last resort, he would, but he stood firmly in opposition to admitting California at all. He issued a grim warning to the Senate: "California will become the test question. If you admit her, under all the difficulties that oppose her admission, you compel us to infer that you … [have] the intention of destroying irretrievably the equilibrium between the two sections." He mocked Clay's call for Union for its own sake: "The cry of 'Union, Union, the glorious Union!' can no more prevent disunion than the cry of 'Health, health, glorious health!' on the part of the physician can save a patient lying dangerously ill," the South Carolinian said.

Webster believed the compromise would preserve the Union, and agreed to support the measure regardless of the consequences he might face in the North. Though he might dispute some details, he thought Clay's proposal was sound and thorough: in addition to admitting California as a free state and strengthening the Fugitive Slave Law, the plan called for the newly acquired territories of Utah and New Mexico to decide for themselves whether to allow slavery or not; banned slave trading but not slavery itself, in Washington, D.C.; said slavery could only be abolished in the District of Columbia if its residents and the State of Maryland approved it, and that owners must be compensated for their slaves; called for the United States to pay debts Texas had incurred before annexation following the Mexican War; assigned disputed land between New Mexico and Texas to New Mexico; and prohibited Congress from interfering with the slave trade in or between slave states.

But Webster understood that the tougher Fugitive Slave Law was the linchpin of the compromise and he focused his remarks accordingly. He realized quickly that the new law mandated harsh and summary enforcement over civil liberties, but he understood also that its very strictness was the only way to ensure Southern support. Webster thought that even the most fervent proslavery lawmakers would recognize the new bill's good-faith concessions to Southern interests.

The proposed law would allow a slave owner or his agent to reclaim a fugitive slave by securing a warrant beforehand or arresting the runaway on the spot. The case for returning the slave to his master would be heard by a federal judge or a court-appointed federal commissioner, who would be paid ten dollars if the certificate of removal was issued, but only five dollars if the claim was denied (abolitionists would later decry this measure as virtually bribing the commissioner to return an individual to bondage). No jury could be called during court proceedings, testimony from the fugitive was prohibited, and the commissioner's decision could not be appealed. In addition, historian Henry Mayer pointed out, "other courts or magistrates were barred from issuing habeas corpus writs or other legal mandates that might postpone or override an order to remand a defendant into slavery." Finally, the law called for stiff penalties—a one-thousand-dollar fine and up to six months in jail—for anyone aiding a fugitive or interfering with his or her return to slavery, a component that chilled and infuriated abolitionists.

Webster's remarks about the Fugitive Slave Law were candid and politically courageous. He was fully aware that he would anger many Northerners and that his hopes for a presidential run would evaporate. But for him, preserving the Union outweighed any sectional loyalties. The new law was necessary, Webster asserted, because Northern legislatures and individuals had shown a "disinclination to perform fully their constitutional duties" to uphold the law "in regard to the return of persons bound to service, who have escaped into free states. In that respect, it is my judgment that the South is right and the North is wrong." Webster also alienated many of his own Massachusetts constituents by criticizing abolitionist societies. "I do not think them useful," he said. "I think their operations for the last twenty years have produced nothing good or valuable." Indeed, despite the fact that "thousands of them are honest and good men, perfectly well-meaning men," Webster contended that the result of radical abolitionism, of "northern agitation," was contrary to its intent. "The bonds of the slaves were bound more firmly than before," he told his colleagues, "their rivets were more strongly fastened" by Southerners who feared a total upheaval to their way of life.

Above all for Webster, though, the Fugitive Slave Law might succeed in holding together a nation that was fraying at the seams. He scoffed at references to "peaceable secession" by some Southerners. "What would be the result?" he roared. "Where is the line to be drawn? What states are to secede? What is to remain American? What am I to be?—an American no longer?" No, he argued, secession would break apart a country that was forged in a furnace fired with courage, sacrifice, blood, and idealism. No one—Northerner or Southerner—should dishonor such achievement, should disrupt the "harmony of the Union," lest "our fathers and grandfathers…rebuke and reproach us; and our children and grandchildren cry out, 'Shame upon us!'"

For weeks after his speech, Webster felt the wrath of abolitionists. They took him to task on the issue and vilified him personally with the venom reserved for traitors and turncoats. Garrison wrote that Webster "had bent his supple knees anew to the Slave Power," and launched a petition drive to convince the Massachusetts legislature to censure the senator whose "degrading" betrayal ranked him beside Benedict Arnold. In his entire career, Garrison said, no speech "had so powerfully shocked the moral sense, or so grievously insulted the intelligence of the people." The *Liberator* also printed a series of poems by Walt Whitman that compared Webster to Judas. And Ralph Waldo Emerson spat, "The word *liberty* in the mouth of Mr. Webster sounds like the word *love* in the mouth of a courtesan." Charles Sumner, who would soon succeed Webster in the Senate, spoke of "Webster's elaborate treason."

Webster was not cowed. In response to constituent letters supporting his commitment to the Union, he reiterated his disdain for the abolitionists and their motives. The Fugitive Slave Law, he said, was satisfactory to all except those whose "business is agitation…whose objects are anything but the promotion of peace, harmony, patriotic good will, and the love of UNION among the people of the United States." He infuriated abolitionists when he responded cavalierly to a statement by Massachusetts congressman Horace Mann (Mann first referred to Webster as "Lucifer descending from Heaven"), who objected strenuously to the Fugitive Slave Law's provision that prohibited runaways from seeking jury trials when they were captured. "A man may not lose his horse without a right to this trial, but he may his freedom," Mann said. Webster countered by ridiculing Mann's analogy, claiming that carried to its logical, if absurd, conclusion, "if Mr. Mann's horse strays into his neighbor's field, he cannot lead him back without a previous trial by jury." Webster's direct comparison of a fugitive slave with a horse provoked the discomfort of even many of his supporters in the debate. While embracing his theme of preserving the Union, even those who agreed with him thought Webster had gone too far in defending the Fugitive Slave Law.

But the die had been cast. Debate continued throughout the spring and summer, but Webster's March 7 speech had put the Compromise of 1850 on a road to passage. Millard Fillmore's ascension to the presidency after President Zachary Taylor's death from typhoid fever on July 9 buoyed proponents due to Fillmore's expressed support for the compromise. Fillmore also chose Webster as secretary of state in his new cabinet, meaning Webster would have to resign his Senate seat; ironically, despite a final speech in support of the measure on July 17, Webster, the compromise's most articulate and passionate defender, would not cast a final vote on its passage in early September.

On September 18, 1850, President Fillmore signed the Compromise of 1850 and thus the new Fugitive Slave Act into law. On October 2, Daniel Webster wrote: "We have now gone through the most important crisis that has occurred since the foundation of this government, and whatever party may prevail, hereafter, the Union stands firm."

Then Thomas Sims came to Boston.

To be certain, Boston had seethed for months *before* the Sims case.

In the immediate aftermath of the Fugitive Slave Law's passage, abolitionists held meetings, raised money, and swore their allegiance to protecting and assisting runaway slaves who found their way to the city. After a sermon on Sunday, October 6, Theodore Parker told his congregation that between four hundred and six hundred fugitive slaves resided in Boston, and it was his parishioners' obligation to aid and protect them. The remark prompted a spontaneous burst of applause and stamping of feet among those assembled. On the night of October 14, more than thirty-five hundred people packed Faneuil Hall and denounced the law as contrary to the Declaration of Independence and the U.S. Constitution. Frederick Douglass expressed fear that even though he possessed his "free papers," some irregularity might be discovered that would send him back to bondage. The meeting led to the formation of the Boston Vigilance Committee, under Theodore Parker's leadership, and within two days, eighty men had joined. By October 21, committee treasurer Francis Jackson's account book showed a balance of more than twenty-seven hundred dollars earmarked to assist fugitive slaves.

All of this happened none too soon. Just a few days later, warrants were issued for William and Ellen Craft, and on November 1, Garrison's newspaper reported that slave hunters, "two prowling villains," had arrived in Boston to seize the Crafts "and carry them back to the hell of slavery." Abolitionists posted placards around the city warning of their arrival. "Since the day of [1776], there has not been such a popular demonstration on the side of human freedom in this region," Garrison wrote. "The human and patriotic contagion has infected all classes." Garrison was sure the slave hunters would be thwarted by "good men and true," including the nearly forty members of the bar who were members of the Vigilance Committee.

But while their success in rescuing the Crafts and, later, Shadrach Minkins, energized the abolitionists—"set the whole public afire," in the words of Wendell Phillips—the Thomas Sims case was different. The Sims case galvanized them and transformed the movement. The bitterness of Sims's capture, the spectacle of his imprisonment, and their own inability to prevent his return—Higginson's lament about their aversion to action—taught abolitionists a lesson in defeat that no victory could teach. Moreover, true to Garrison's prophecy, the Sims case changed the slavery debate in Boston and bolstered the city's influence nationwide, and even internationally, in the abolitionist movement.

In the most important issue the nation faced at the outset of the second half of the nineteenth century, Boston would lead the way.

—⚏—

The first sign that the Sims case had shaken Boston to its core came just two weeks after the fugitive slave's departure, when, on April 24, the Massachusetts legislature, on its twenty-sixth ballot, finally elected radical—and fanatical—antislavery candidate Charles M. Sumner to the United States Senate (senators were not yet elected directly by the people). The stunning selection of the man to replace Daniel Webster left "half the [Massachusetts population] rejoicing and half of it embittered," Allan Nevins pointed out. Abolitionists celebrated with bonfires, bell ringing, cannon firing, and public meetings. "This is a very important day in the history of Massachusetts," crowed John Langdon Sibley in his diary. "[Sumner's election] has been done notwithstanding all the money & influence of Boston, nearly all the newspapers, Daniel Webster's personal influence, talents, friends…and all the patronage which can be furnished from Washington." But among the merchants, the feeling was different. "On State Street," Nevins recounted, "faces were long and scowls were black." Or, as Edmund Quincy wrote of the "State Street reaction" on April 28, 1851, from Boston: "If you could have heard the *swearing,* your hair would have stood on end."

Nonetheless, the election of Sumner, who along with Garrison and John Brown would eventually be categorized among the most radical and influential American abolitionists, likely would never have happened without the Sims episode. "The election of Charles Sumner…practically followed from [Sims's misfortune]," Thomas Higginson wrote.

Indeed, Sims's capture and dramatic return to slavery became the stuff of legend in Boston, and along with Sumner's election, set in motion a chain of actions that would establish Boston as the philosophical center and conscience of the antislavery movement. Abolitionists and Underground Railroad participants assumed great risk in New York, Rhode Island, Pennsylvania, Ohio, and other states; but by 1851, the antislavery heartbeat pulsated most powerfully from Boston, pumping a combination of ardor, militancy, and influence across the North, and a constant stream of invective and contempt toward the South.

Boston Vigilance Committee members, finally taking action that must have delighted Higginson, helped more than three hundred fugitive slaves escape in the three years after Sims's return to bondage, providing funds, food, clothing, and safe passage along the Underground Railroad network that wound its way through Concord and Lincoln, snaked northward through New Hampshire and Vermont, and eventually crossed the border into the rugged forests of Canada. In 1853 Vigilance Committee member Lewis Hayden, himself a fugitive, reported that he had as many as thirteen runaways in his house "of all colors and sizes." Austin Bearse captained two vessels, the *Moby Dick* (presumably named for Herman Melville's novel; Melville became a strong supporter of the Vigilance Committee and good friends with Richard Henry Dana) and, later, the *Wild Pigeon*, pleasure craft that doubled as escape boats helping runaways reach ports on Massachusetts's north shore and in New Hampshire.

Antislavery partisans became increasingly bolder, not only helping runaways escape, but continuing to preach in America and abroad on the evils of slavery and the "slaveholding government," as Wendell Phillips referred to the South. Weymouth-born Maria West Chapman, who headed the Boston Female Anti-Slavery Society and sat on the executive committee of the Massachusetts Anti-Slavery Society, vigorously sought contributions for antislavery causes from European elites during an extended trip to Paris. A new tenacity inspired the abolitionists. They used the word "revolution" again and again, and Thomas Higginson summarized their passions at the New England Anti-Slavery Convention in 1855: "What we want is not to dream of a land of freedom somewhere at the west, but to *make* a land of freedom *here*...not to send slaves to Canada, but to make Canada on the spot where we stand."

Such work, Higginson pointed out, found a natural home in Boston. "It is not done without danger; it is not to be done without revolution; for the instant you begin to do it, a revolution has begun in you. Where on earth are there such materials for revolution as here?"

It wasn't just the abolitionists who were newly energized by recent events. The Massachusetts Senate passed a resolution asking the state's senators and representatives in Congress to repeal the Fugitive Slave Law on moral and constitutional grounds. Calling the law "unconstitutional, inhumane, and wicked," the Senate took greatest umbrage in the irony of innocent blacks forced to flee to England. "They seek in a monarchy asylum from the injustice and cruelty of a republic!" The Senate resolution also reserved harsh words for slave hunters. "[He] profanes the soil of Massachusetts, seeking whom he may devour. His presence spreads terror among the colored people of our state...to our judgment, the *illegal* kidnapper on the coast of Africa, and the *legal* man-hunter in Boston, belong to the same class of felons." Without reservation, the Senate declared that the Fugitive Slave Law was "alien to the spirit of the Constitution...and abhorrent to the feelings of the people of this Commonwealth."

The Fugitive Slave Law mobilized Boston's influential writing community, too, whose works had contributed to the city's designation as the Athens of America a decade earlier. Emerson, Thoreau, Melville, Hawthorne, Longfellow, Bronson Alcott (and later, his daughter Louisa May), all spoke and wrote against slavery, their words ringing across the country and across the world. Emerson told the citizens of Concord that the Fugitive Slave Law was an "ignominy which has fallen on Massachusetts, which robs the landscape of beauty, and takes the sunshine out of every hour." He was ashamed of Boston's official behavior in the Sims case—"the reverse of what it should have been; it was supple and officious...it should have placed obstruction at every step"—and maintained that it was a moral duty to break an immoral law "at every hazard."

Yet Boston's most significant and noteworthy literary figure in the antislavery cause was not a writer but a publisher. John P. Jewett, Vigilance Committee member and head of a prestigious Boston publishing house that bore his name, decided to take a chance on an author whose antislavery fiction had been serialized in a weekly Washington paper called the *National Era*. In 1852 Jewett published Harriet Beecher Stowe's *Uncle Tom's Cabin* in book form. "She applied to several Boston publishers, but they were afraid to have anything to do with such a dangerous anti-slavery production," Jewett remarked in a later interview. "Unsuccessful elsewhere, Mrs. Stowe and her husband came to me. My sentiments in regard to slavery were pretty well-known in Boston...the anti-slavery aspect of *Uncle Tom's Cabin*, so far from being a bugbear, was a recommendation to me." Jewett's personal attitude aside, he harbored some reservations about the commercial viability of the book. "The only question with me then was whether the book would sell," he said. "My wife, on whose judgment I had frequent occasions to rely...declared that 'Uncle Tom' would make a book that would sell largely."

But not even Mrs. Jewett could have anticipated the impact of

Uncle Tom's Cabin. A nineteenth-century literary phenomenon, the book became the first American novel to sell more than a million copies. Jewett recalled that within two days, five thousand copies of the novel were sold, ten thousand within a week, and more than three hundred thousand copies by the end of 1852. "So large were the orders for the book, that from the day I first began to print it the eight presses never stopped, day or night, save Sundays, for six months," Jewett recounted, "and even then there were complaints that the volumes did not appear fast enough."

Stowe's evocative writing style, sympathetic characters, and almost religious attack on the institution of slavery moved readers in a way nothing else had. Frederick Douglass hailed the book as "plainly marked by the finger of God" and "a flash to light a million camp fires in front of the embattled hosts of slavery." Just as influential were the stunning sales in Great Britain and its colonies during the first year of publication, which exceeded 1.5 million copies; Stowe's relationship with British writers and reading groups—she made three transatlantic trips during the 1850s to promote the book—helped fuel sales and trumpeted the antislavery message on the other side of the Atlantic. During its commercial lifetime, *Uncle Tom's Cabin* would sell more than 3 million copies in the United States and an equal number overseas.

The popularity of the novel "finally took the sting of fanaticism out of abolitionism," author Henry Mayer wrote, and "gave incalculable weight to the idea of emancipation as a moral and historical inevitability."

Two other widely publicized events during the mid-1850s reinforced Boston's position as the nation's antislavery leader. While *Uncle Tom's Cabin* took the "sting of fanaticism out of abolitionism" upon its publication in 1852, the cumulative impact of these later incidents instilled or awakened deep antislavery passions in thousands of people who had previously remained neutral about, or even shunned, abolitionism.

The first occurred three years after the Thomas Sims case. After helping hundreds of runaways flee to Canada, after establishing herself as a haven for escaped slaves seeking refuge, Boston sent her second and final slave back to captivity midway through 1854. The mood among Boston abolitionists was already darkened by the imminent passage of the Kansas-Nebraska Act (it became law on May 30). The act repealed the Compromise of 1820 (also known as the Missouri Compromise) and stated that the future of slavery in the territories would be decided by popular vote. Northern antislavery forces vehemently opposed the measure, fearing (justifiably, it turned out) that Southern proslavery sympathizers would pour across the Kansas territorial border—Nebraska was too far north to attract slave owners—to vote in favor of the institution.

Thus, when twenty-three-year-old Anthony Burns was arrested in Boston on May 24, on a warrant that he was the escaped slave of a Virginia master, abolitionists did more than howl in protest. Burns's incarceration occurred "at the most combustible moment imaginable," Henry Mayer wrote. This time, Higginson led a group of rioters, armed with axes, on a courthouse assault. "We hammered away at the southwest door...before it began to give way," he wrote. A few men squeezed inside and were met by a half-dozen policemen wielding clubs, "driving us to the wall and hammering away at our heads." A shot was fired—it was impossible to say by whom—and a guard named Batchelder was killed. Higginson and his men were beaten back, but earned the respect of their colleagues for their efforts (Henry David Thoreau called Higginson "the only Harvard Phi Beta Kappa, Unitarian Minister, and master of seven languages who has led a storming party against a federal bastion with a battering ram in his hands"). Burns remained imprisoned, and after his trial, he was marched down State Street to the docks in a route eerily similar to the one Sims had followed.

This time, though, more than fifty thousand Boston residents jammed the streets and rooftops on Friday afternoon, June 2, 1854, to protest the escaped slave's return to bondage. As Burns marched toward Long Wharf, surrounded by one thousand U.S. soldiers and militiamen, the Brattle Street Church bell tolled, the crowd booed, hissed, cursed, and cried, "Kidnappers, Kidnappers!" Black bunting draped office buildings in Boston's mercantile and financial districts, and the accompanying symbolic props were telling. From one building a coffin was suspended with the word "Liberty" printed on its side; at the Merchants' Exchange, a petition calling for the repeal of the Fugitive Slave Law was signed by many of Boston's commercial elite, proving that "the most solid men of Boston...are fast falling into the ranks of freedom," Theodore Parker wrote. A colleague wrote excitedly to Higginson that the petition drive was organized by none other than John Pearson, the owner of the Brig *Acorn* that had transported Thomas Sims back to slavery.

Pearson's turnabout delighted the abolitionists and illustrated the philosophical transformation that was occurring among Boston Unionists and Whigs. "Pearson's change of heart...his going over to the abolitionists a repentant sinner made a sharp and forceful political statement," historian Albert J. von Frank wrote. "It was the most visible break in the ranks of wealthy Boston...and a sign of more to come." Indeed, many Webster Whigs, among the strongest pro-Union voices in the country, felt betrayed by the South; yes, they had commercial interests and economic ties to consider, but most found both slavery and the Fugitive Slave Law distasteful. Garrison biographer Henry Mayer pointed out that when Thoreau wrote of the Burns case "My thoughts are murder to the state," he voiced the common anger of both abolitionists and businesspeople. As textile merchant Amos Lawrence commented on the Burns case in June of 1854, "We went to bed one night, old fashioned, conservative, compromise Union Whigs and waked up stark mad Abolitionists."

And for those whose minds and attitudes weren't changed by the Burns affair, they were finally convinced by another stunning development almost two years later to the day.

Again, Boston was at the center of the storm.

With the Kansas situation deteriorating, with North-South sectional strife approaching a boil, Boston and Massachusetts found themselves enmeshed in one of the most dramatic events in American history, one that ricocheted from Washington to Boston to South Carolina, through the cities and factories of the North and the plantations and small towns of the South, and even across the Atlantic to London, Scotland, and Paris. It shattered the fragile truce between North and South, cemented the reputation of Boston abolitionists as the South's most bitter enemies, and ended any chance to settle sectional differences peaceably.

Many factors conspired to cause the Civil War, but what made war unavoidable was the brutal caning of the abolitionist U.S. senator Charles Sumner of Massachusetts by proslavery South Carolina congressman Preston Brooks. Early in the afternoon of May 22, 1856, Brooks strode into the U.S. Senate chamber in Washington, D.C., and began beating Sumner with his cane; again and again Brooks struck, more than thirty times across Sumner's head, face, and shoulders, until the cane splintered into pieces and the Massachusetts senator lay unconscious, covered in blood.

It was a retaliatory attack. Forty-eight hours earlier, Sumner had concluded a venomous speech on the Senate floor titled "The Crime against Kansas." His caustic remarks had spanned two days, during which time he levied personal slurs against Brooks's cousin, South Carolina senator Andrew Butler, and insulted the entire South for its proslavery stance, particularly its attempts to incite violence in Kansas as a way to influence its statehood vote in the direction of slavery.

Brooks's reasons for flaying Sumner were immaterial to the North. The South Carolina lawmaker unleashed a firestorm that could not be extinguished. Both antislavery Northerners and proslavery Southerners pounced on the caning to support their views: the North to argue that the South could no longer be reasoned with on the most important issue facing the country; the South to declare that Sumner's reckless Kansas speech had unmasked the North's true goal, which was to destroy the South's economic system and its way of life. Northern papers, even those that acknowledged and denounced the acerbic tone of Sumner's words, blasted Brooks and the South for resorting to violence, many suggesting that the South Carolinian's actions were symbolic of the South's approach in the slavery debate. "The outrage in the Senate...is without parallel in the legislative history of the country," noted the Republican-leaning *Boston Atlas* in an editorial. "We almost forget the private injury of Mr. Sumner in the broad temerity of the insult which has been offered to the country, to Massachusetts, to the Senate."

Yet the true measure of the caning's impact was best reflected not by editorials, but by the reactions of ordinary people and elected officials, and its effect upon political strategies and maneuvering that further inflamed sectional tensions between the regions. "For most Northerners," Sumner biographer David Donald wrote, "news of the attack upon Sumner came as an electrifying shock," and produced "a deep sense of outrage." Hundreds of well-wishers, including children, wrote Sumner to express their sympathy. "The instant papa told me," one Massachusetts girl wrote, "it seemed exactly as if a great black cloud was spread over the sky." Richard Henry Dana's daughter, Mary, wrote, "Mr. Brooks is a very naughty man and if I had been there I would have torn his eyes out, and so I would do now if I could." A Boston man added: "Indignation at the brutal attack upon you is on every lip, and fills every heart." But the writer astutely prophesized the positive outcome of Sumner's beating. "It seems to be the last feather that breaks the camel's back of [Northern proslavery supporters'] sympathy with slavery."

Sumner's support did not stop with letter writing and certainly did not end at the Massachusetts border—the caning enraged and energized the entire North. Huge rallies and protest meetings, often with more than five thousand people in attendance, were held in Boston, Albany, Cleveland, Detroit, New Haven, New York, and Providence. Republican strategists distributed more than a million copies of Sumner's "Crime against Kansas" speech as a thirty-two-page pamphlet. They delivered speeches, citing the Brooks assault as the rallying event to unify Democrats, Whigs, and Republican abolitionists in the North.

The caning of Charles Sumner destroyed any pretense of civility between North and South. It forever altered the slavery and sectional debates, and it stands as a moment in time that redefined the nation. In the North, the Sumner beating cemented the abolitionist view that slaveholders were barbarians, but of even greater consequence, it convinced moderate Northern voices that the South could no longer engage in reasonable debate about slavery and sectional differences. Even those moderates who deplored Sumner's language in the Kansas speech were left with little choice but to stand shoulder-to-shoulder with the stricken senator and condemn the bloody beating that Brooks had inflicted upon him. Just as significantly, the newly formed Republican Party used the caning to seize dominance from their Democratic and Know-Nothing rivals, the latter of whom adopted an anti-immigrant, anti-Catholic platform. It was the caning of Charles Sumner that drew thousands into the party that nominated Abraham Lincoln in 1860, after the Illinois lawyer had unified them with a cohesive voice and direction.

Abroad, the caning shocked the British Isles and the European continent, partly due to Charles Sumner's extended trips overseas during his three-year convalescence after the incident. "The feeling on the subject of Slavery is very strong," Sumner wrote from Paris in 1857. "All consider it Barbarism."

What the caning illustrated most clearly, as David Donald noted, was that the North and South "no longer spoke the same language, shared the same moral code, or obeyed the same laws...thinking men began to wonder how the Union could longer endure."

Or, as Ralph Waldo Emerson gravely observed on June 6, 1856: "I do not see how a barbarous community and a civilized community can constitute one state. I think we must get rid of slavery, or we must get rid of freedom."

In October of 1858, Mississippi senator Jefferson Davis visited Boston and delivered a rousing speech on states' rights and individual liberties at Faneuil Hall. Davis called on Boston, as a staunch proponent and defender of the Constitution, to uphold the Fugitive Slave Law and resist "political agitators" who sought to disobey it.

But it was too late.

While some conservative businesspeople applauded Davis lustily —after a financial panic and recession in 1857, they were looking to rebuild their ties with Southern agriculturalists—abolitionist fever gripped Boston like a vice. As a whole, the city was in no mood to hear, let alone embrace, Davis's message. Instead, most echoed Theodore Parker's words when he said, "I hate slavery—not merely in the abstract. I hate it in the *concrete*. I hate *Slave-hunters, Slave-breeders, Slave-sellers, Slave-holders*...hate them as I hate robbers, murderers and pirates, and shall seek to rid the world of such a nuisance as fast as I can." Then, in 1859, Thomas Higginson and Parker became two of the "Secret Six" from Boston who financed John Brown's failed raid on the federal armory in Harper's Ferry, Virginia, a brazen and lawless act that brought the nation to the brink. One year later, the election of Abraham Lincoln pushed it over the edge. Southern states began to secede one by one; Jefferson Davis, whose last-gasp pleas for moderation had fallen on deaf ears in Boston in 1858, became president of the Confederate States of America in February 1861. Two months later, the nation was at war.

The antislavery cause transformed Boston during the 1850s. The Sims case, the Burns case, the Sumner beating; the strength of its opposition to the Fugitive Slave Law; the passion and tenacity of its abolitionists; the power of its literary voices—authors, publishers, and poets; these all converged during one of the most important decades in American history to thrust Boston onto the national and world stage as the center of antislavery leadership and progressive thought. On the most compelling and intertwined issues of the day—the future of slavery and the fate of the Union—the country looked to Boston: the North with admiration, the South with disdain.

The abolitionist movement alone could have propelled Boston Town into a world-class city. But far more occurred in Boston during the 1850s to raise the city's profile, particularly in the areas of commerce, transportation, engineering, immigration, and physical expansion. Like the abolitionists, leaders in these fields had grand ideas and visions of masterful accomplishments. Once they got started, there would be no turning back.

They celebrated the first of these major achievements in the fall of 1851, just a few months after Thomas Sims was returned to slavery.

Again, the whole country looked on; Canada, too.

CHAPTER 2

The Great Railroad Jubilee

You can stretch forth your iron arms, reach the remotest cities of the Union, and bring hither their wealth and their productions.

—*President Millard Fillmore, at the Boston Railroad Jubilee, September 1851*

SEPTEMBER 17, 1851. One year after he had signed the controversial Fugitive Slave Act into law, seven months after he asserted that Boston's reputation had been "stained" by the Minkins rescue, and five months after he authorized federal troops to assist in the return of Thomas Sims to slavery, President Millard Fillmore rode tall astride a black cavalry charger, gazing at the resplendent assembly spread before him on Boston Common. Handling his horse with graceful ease, Fillmore high-stepped the steed between dozens of rows of military regiments, their colors held high, inspecting the men who stood at attention under a red-streaked, early-evening sky.

Thousands of cheering Boston residents thronged the gently rising hill that nearly encircled the field, waving flags and handkerchiefs. Echoes of booming cannon, discharged minutes earlier to announce Fillmore's arrival on the Common, hung in the air. The president rode along the whole front, saluted by each company as he passed— artillery and light-infantry regiments, rifle brigades and color guards, all part of Massachusetts's volunteer militia. Then the line broke into columns and marched in review before the commander in chief, and after circling the field, formed into line again. Later, President Fillmore declared that the crisp display was the finest he had ever witnessed. Bostonians who watched the spectacle agreed.

Yet these troops were not gathered on Boston Common to commemorate a military victory or honor comrades who had sacrificed their lives in battle. Fillmore did not review them as a prelude to sending them into harm's way. Rather, the president, the militia, the thousands of spectators who gathered on the Common were celebrating the "peaceful and beneficent triumphs of science and skill," according to the Boston City Council report later written on the event.

This was day one of a three-day citywide and region-wide celebration known as the Great Boston Railroad Jubilee, organized to mark the completion of railway lines and the beginning of service connecting Boston with Montreal, Canada, and the West (in 1851, defined as the Great Lakes and Chicago), as well as the establishment of a new line of ocean steamships to broaden Boston's commerce with England. Boston would now serve as the most cost-effective and efficient nexus, the link between ship and rail, for goods transported from Liverpool to Montreal. No one seemed to notice, or care, that including the shipping component as part of the celebration lent an incongruity to an event labeled a "Railroad Jubilee." All were focused on the exuberance of the occasion, and as the City Council report noted, "however extensive and brilliant may have been the public pageants on other occasions, no one, it is believed, has, on this Continent, surpassed, if any have equaled, that of the 17th, 18th, and 19th of September."

His travel schedule over the last few days had left President Fillmore exhausted, but the jubilant response he received from Massachusetts citizens exhilarated him. He had departed from Washington two days earlier, accompanied by Interior Secretary Alexander Stuart and War Secretary Charles Conrad; the presidential party traveled by train to New York, then by steamer to Newport, Rhode Island, where they arrived on the morning of September 16 and spent the day. The following morning, Fillmore and his entourage boarded another boat for the short ride to Fall River, Massachusetts, where they climbed aboard a "very handsomely decorated" train for the ride to Dorchester. As the locomotive pulled the presidential train into the Harrison Square station house at 10:00 a.m., a cheering "immense multitude, on foot, on horseback, and in carriages," was awaiting its arrival.

After brief remarks, Fillmore took his seat in a carriage heading a procession that wound its way through Park Street to Neponset, up Adams Street, toward Meeting-House Hill. All along the way, thousands lined the roadways, applauding and waving handkerchiefs. President Fillmore gratefully acknowledged the cheers; he knew better than anyone the furor he had created in Massachusetts during the Thomas Sims fugitive-slave case and had not been sure what kind of reception he would receive in the state.

As the procession approached the Boston line, Fillmore saw the broad avenue of Washington Street packed with thousands of people; lines of flags stretched from tree to tree and house to house. Cannon boomed and music blared. Mayor John P. Bigelow greeted President Fillmore with much pomp and fanfare, and Fillmore, in turn, commented upon the swiftness of his journey from Washington to Boston, when compared with George Washington's similar trip seventy-five years earlier. "Why is it that the distance which it took him eleven days to travel over, and that, too, when a most critical state of affairs called for the utmost speed, has now been passed over by me, as a matter of pleasure, in almost as many hours? It is owing, in great part, to the intelligence of your citizens, who have also opened avenues of commerce to the western world, which is now, through them, pouring into your lap her richest treasures."

As the procession wound its way toward the city center, the sidewalk crowd became denser and more vocal, greeting the president with full-throated cheers. Fillmore noticed the number of signs that paid tribute to the Union as well, as though Boston wanted to assure him that its opposition to the Fugitive Slave Law did not impact her loyalty to the Union. One sign read, "President Fillmore—the President of the Nation, and Not of a Party," and another displayed the motto, "In Our Union Is Our Strength."

Fillmore firmly believed the sentiments and believed further that the miracle of railroads could help unite a fractured nation. The Boston Railroad Jubilee, he hoped, would resonate well beyond the borders of Massachusetts. It was a symbolic event, one that illustrated how railroads could increase understanding among people of all regions, reduce prejudice and ignorance, and—a presidential concern even as early as 1851—avoid civil war.

—〰—

Fillmore had nearly skipped the jubilee. A full agenda, punctuated by several domestic and international crises during the summer—including an American mercenary-led uprising in Cuba intent on overthrowing Spanish colonial rule and establishing an independent republic—made him reluctant to leave Washington. When Mayor Bigelow's invitation to the jubilee arrived on August 24, the president delayed making a decision while the Cuba crisis worsened. "I fear I cannot go to Boston. This Cuban matter may prevent [it]," he confided to Daniel Webster.

But things changed swiftly. Prominent Bostonians pleaded for Fillmore to attend the jubilee, believing it would bolster the Whig Party in Massachusetts and help the city expunge the nation's collective memory of the fugitive-slave debacles of the spring: law-and-order Democrats and Whigs continued to be appalled at the abolitionists' radicalism; antislavery forces in other states were shocked that Boston had allowed Thomas Sims's return to bondage. City Councilman H. M. Holbrook maintained, "Politically, we are in a peculiar, as well as, critical position in this State." While these entreaties evidently influenced Fillmore, a late calming of the Cuban crisis and a September 12 cabinet meeting at which most of his advisers "thought, upon the whole, I had better go," ultimately convinced the president to change his mind. He also feared political fallout if he remained in Washington. "The motives for my declining were likely to be misunderstood and misrepresented," he wrote to Webster, "[plus] this change in public affairs leaves one at liberty to attend."

Political and personal reasons notwithstanding, Fillmore's decision to attend the jubilee was no doubt influenced by his being a longtime devotee of railroads. The president frequently wove together the themes of commerce, Unionism, and peace in his speeches and public statements. Fillmore and the Whigs "hoped to forge a national brotherhood on the back of the steam train," historian Michael Connolly observed. "The more quickly men could travel from Boston to Mobile, Maine to Alabama, North to South, the less likely they were to succumb to misunderstanding and violence." Fillmore persistently pushed for any technological advance that would break down the barriers of distance and time that separated citizens from each other. He and his fellow Whigs "were attempting to create a nineteenth-century nation out of an eighteenth-century experiment," Connolly noted. "With their rigorous schedules, military look and efficiency, and scientific exactitude, railroads were more conducive to stable, orderly nationalism than any political philosophy or intellectual theory."

Moreover, railroads could democratize America through association. In sentiments Fillmore shared, Daniel Webster said a few years prior to the jubilee, "The rich take the train because it is quicker, the poor because it is cheaper...in the history of human inventions there is hardly one so well calculated as that of railroads to equalize the condition of men...men are thus brought together as neighbors and acquaintances, who live two hundred miles apart." In more magisterial imagery, Massachusetts orator Edward Everett used the occasion of the jubilee to ascribe to railroads almost supernatural qualities: "By the magic of these modern works of art, the forest is thrown open—the rivers and the lakes are bridged—the valleys rise, the mountains bow their everlasting heads."

With railroads offering so much potential to bind the nation's sectional wounds, President Fillmore viewed his attendance at the Boston jubilee as both a political and moral necessity, a gesture imbued with deep historical symbolism, for his presidency and his country.

"Perhaps," Michael Connolly observed, "the president could reunite Massachusetts Whigs, as well as a bickering nation, around the miracle of railroads."

The Boston jubilee was the culmination of twenty years of breathtaking technological progress.

The first shovelful of earth was moved in the Massachusetts public railroad system in 1831, a locomotive engine was first introduced in 1834, and the earliest completed lines—or "roads" in the contemporaneous terminology—opened for travel in 1835 (the Boston & Providence in June and the Boston & Worcester in July). A hundred million dollars in both state and private investment (the equivalent of more than 10 billion dollars today), and twelve hundred miles of track later, Boston and Massachusetts were the indisputable leaders in rail travel and commerce. Within a radius of sixty miles from the State House, more than 1 million people resided, nearly all of whom were in convenient proximity to railways that connected with Boston. Seven major rail lines served Boston, "diverging irregularly to all the points of the compass, except on that side which fronts on the ocean," the City Council report pointed out. All the roads were constructed upon a uniform track gauge, meaning rail carriages could be transferred from line to line when necessary, to move passengers and freight. In his circular to Boston citizens promoting the Railroad Jubilee, Mayor Bigelow announced that in 1850 alone, 9.5 million passengers and 2.5 million tons of freight traveled over Massachusetts rail lines alone.

Some rail lines began offering reduced fares for short, daily trips between Boston and neighboring or nearby towns, which provided people the opportunity to work in the city and live outside it; so long as passengers carried no luggage, they were charged "commuted fares" which gave way to the term "commuter." Historian Charles Kennedy pointed out that the first Boston commuter service began in 1839, between Boston and Dedham, part of the Boston & Providence line's service. The traffic was light; in fact, for a time, the train consisted of a single coach that was hooked onto the main-line trains, and the cost was still too high for everyday workers to travel by rail. By the mid-1840s, when the Boston & Maine built its own tracks into Boston, "it immediately assumed the leadership in promoting the development of suburbs by lowering its fares," Kennedy noted. The number of Boston commuters multiplied. One reporter estimated that by 1848, one-fifth of Boston's businesspeople lived in the suburbs and commuted by rail. In 1855 the Boston & Maine estimated the number of commuter "season-ticket holders" at sixty-five hundred, with more people commuting over B&M than any other road in Boston.

But the true measure of Boston's rail success was the role it could now play in moving cargo to and from the Great Lakes, up and down the East Coast, and, with its port access, to and from England and Europe, establishing the city as a regional and national transportation hub and a potential commercial juggernaut. "We are now about to realize," Mayor Bigelow noted, "the full benefits of these great enterprises, in the perfecting of which we have expended so much capital." Estimates put the imports and exports of the Great Lakes harbors alone at more than $200 million in 1851, a figure that officials believed would double in six years. Goods shipped to and from Canada topped $50 million that year. Custom House records showed that merchandise shipped to Canada for the six months ending June 30, 1851, quadrupled that of the six months ending January 1, 1851.

And Boston possessed other advantages to augment its new railroad muscle. "Her harbor is one of the finest in the world," Bigelow pointed out. "Her wharves and storage accommodations are equal, if not superior, to those of any other city, and capable of indefinite extension…the enterprise and integrity of her merchants are well known. The lines of railway to which we have alluded, all centre in her and radiate from her." Cargo from Liverpool, England, could reach Montreal in twelve days, using Boston as the transfer point between ship and rail.

Further, Bigelow added, the fact that the St. Lawrence Seaway was made impassable by ice for five months of the year, and Boston Harbor was virtually always open, "must make Boston…the port of entry for the Canadas, thus opening to us a business, the extent of which we have not begun to realize."

Bigelow spoke for many Bostonians when he added: "It seems to us, then, that Boston has every facility for becoming a great exporting as well as importing city."

While city fathers organized the jubilee mainly to celebrate Boston's railroad leadership, it wasn't just railroads that captured the imaginations of residents. Faster steamer shipping from England to Boston was one accomplishment, but by the time of the jubilee in 1851, Boston was basking in the recent success of another kind of vessel: Donald McKay's sleek, speedy clipper ships, constructed in his East Boston yard.

The clippers marked a giant leap forward in American shipping. Capable of sustained speed of more than twelve knots, they were faster than traditional ships, which averaged between six and eight knots, making them ideal to transport cargo and passengers more cost-effectively from the East Coast to the gold fields of California and other West Coast ports of call.

One of McKay's clippers, *Flying Cloud*, had riveted the world during the summer of 1851, when it set a new world's record sailing from New York to San Francisco: eighty-nine days, twenty-one hours, around Cape Horn at the tip of South America, whose treacherous seas and high winds often destroyed ships or delayed them for weeks. When McKay finished building *Flying Cloud* in April of 1851, the *Boston Daily Atlas* reported that "her admirers are sanguine that she will outsail any vessel in the world," a prediction that was validated when *Flying Cloud* dropped anchor in San Francisco on the morning of August 31. East Coast papers trumpeted the voyage as evidence of "Yankee superiority" in shipbuilding and ship handling.

McKay's precision-run East Boston shipyard was yet another tribute to Boston's craftsmanship, propensity for progress, and dedication to leadership. "The rush to complete the orders for the new clippers made each day a ritual of controlled chaos," author David W. Shaw described. "Most every man working on the ships appreciated the magnitude of the building and worked all the harder at turning trees into vessels of unparalleled swiftness."

It was less than three weeks after *Flying Cloud's* record-setting voyage that President Fillmore joined Boston officials and citizens to celebrate the city's rail and steamer ship achievements—Boston was a city that now boasted seven rail lines, five bridges, and two ferries that transported tens of thousands of people in and out of its borders every day, and a commercial hub that would serve millions of others on both sides of the Atlantic. Fillmore was not exaggerating when he told the Massachusetts legislature on the afternoon of the jubilee's first day: "It is a gratification to me to be permitted to look into the institutions of this State, the most flourishing, perhaps, of any in the Union."

Fillmore also lauded Massachusetts's accomplishments in transportation as fostering a national identity. The state had "stretched out its railroads to the North and invited her Commerce," he had said, "and is now pouring tribute into your lap." In so doing, the State would enjoy "rich blessings," not only financially, but through the ability to rapidly spread her knowledge and assimilate with new people and new geographic territories. In addition, Fillmore told the assembly, other states could take a lesson from Massachusetts's ingenuity. "You have taught sister States that although you do not possess the power of inviting commerce by canals, you can yet stretch forth your iron arms, reach the remotest cities of the Union, and bring hither their wealth and their productions."

Cloudless skies, warm breezes, and even larger crowds marked the Railroad Jubilee's festivities on the second and third days. Among the highlights was the arrival of Canadian leader James Bruce, Lord Elgin, the governor general of British North America, and his entourage, in the late afternoon of the second day. The Canadians were invited on behalf of the mayor and governor by a contingent of Boston dignitaries who visited Canada prior to the jubilee. On the morning of day two, Fillmore joined city, state, and federal dignitaries in a massive Boston Harbor procession of ships, "one of the most beautiful and exciting regattas ever witnessed in Massachusetts Bay." At just after 5:00 p.m., Lord Elgin arrived by train, where Mayor Bigelow welcomed him to "our festival [which] may be considered, in some sort, as the celebration of a conjugal union between Canada and the Ocean."

Lord Elgin met President Fillmore at the historic Revere House, and later Mayor Bigelow hosted a dinner at his mansion on Temple Street and then a grand military ball at Union Hall. The evening was capped with an exhibition of fireworks in front of the Revere House in honor of President Fillmore and Lord Elgin. Thousands of residents watched the display and thousands more enjoyed a second brilliant fireworks show that originated in East Boston.

On the third day, a giant parade—eleven divisions' worth of brass bands, military brigades, and prominent guests—marched through Boston, beginning at City Hall on School Street, winding its way north down Tremont, Court, and Cambridge streets to Haymarket Square, and then wheeling onto Blackstone, through South Market onto State Street, then Washington, Dover, and Tremont, before entering the Common at the corner of Park Street. Boston streets had been cleared of carriage traffic and sprinkled with water to tamp down dust and grime. Sidewalks were jammed with spectators, "compact yet perfectly orderly," as were virtually every window, balcony, and portico, and even many roofs. Organizers estimated the length of the procession at three and a half miles and claimed it took two hours for the entire parade to pass any given point.

The procession offered Boston an opportunity to strut its transportation leadership and provided its merchant community a chance to voice its business acumen and its support for the Union. Virtually every building was adorned with banners and signs welcoming President Fillmore (who, recovering from a mild ailment, watched the parade from a window of the Revere House, but did not participate), proclaiming loyalty to the Union, celebrating the trading link between the United States and Canada, or embracing the virtues of railroads. One Dover Street business display featured a representation of a steam engine, with the inscription: "The Great Peace Maker—Steam Power, One of the Powers That Be." On Washington Street, where colorful flags and streamers covered stores and businesses, one plain white flag captured the essence of the jubilee with the words, "Boston and Canada United, 1851."

Boston's vibrant merchant community was on display in the "Procession of Trades," including more than fifty separate groups, each representing a branch of industry. Iron workers, hatters, lathe turners, bookbinders, express men, riggers, carriage makers, and bakers; masons, carpenters, house painters, and bellows makers; upholsterers, printers, granite cutters, and silver smiths—all paraded carrying signs and banners and examples of their work.

The attitude of the marchers was best reflected by one banner that draped a carriage driven by a furniture maker: "There's no such word as can't."

A century before the word "marketing" came to mean the promotion of a cause or a business, Boston used the Railroad Jubilee to showcase its offerings to potential trading partners. It did not matter that Massachusetts was burdened with "sterile soil, a rugged surface, a stern climate, and a deficiency of navigable streams," Bigelow said. "Our iron pathways are our rivers, and they more than compensate for the deficiency of natural channels." Railroads were far superior to waterways and marked the way of the future, according to Bigelow. Water transport was subject to the whims of nature; railroads provided far more control over the movement of goods and people. And with the completion of the Boston–Great Western–Canadian lines, railroads rolled into Boston "laden with the products of a continent."

As night closed over the city on September 19, 1851, the final day of Boston's Railroad Jubilee, thousands of Bostonians roamed the streets, still celebrating the historic event. Railroad connections to the Great Lakes and Canada meant that Boston had established itself as a leading importer and exporter of passengers and goods, which in turn would drive its economic might, cultural influence, and political power. In a speech to a Boston audience seven years earlier, Ralph Waldo Emerson had envisioned railroads becoming "a magician's rod in its power to evoke the sleeping energies of land and water." Now, with Boston's ability to harness the power of railroads from the Atlantic shore to Montreal, Emerson's metaphor seemed apt.

But it was more than that. The railroads symbolized the city's promise. It was the beginning of the second half of the nineteenth century, and the Boston Railroad Jubilee had ushered in a new era of technological achievement in which Boston was at the vanguard.

—ꟽ—

Bostonians relied on locomotive-powered speed and efficiency to reach beyond their borders, but in the years following the Railroad Jubilee, they turned to a different source to provide the power for another kind of railroad system that revolutionized transportation *within* the city limits—the horse.

With the success of long-distance rail transportation and Boston's population growth as their inspiration, investors rushed to form street railway companies—or horse railways as they were commonly called—in which horse-drawn carriages (known as "horsecars") rode along tracks laid upon city streets. Each railway was incorporated by special act of the legislature; each charter granted specific privileges in the streets and authorized the city to impose certain restrictions. For example, the Union Railway, chartered in 1855, provided horse-railroad service from Bowdoin Square in Boston to the Cambridge-Watertown line. The company leased the roads for ten years at a cost of twenty-five thousand dollars per year, according to its first annual report. The Cambridge Railroad Company, chartered in 1853, operated a line from Bowdoin Square to Harvard Square for the same annual cost. The Metropolitan Railroad Company laid most of its track in the downtown center, commencing near the Granary Burial Ground and then proceeding along Tremont, Washington, and Boylston streets; but it also stretched its lines along the Washington Street "neck" that connected Boston with Roxbury, and provided service to the South End, Roxbury Crossing, and the Roxbury Post Office beyond Dudley Street.

Between 1852 and 1888, when Boston first electrified its street railroad and trolley system, companies laid more than 560 miles of track for the horse railroads, according to Walter S. Allen, who served as secretary to the Special Street Railway Commission of 1897.

The horse railways transformed Boston from a city made up almost exclusively of pedestrians to a growing metropolis that soon encompassed the independent towns of Roxbury, Dorchester, and West Roxbury, as well as Cambridge, Brookline, Chelsea, and other nearby towns. (Prior to the horse railways, a small and mostly affluent proportion of the population owned private carriages; similarly, the horse-drawn omnibus, an urban version of the stagecoach, held few passengers and was very expensive.) "This continuous expansion of surface transportation had a cumulative effect upon the city," historian Sam Warner noted. "The pace of suburbanization, at first slow, went forward with increasing acceleration, until by the 1890s, it attained proportions of a mass movement."

In addition to consumer demand, another factor that drove the formation of the horse railroads was the rapid return on investment for entrepreneurs. Speculators were used to waiting a long time to realize profits on large-scale land-use projects. "To real estate men, the simple procedure of placing a coach on iron rails seemed a miraculous device for the promotion of out-of-town property," Warner said. Companies scrambled for franchises, granted by the Boston Board of Aldermen, and for charters of incorporation granted by the legislature.

As with any new transportation technology, the horse railroads had their problems. Safety and congestion were paramount concerns, as Boston's downtown streets were simply too narrow to carry all the needed cars. But despite early snags, the horse railroads provided the template for mass transit in Boston, only the second city in the country to benefit from the concept (New York's first horse railroad began operating in 1852, a year before Boston's). Within a few years, Sam Warner noted, the main streets of the old city "had become the new horsecar thoroughfares."

Besides changing the face of transportation in Boston, the horse railroads allowed Bostonians to move more easily within the city, and to live outside of Boston's borders and work in the city. This drove up the cost of property along the horsecar lines, resulting in a real estate boom in Boston. Wealthy investors enjoyed this surge, but more moderate earners who could not afford homes downtown were forced to move into the towns of Dorchester, Roxbury, and West Roxbury, or into the fledgling rural communities that surrounded Boston. Meanwhile, poor immigrants were flooding into Boston's destitute neighborhoods, such as the North End, and the horse railroads provided the transportation that permitted them to work at locations across the city. Indeed, the horse railroads also helped change the demographic face of Boston.

In the fall of 1851, one man came to represent that changing demographic face. He was not well known at first, though he eventually captured a few headlines as well as the imagination of the city. Some supported his cause, most did not. A broad cross-section of the population feared him, or more accurately, feared what he represented.

In the annals of Boston history, he has long become a footnote. But he began a seismic cultural, social, and political shift that would redefine Boston for decades. In a city of hallowed names—Adams, Revere, and Hancock; Longfellow, Emerson, and Thoreau; Garrison, Douglass, and Higginson—his hardly bespoke prominence or accomplishment.

But he *was* a pioneer.

And Bostonians would feel the full impact of Barney McGinniskin's trailblazing for years to come.

CHAPTER 3

The Irrepressible Irish

The strongest wind cannot stagger a Spirit...A just man's purpose cannot be split on any material rock, but itself will split rocks till it succeeds.

—*Henry David Thoreau, on the perseverance of the Irish*

OCTOBER 6, 1851. When members of the Boston Board of Aldermen approved Barney McGinniskin's petition—or more accurately, Mayor Bigelow's petition on behalf of McGinniskin—they knew their decision would generate great controversy. A small percentage of Bostonians would agree with their actions, but most would condemn the vote unequivocally.

Controversy was one thing; it could be anticipated and managed. What the aldermen could not know, though, was the far-reaching historic implications of their decision (had they an inkling of what the future would bring, they almost certainly would have enthusiastically denied the petition). These ramifications would not become evident overnight, though Bostonians certainly recognized immediately that significant change was afoot in their city; but the near-unanimous vote (there was one dissenter) of the Board of Aldermen represented the kind of watershed moment that forever changes a community's face, personality, and direction.

Though monumental in its symbolism, the aldermen's action was described simply and routinely: the board confirmed Mayor Bigelow's nomination of Barney McGinniskin as the first person of Irish heritage ever selected as a Boston police officer.

It was a decision that reverberated throughout Boston in 1851, and over the next fifty years, would redefine the city's power structure.

Forty-two-year-old Bernard "Barney" McGinniskin was many things, none of them extraordinary or newsworthy: an immigrant who had lived in Boston for more than twenty years; a former driver of a horse-drawn omnibus; a grain-store employee working for one of Boston's leading merchants; a Catholic; a resident of the North End. But after the aldermen's vote on a fall evening in 1851, he added the ground-breaking designation of "first police officer of Irish descent" to his biography, which thrust him into a debate about the city's future, helped him achieve iconic status among thousands of Irish who had arrived during the past decade, and eventually redefined the reputation of, and thus the expectations for, his entire ethnic group.

Like many of his countrymen, McGinniskin's road was not an easy one; not only was he Irish, a difficult-enough handicap at the time, but his nomination was wrapped in a political maelstrom. The Whig ascendancy in Massachusetts had been broken in the state election of 1850, and further eroded with Daniel Webster's seventh of March speech supporting the Fugitive Slave Law and Thomas Sims's return to slavery; this resulted in a controlling coalition of Democrats and Free-Soilers in the legislature. While statewide the Whig Party was peril-ously close to collapse, Boston Whigs still held the mayor's office and a majority of Boston's Common Council (the "lower house" in the city's bicameral legislative structure) and Board of Aldermen. Boston Whigs believed that conservative Irish Democrats—who opposed aboli-tionism and were unhappy with the reform movement—might be persuaded to join an opposing alliance. Whether it would be called Whiggery or something else was immaterial. "As part of the intended *rapprochement*," historian Roger Lane concluded, "it was proposed, in June of 1851, to add an Irishman to the police."

A number of businessmen signed a petition on McGinniskin's be-half, and Mayor Bigelow asked City Marshal Francis Tukey to conduct a background check, which Tukey did on June 2, 1851, just weeks after the marshal had mustered the militia to escort Thomas Sims back to slavery. A week later, after interrogating McGinniskin, Tukey reported back that the Irishman "has a family, has been in this country 22 years, and ... has the reputation of being a temperate and quiet man." Bigelow nominated McGinniskin to the force in September, and the Board of

Aldermen gave its preliminary approval on September 19; a lone alderman asked for reconsideration for the October 6 meeting on the
grounds that McGinniskin was a "poor Irish specimen, was intemperate, and that his appointment had been smuggled through the Board."

Mayor Bigelow delivered a stinging rebuke to this argument. In
a speech later reported as far away as London, the mayor noted that
the motion for reconsideration was made "on the grounds that it is a
dangerous precedent to appoint a foreigner to stations of such trust."
Yet, Bigelow pointed out, the city was represented in the legislature
by persons "born on the other side of the ocean." Bigelow himself had
served in the General Court with two Irishmen, "and both possessed,
in a remarkable degree, the confidence of the people, who elected
them to many offices of important trust." Moreover, the city crier,
David Hill, a veteran of the Mexican War, had been appointed without reference to his Irish birth, as had the late constable Michael Ri-
ley. Recalling to memory a French hero of the American Revolution,
Bigelow admonished: "An American who cherishes the narrow prejudice referred to should blush at teaching his children to honor the
name of Lafayette, as being next to that of the Father of his country."
McGinniskin, Bigelow pointed out, "presents recommendations from
some of the best men in our community," and based on Tukey's inves-
tigation, "he stands the scrutiny of our lynx-eyed City Marshal."

Nonetheless, in the weeks after McGinniskin's appointment, and
even after he began work on November 3, it was Tukey who became
the leader in the fight against the Irishman joining the police force; he
did so in defiance of the mayor and apparently as a spokesman for the
force. "Although it was true that Irishmen had served the city earlier,
the men were convinced that their own department was something
different," Roger Lane wrote. And while Tukey's men often aided the
residents of Irish districts with gifts of firewood and other necessities,
and organized a regular charity for the benefit of poor Irish residents,
"the gap between a rough compassion and acceptance onto the force
was not easily bridged."

In an open letter to the press, published on the day of the state elections, Tukey objected to McGinniskin's credentials, calling him a
threat to the status of every other member of the police force. He
was a "common cabman" from Ann Street in the North End, one of

the most notorious locations for brothels, rough taverns, and crime. (Ann Street was later changed to North Street as residents sought to alter the neighborhood's reputation.) Ten years earlier, he had been convicted of a criminal offense as a participant in a brawl at St. Mary's Church on Endicott Street in the North End. And although Tukey denied any prejudice, he objected to McGinniskin's "outrageously Irish" behavior upon arriving for work for the first time on the afternoon of November 3, announcing himself to the night force as "Barney McGinniskin, fresh from the bogs of Ireland!"

Tukey's protests notwithstanding, his objections also appeared personal in nature. McGinniskin was both an Irishman and a former omnibus driver, and Tukey had had problems with both since his appointment as city marshal in 1846.

Poor Irish immigrants who had flooded the city in the wake of the Irish famine in the late 1840s accounted for numerous petty crimes such as thievery, public drunkenness, disorderly conduct, and assault, and Tukey was involved in apprehending many of the miscreants. During one brawl in the North End—"a disgraceful disturbance among the Irish population of that neighborhood," according to one press account—Tukey was knocked down several times and suffered an eye injury. The so-called Hamilton Street rioters were eventually sentenced to one year in prison for the assault on Tukey and two other police officers. On another occasion, Tukey paraded notorious Irish pickpocket John McDonald, handcuffed, before his officers in the station house and implored the police to watch for him in the future, and to roust him from the city if they spotted him in a crowd. Tukey also objected to the blatant disregard on the part of the Irish for the state's laws prohibiting the sale of liquor on the Sabbath. One Sunday, armed with warrants, Tukey approached the Jefferson House tavern on Ann Street. He found a notice posted on the front door that read: "This establishment is closed until Monday. P.S.—Those whom we have agreed to supply with WATER will be served at the pump, at the back door." Tukey proceeded around back and found the "pump" in full operation, providing beer and liquor to dozens of patrons. He ordered the tavern closed immediately.

Tukey had little patience for omnibus drivers either, whom he often accused of transporting customers intent on breaking laws and of recklessly driving their teams through city streets. In 1846, for ex-

ample, Tukey investigated the claims of two passengers, one carrying
nine hundred dollars and one sixty dollars, who took a cab to a house
of "ill-fame...where they were furnished with champagne till they
were no longer masters of themselves," according to one account. The
man with the smaller amount of money was robbed by prostitutes;
"the other, more cunning than his friend, had preserved his money by
concealing it in his boot before his brains had been stolen from him."
Tukey investigated the case, cited the cabdriver for deliberately transporting passengers to an illegal brothel, and arrested and locked up
the prostitutes. On another occasion, two years later, Tukey spotted
an unattended omnibus on a busy street. He climbed into the driver's
seat himself and was attempting to guide the horses, when the team
"took off at a more rapid pace than the law allows." Tukey cited the
Irish driver, but the driver turned around and entered a complaint
against Tukey for "fast driving." In a public blow to his ego and his
authority, Tukey pleaded guilty and was fined one dollar plus court
costs, for a total payment of four dollars and fifty-five cents.

McGinniskin's ethnic heritage and work history as a cabman
made him unfit for duty, in Tukey's eyes, and the marshal refused to
assign duties to the new officer. McGinniskin quickly sought public
support in his efforts to counter Tukey's tactics. In a lengthy press
statement, he reminded Boston residents that Tukey had offered a
favorable report on his character when Bigelow asked for the background check. He did not deny his "from the bogs of Ireland" remark
when he entered the police station, but took issue with Tukey's char-
acterization that he had uttered the phrase in an "impudent, insulting
manner, evidently with the intention of provoking a quarrel." On the
contrary, McGinniskin said, "I did so in a good-humored way, with
the intention of placing myself at once on a free and friendly footing
with my fellow members of the night police." His fellow officers must
have agreed, McGinniskin said; "the manner in which I was received
indicated that my greeting was taken in the kind and good-natured
sense in which it was intended." As for his arrest at St. Mary's a decade
earlier, McGinniskin argued that he was attempting to quell a fight
that broke out when police apprehended him. "For this I was indeed
tried and fined ten dollars by the Court," he said, "but this...affords
no evidence that my motives were not good or that I am of a riotous
or quarrelsome disposition." Of far greater import, he said, was his
long work history and the numerous recommendations he had re-

ceived from prominent Boston businesspeople. "These facts I regard as sufficient to repel the charges against me, and to vindicate my character," McGinniskin wrote.

For the next six weeks, both sides were at an impasse. Tukey refused to assign McGinniskin to work, and without authority, essentially removed him from the police force. Mayor Bigelow had been defeated in the November election, and the marshal was hoping the new mayor, former Common Councilor Benjamin Seaver (whom the police had supported en masse), would officially fire McGinniskin after inauguration day in January. But Seaver resented the blatant politics Tukey employed; upon taking office, he vetoed Tukey's decision, and ordered the marshal to reinstate and assign McGinniskin. The *Boston Atlas* saluted Seaver for standing up against the "usurpation of the City Marshal, who clearly has no more right to discharge a police officer than the City Treasurer or Physician...Marshal Tukey is an efficient and competent officer, but he should remember that he is a subordinate officer of the Government."

And so by January of 1852, Barney McGinniskin—Irishman and Catholic—was a working member of the Boston police force. He not only sought his appointment, but when it was challenged by the city marshal, he fought back and won.

In so doing, McGinniskin injected hope among his Irish brethren in Boston, a people who had known mostly despair in the past several years. For the Boston Irish, McGinniskin's appointment was a signal that the poor and downtrodden could prevail, despite enormous odds. For Boston itself, McGinniskin's achievement represented something else: the beginning of a new era.

Well before they reached Boston, the Irish had journeyed to what must have seemed the gates of hell. Most had their characters forged in a crucible of want; most felt the brush of death's fingers before escaping their tortured homeland, and then suffered terrible hardship and deprivation on their voyage across the Atlantic. The near-inhuman conditions they endured on their journey to Boston is an essential component of the Irish experience in the city—their ordeal instilled in them a deep resolve to overcome the obstacles that awaited them on their arrival.

Barney McGinniskin journeyed from Ireland in 1829, among the earliest Irish immigrants to land in the New World. But most of his countrymen came to the United States in the decade before his appointment as a police officer, and the majority of those crossed the ocean just a few years prior to 1851, desperate to claw their way from the scourge of starvation brought on by the great famine. A blighted potato crop coupled with the British government's apathy, outright hostility, or active genocide—depending on one's historical interpretation and perspective—produced six terrible years between 1845 and 1851, during which more than 1 million Irish men, women, and children died from the effects of prolonged hunger and disease, and 1 million more fled across the ocean on contagion-ridden ships.

The wretched conditions and misery inside Ireland bordered on the incomprehensible, yet help explain both the desperation and fortitude of Irish peasants when they arrived in the United States. Under Ireland's corrupt landlord-tenant system, Irish peasants were virtually enslaved to wealthy British landowners; they worked the land and grew the crops, and turned most food and any profits over to the landlords. After several years of the potato-crop failure, most Irish families were unable to pay their rent—hundreds of thousands were evicted from their homes and left to wander the countryside in a hopeless search for food. "Ejectment is tantamount to a sentence of death by slow torture," stated a special report to the British House of Commons in 1846. Turned off the land, evicted peasants wandered "begging, miserable, and turbulent," according to author Cecil Woodham-Smith in *The Great Hunger*, his classic history of the famine.

Disease and death ravaged the country. Irish peasants succumbed and died by the thousands on country roads and in ditches, in the slums and alleyways of towns, in the bogs, on the hillsides, in hovels, and often in ground-holes they had dug in a vain search for grubs to eat or as protection against the elements. "They died of starvation, of dysentery, of typhus and relapsing fever, of hypothermia brought on by exposure to wind and rain," explained author John Percival. "The corpses in some places were so numerous that they were loaded onto carts and dumped into coffinless pits. In remoter areas the dead were never buried; their bodies rotted into the earth or were torn to pieces by dogs."

Sir Charles Trevelyan, assistant secretary of the British Treasury and the civil servant in charge of famine relief in the United Kingdom, doubted the seriousness of the famine and refused to alter the government's policy of prohibiting exports of wheat and other grains, which he feared would create food shortages within England. Yet Ireland was part of the United Kingdom. Would food sent to Ireland qualify as *exports?* Trevelyan, whose philosophy also included a limited view of the responsibilities of government in general, believed the answer was yes. "This perception, when it became widely known in Ireland, made a nonsense of the idea of equal partnership between one part of the United Kingdom and another," John Percival noted. "Some parts, particularly the English parts, were more equal than others."

Ironically, much of the food that Ireland was able to grow was exported back to England, demanded by English landowners of Irish property to sell on the open market. A Limerick merchant and ship-owner, Francis Spaight, recorded the exports flowing through the port of Limerick from June of 1846 to May of 1847; these included more than 387,000 barrels of oats and 46,000 barrels of wheat. "Perhaps the most disgraceful aspect of the Famine was that in each of its six years there was probably enough food exported out of Ireland to sustain the nation, certainly enough to have saved the million who died," author Edward Laxton wrote. "The bulk of the agriculture produce, most of the cattle, butter, wheat, barley, vegetables, went to markets in England. They were not disposed towards introducing food tariffs, and the starving Irish could not afford the market prices." Years later, Dublin-born playwright George Bernard Shaw highlighted the perverseness of the situation, and summed up much of the hatred the Irish felt for the English, with this exchange in his play *Man and Superman:*

> MALONE   My father died of starvation in Ireland in the Black 47. Maybe you've heard of it?
> VIOLET   The Famine?
> MALONE   No, the starvation. When a country is full of food and exporting it, there can be no famine.

As blight destroyed the dietary mainstay for half the Irish population, the British government's responses were woefully inadequate. (Trevelyan took his family to Italy on holiday at one point during the crisis.) This, despite the reports of British officials dispatched to Ireland to assess the famine situation. "I confess myself unmanned by the intensity and extent of the suffering," one military inspector wrote. "I witnessed more especially among the women and little children, crowds of whom were scattered over the turnip fields like a flock of famishing crows, devouring the raw turnips, mothers half naked, shivering in the snow and sleet, uttering exclamations of despair while their children were screaming with hunger. I am a match for anything else I may meet with here, but this I cannot stand." A British magistrate writing to the Duke of Wellington described the heartbreak of walking into an Irish village that appeared deserted, only to find starving peasants shivering in corners of shacks and hovels. "In the first, six famished and ghastly skeletons, to all appearances dead, were huddled in a corner on some filthy straw, their sole covering what seemed a ragged horsecloth," Nicholas Cummins wrote. "I approached with horror, and found by low moaning that they were still alive—they were in fever, four children, a woman, and what had once been a man. It is impossible to go through the detail." His letter was published in the *Times* on Christmas Eve, 1846. Other peasants stumbled from their dark hiding places, and within minutes, Cummins reported, "I was surrounded by at least 200 such phantoms, such frightful specters as no words can describe, [suffering] either from famine or from fever. Their demoniac yells are still ringing in my ears and their horrible images are fixed upon my brain."

The winter of 1847–48 was one of the most severe in Irish memory: heavy snow fell in early November and continued for months; icy gales and bitter cold gripped the British Isles. The hunt for food became even more desperate for Irish peasants, who struggled through deep snowdrifts and impassable roads. In addition, the British government passed the Poor Law Extension Act of 1847, which put the burden of paying for what little relief there was forthcoming from England on to Irish landlords. The landlord's inability or unwillingness to pay heavy relief taxes imposed by the new Poor Law led to another wave of peasant evictions.

"Without land to work, firewood to burn, or food to eat, the poor people of Ireland died by the tens of thousands of hunger, exposure, and disease," historian Thomas O'Connor wrote. "For many, especially in the Catholic southern counties where the devastation was the worst, there seemed to be no future at all. The land was ruined; food was unobtainable; work was unavailable; and eviction was inescapable."

—ɯ—

If the British government's response to the Irish catastrophe represented moral negligence, the city of Boston, with its already significant Irish Catholic population, reacted in much the opposite way;
its residents quickly demonstrated their beneficence on behalf of the
Irish people. Boston Catholics donated more than $150,000 to famine
relief, according to Thomas O'Connor, as Bishop John Bernard Fitzpatrick called upon his congregation to share their "last loaf of bread"
with those sad souls whose "wild shrieks of famine and despair" could
be heard across the Atlantic.

Non-Catholics made substantial contributions to the Irish people, too. In a first-of-its-kind request, a group of Boston businessmen
petitioned the United States Congress on February 22, 1847—the
anniversary of George Washington's birthday—to allow the use of
certain warships to deliver provisions and food to famine-stricken
Ireland. Congress gave its assent, and one of the ships it authorized
was the *Jamestown*, a sloop based at the Charlestown Navy Yard. The
Jamestown was commanded by forty-three-year-old Captain Robert
B. Forbes of Jamaica Plain, a member of one of Boston's best-known
families. Boston merchants and Boston abolitionists joined together
to organize fund-raising drives, and on March 17, Saint Patrick's Day,
members of the predominately Irish Laborers Aid Society of Boston,
volunteering their time, began loading more than eight thousand barrels of meal, bread, beans, corn, beef, pork, peas, potatoes, rice, wheat,
fish, and clothing and other supplies, valued at nearly thirty-six thousand dollars.

On Sunday, March 28, at 8:30 a.m., amid the hearty cheers of hundreds on the dock and "with a fine breeze at the northwest and clear,
cold weather," Forbes sailed the 157-foot *Jamestown* out of the Navy
Yard, her stores laden with cargo, her twenty-two deck guns having
been removed to allow more room for the humanitarian aid, her three
topsails unfurled. From her mizzen peak flew the Stars and Stripes
and from her royal mast snapped a white flag with a green shamrock
at its center. Her destination was County Cork. The *Boston Investigator* reported with pride: "There is something so great and honorable in
the fact that this country, besides its very numerous individual contributions for the assistance of the suffering Irish, has sent out a national
ship loaded with provisions for their relief, that we must place it on

the record!" Indeed, historian James Tertius de Kay wrote a century and a half later, "To this day, the resolution authorizing the use of [government-owned] ships by private individuals remains unique in the history of Congress."

After snow, sleet, dense fog, and a succession of "rainy, dirty weather and variable winds," Captain Forbes reported that the *Jamestown* reached Cork's outer harbor, at the town of Cove, on April 12, 1847, "exactly 15 days and 3 hours from the Navy Yard, Charlestown, without having lost a rope yarn," to the cheers of throngs along the shore, while an Irish band played "Yankee Doodle." Forbes and his crew were greeted by a jubilant reception committee "before the anchor had fairly bitten the soil." The next morning, the *Jamestown* was towed to the dock, dwarfed by the hills of Cork seemingly rising from the water, as men in small boats shouted their greetings, while on shore, "the good people cheered and the ladies waved their muslin in welcome of our arrival." The *Cork Examiner* headlined its story: "Arrival of the Jamestown: American sloop of war in Cove with provisions for the destitute Irish." The paper reported that "the South of Ireland in particular, and the whole of Ireland in general" looked forward to *Jamestown's* arrival "with great anxiety." To the extent it could under the circumstances, "the town itself wore a most gay and exciting appearance, the quays and heights being thronged by thousands desirous to see and greet the illustrious stranger."

On Wednesday, the fourteenth, the *Jamestown* crew began to discharge her precious food cargo, and Forbes, escorted by a Catholic priest, ventured into Cork. He was stunned by what he saw. "I went…only a few steps out of one of the principal streets into a lane: the Valley of the Shadow of Death, was it? Alas no, it was the valley of death and pestilence itself," he wrote. "I saw enough in five minutes to horrify me; hovels crowded with the sick and dying…some called for water…and others for a dying blessing…we proceeded to a public soup kitchen where hundreds of spectres stood without; begging for some of the soup which I can readily conceive would be refused by well-bred pigs in America. Every corner of the street is filled with pale, careworn creatures, the weak leading and supporting the weaker; women assail you at every turn with famished babies imploring alms."

The *Jamestown* remained in Ireland for more than a week and, its mission of mercy complete, arrived back in Boston on May 17, 1847.

While more than five thousand ships carried Irish emigrants away from their stricken home country during the great famine, the *Jamestown* from Boston was one of a handful that traveled in the other direction to bring relief. Forbes later wrote, "This expedition will be remembered in the history of philanthropy; and as the servant of the generous people of Boston, of Massachusetts, and parts of New England, who gave their mite to the alleviation of the suffering poor of…Ireland."

Despite the scenes of hunger and despair he had witnessed, Forbes was grateful for the role he played in helping the Irish peasants. Later in 1847, he wrote: "I shall ever look back on the voyage of the *Jamestown* as the happiest event of my life."

One act of mercy the *Jamestown* was not equipped to undertake was the transport of starving Irish back to Boston. Forbes had made that clear prior to the ship's departure for Ireland; the *Jamestown's* volunteer crew simply had no expertise in caring for the sick and starving, nor could he possibly take every person who wanted to escape the famine's clutches. And he simply would not make the decision about who would go and who would remain behind. "The ship will not take back any emigrants," Forbes insisted.

Those Irish who were able to scrape up fare for other voyages traveled to the New World in cramped, filthy, disease-infested ships; in many cases conditions were as bad aboard ship as they were in the ravaged country left behind. The vessels that carried these desperate travelers to British North America (Canada), New York, and Boston were labeled famine ships by some observers. Others referred to them, chillingly, as coffin ships.

On November 25, 1850, while traveling to America aboard the *Washington*, with more than nine hundred passengers, mostly Irish, on board, Vere Foster wrote the following: "Another child, making about 12 in all, died of dysentery for want of proper nourishing food and was thrown into the sea, sewn up, along with a great stone, in cloth." With no clergy on board to perform a funeral service, crew members sang a sailor's song and threw the child overboard "at the sound of the last word of the song, making use of it as a funeral dirge."

Foster was a wealthy philanthropist who took a special interest in the plight of the Irish emigrants. He had even helped several reach

America by paying their fares, according to author Edward Laxton. "Concerned about bad reports of emigrant travel, he resolved to discover for himself the quality of life aboard a famine ship," Laxton wrote. Foster kept a meticulous diary which he sent to a minister at the Board of Trade in London, and later published a helpful guidebook for emigrants that offered tips for surviving on board and on shore. But his efforts for political and social reforms on the ships fell short. "Famine emigrants continued to suffer at the hands of corrupt captains, owners, or agents," Laxton pointed out.

In one of the era's worst examples of criminal negligence, seventy-two Irish emigrants were killed—one Boston newspaper said "murdered"—on the night of December 1, 1848, on board the steamer *Londonderry*, transporting passengers from Sligo, Ireland, to Liverpool, for eventual passage to America. A violent storm rocked the ship, driving the 150 passengers below into the small forward cabin for protection; only one ventilation aperture provided air for the congested room. In a disastrous decision, one mate—in an attempt to protect the compartment from water rushing over the sides of the ship—closed the ventilation opening and nailed a piece of tarpaulin over it. The violence of the storm masked the screams of the passengers below as they began suffocating. When the storm finally passed, one mate went below and witnessed the "full nature of the catastrophe" according to one steerage passenger who had forced his way out of the fetid cabin. "There lay, in heaps, the living, the dying, and the dead, one frightful mass of mingled agony and death, a spectacle enough to appall the stoutest heart," he wrote. Men, women, and children were huddled together, "blackened with suffocation and distorted by convulsions…after some time the living were separated from the dead."

Nearly half of the ship's passengers had perished in the airless cabin, frantically climbing over each other as they tried to reach the aperture, tearing at the nailed door in vain as they attempted desperately to escape. "It was evident," the eyewitness reported, "that in the struggle, the poor creatures had torn the clothes from each other's backs, and even the flesh from each other's limbs."

A coroner's jury found *Londonderry's* captain, Alexander Johnstone, first mate Richard Hughes, and second mate Ninian Crawford guilty of manslaughter, and, according to one newspaper report, "expressed in the strongest terms, [the jury's] abhorrence of the inhuman conduct of the other seamen on board."

Despite the legal action in the *Londonderry* case, sailing conditions were rarely monitored, and Irish emigrants were often denied the food and water promised with the price of their tickets. Sickness and disease were rampant; the most lethal of these was typhus. While awaiting passage from Liverpool, thousands of Irish emigrants contracted the disease from infected lice, which infested the city's cheap lodging houses. Liverpool shared the distinction of being a "fever port"—though few realized it at the time—as did a number of Irish ports, notably Cork and Sligo, and this would have deadly consequences for Irish emigrants.

Crowded conditions on board the famine ships hastened the rapid spread of typhus and other afflictions. The ships became fever and disease factories. The allotted space for each adult was about eighteen inches of bed space; for children, about nine inches, according to John Percival. The cramped living conditions, coupled with the fact that people had no means of changing their clothing or their bedding, provided the ideal breeding conditions for the spread of body lice and typhus. "If one passenger had contracted the disease before he came on board, others soon caught it," Percival pointed out. "Typhus was often called 'ship fever' precisely because it was so common in these overcrowded and dirty conditions." On some ships the first deaths occurred within a few days at sea and multiplied as the voyage continued. Percival detailed the journey of the *Virginia* from Liverpool, on which a staggering 158 passengers died from typhus.

Dysentery also claimed many lives. Bad or undercooked food and contaminated water caused outbreaks of this disease on almost every ship. Most passengers had access to little more than a bucket for their waste. "When the hatches were closed, as they often were in heavy weather, the stench in the hold must have been appalling," Percival noted. "Conditions do not bear thinking about." Wrote one commissioner of emigration in the United States: "If crosses and tombs could be erected on the water, the whole route of the emigrant vessels from Europe to America would long since have assumed the appearance of a crowded cemetery."

Nonetheless, without interruption, westward these ships came to America and Canada. The British government tried to encourage emigration to its North American colonies by significantly reducing the price of a ticket to Canada in comparison to passage to the United States. But, while thousands of Irish emigrants did settle in

Canada, the majority had no desire to do so—their hatred of the British made settling in British North America repugnant to them. "The native Irishman had become convinced that no justice or opportunity could exist for him under the Union Jack," Cecil Woodham-Smith wrote. Or as one Irishman wrote from Boston: Canada represented little more than "a second edition of Ireland, with more room." Most Irish either boarded another ship from Canada to Boston or New York—they were often referred to as "two boaters"—or simply entered the United States by way of an overland route.

"With an almost frantic longing, they wished to go to the United States," Woodham-Smith wrote.

With disease rampant among Irish immigrants, Boston took precautions. The city required a bond from the ship's captain or the vessel's owner of one thousand dollars for each sick, aged, or incapable passenger. So great was the typhus fear that Boston often refused to allow ships carrying sick passengers to enter the harbor. In June of 1847, for example, city authorities turned away the British brig *Seraph*, from Cork; she had 118 cases of fever on board, and according to Woodham-Smith, her passengers were in such a state of starvation that the British Consul had to go down to the pier with supplies of food. When *Seraph* was ordered to St. John, New Brunswick, or some other British port, the passengers made a rush and tried to "insist on landing," but were driven back into the ship by Boston police and militia. In some cases, Boston required the captain to dispatch sick passengers at a Deer Island hospital before allowing the ship to dock at city wharves.

A Massachusetts Senate report noted that in January of 1847, one vessel carrying 657 immigrants—mostly Irish—came into port, and 60 people were immediately sent to Deer Island "in a very sick and filthy condition." Another 25 bodies, those of would-be immigrants who died during the voyage, were removed and given a pauper's burial.

It wasn't just criminal negligence, sickness, fever, and starvation that stamped the coffin ships with their gruesome name. Crews battled onboard fires and vicious North Atlantic storms, and, when ships began leaving Ireland year-round during the famine years, ice fields and icebergs became a terrifying reality.

One of the most heart-wrenching of these disasters occurred shortly after the *Ocean Monarch* left Mersey in September of 1848, when 173 Irish passengers perished, this time despite efforts on the part of the crew to save them. A few hours outside of port, a fire broke out in a belowdecks cabin; in less than five minutes flames had enveloped the stern. Captain James Murdoch pleaded for calm, but his orders could not be heard in the noise and confusion. Passengers fled from the stern and crowded in the forepart of the vessel, their "piercing, heart-rending shrieks for aid carried by the breeze across the dark blue waves," Murdoch's official statement read. Then the unthinkable occurred: passengers, many of them women with children in their arms, began jumping overboard to escape the flames. "They sunk to rise no more," Murdoch said. "Men followed their wives in a frenzy, and were lost." Groups of men, women, and children clung to each other in the water, but most could not swim and were swallowed by the ocean. "In vain did I entreat and beg of the passengers to be composed," Murdoch said. "I pointed out to them that there were several vessels around us, and that if they preserved order, they would all be saved—It was of no avail."

Murdoch tried to maneuver the ship to "get her head to the wind" and thus, if possible, confine the flames to the stern, but his efforts were useless. The foremast went over, snapped the fasteners of the boom, and carried the load of passengers who had gathered atop it into the water "amid the most heart-rending screams both of those on board and those in the water." Crew members managed to get two lifeboats prepared, but as their lashings were cut, the flames reached them and consumed both of them. "On seeing this, the passengers were more unmanageable than ever," Murdoch lamented. "The shrieks of terror and alarm baffle all description." More passengers jumped overboard and Murdoch could not stop them. "Seeing the awful sacrifice of life which was going on despite every effort which I made, I gave directions to throw overboard every movable article so that those who had left the ship might cling to them until help arrived."

A private yacht arrived first, lowered a lifeboat, and rescued as many passengers as possible. Murdoch ordered another group of passengers to jump overboard and cling to a wooden spar—a beam that supported the rigging—and this time many obeyed his instructions. "I was surrounded on all side by flames," he reported, "and seeing no possible chance of escape if I remained longer, I followed the spar

I had sent overboard." A half hour later, Murdoch and many other passengers—some in the water hugging wreckage and others still on the ship—were rescued by several ships that had steamed to the deadly scene. Frightened and freezing passengers were taken to Liverpool, where "they presented a sad and pitiable spectacle," Murdoch recalled. "Many...were almost in a state of nudity. Some had their heads bandaged, some their arms, legs, and other parts of their bodies bound up, having been injured by their contact with spars in the water, by knocking against boats, and in other ways."

The Liverpool mayor quickly put together a committee to raise funds for the emigrants who had lost everything when the *Ocean Monarch* went down. And, Murdoch pointed out, "the agents of the ship will provide a free passage for those steerage passengers wishing to proceed to America."

Fire was one hazard; ice another. Four ships carrying Irish emigrants went down after colliding with ice in 1849, and hundreds were killed, either drowned or crushed between ice floes. One of the most tragic of these was the sinking of the *Maria*, sailing from Limerick to Quebec in May of 1849, which hit an iceberg at night just fifty miles from the Canadian coast. She sank rapidly. Nine passengers jumped on to the ice as the ship went down and three crew members grabbed a lifeboat, but the remaining 109 passengers died. "The whole of her bows stove in and the next moment the sea was rushing into the hold," one newspaper account reported. "A piercing shriek was heard from below, but it was only for a few moments' duration, as the ship went down almost immediately." The daily shipping newspaper, *Lloyd's List*, reported in July of 1849: "The immense field of ice that has been encountered in and near the Gulf of St. Lawrence this season has not been equaled for many years." The paper noted that "scarcely five minutes" elapses from the moment a ship strikes ice to its foundering.

If the ice didn't get one of the emigrant ships, gale-force winds or hurricanes often did. On October 7, 1849, Massachusetts Bay recorded one of the period's greatest disasters when the brig *St. John*, traveling from Galway, Ireland, encountered a vicious storm as it approached Boston Harbor. The captain dropped anchor and attempted to ride the storm out. But its anchors failed to hold, and the ship was smashed on the rocks off the coast of Cohasset. The crew abandoned ship and left behind 120 passengers to fight for their lives, perhaps no more than a mile from land. Only 10 were able to survive by clinging to debris from the disintegrated ship.

Most of the bodies washed ashore at Cohasset Harbor, including those of Patrick Sweeney of Galway, his wife, and their nine children. Forty-five bodies were never identified and were buried in a mass grave in the Cohasset Central Cemetery. "As we passed the grave-yard, we saw a large hole," Henry David Thoreau wrote after a visit to see the shipwreck and its aftermath. "[It] was like a cellar, freshly dug there."

Thoreau was struck by the number of spectators searching for relatives, looking through bodies, examining the fragments of the wreck. "Some were lifting the lids of coffins and peeping under the cloths— for each body, with such rags as still adhered to it, was covered loosely with a white sheet," he wrote. Sometimes, Thoreau noted, there were two or more children or a parent and child in the same box. "On the lid would perhaps be written with red chalk, 'Bridget such-a-one and sister's child.'" Thoreau also commented on the irony of these emigrants, who had suffered so much already, losing their lives so close to their goal. "All their plans and hopes burst like a bubble! Infants by the score dashed on the rocks by the enraged Atlantic Ocean!" he wailed.

Yet Thoreau also captured the courage of the many Irish emigrants who survived the horror of the famine and the frightening conditions aboard the coffin ships to reach the New World. "The strongest wind cannot stagger a Spirit," he wrote after witnessing the aftermath of the *St. John* tragedy. "It is a Spirit's breath. A just man's purpose cannot be split on any material rock, but itself will split rocks till it succeeds."

Literally and otherwise, the Irish who settled in Boston after their perilous journeys eventually split tons of rock—and dug trenches, carved canals, laid rails, packed roads, sunk pilings, framed buildings, halved hills, hauled dirt, filled bays, expanded the city, and fought and died by the thousands as part of Massachusetts regiments in a bloody civil war that ultimately saved their adopted nation.

The Irish did not merely descend upon Boston; they *inundated* the city, a swarm of humanity that crammed every nook, cranny, cellar, tenement, and shanty in the North End and along other waterfront neighborhoods. For four defining years, 1846 through 1849, which encompassed the cruelest period of the great famine, enough Irish arrived in Boston to irrevocably alter the city's demographic and religious profile, and transform it from an influential but quaint large town to a growing and overcrowded ethnic city. It was the immigration pattern during these years that led to Barney McGinniskin's appointment as the first Irish police officer in Boston history in 1851.

According to the Report on the Census and Statistics, in the nine years prior to 1845, about fifty thousand emigrants arrived in Boston, two-thirds of them on ships and the others making the overland route from Canada; in 1845 foreign-born residents made up about one-third of Boston's overall population.

Then the numbers increased exponentially.

Between 1846 and 1849, one official Boston city report estimated, 125,000 foreigners arrived, three-quarters of whom were Irish laborers. By 1850, the City Census showed a total Boston population of 138,700, of whom 63,300, or 43 percent, were foreigners, the vast majority of them Irish. By the early summer of 1847, Boston was overrun with destitute Irish immigrants; "groups of poor wretches…resting their weary and emaciated limbs at the corners of the streets and in the doorways," reported the *Boston Transcript*. Some native Bostonians called the arrival of so many poor Irish the "Celtic locust swarm" and others despaired that the newcomers were transforming Boston into the "American Dublin." The Alien Commissioners in Boston expressed frustration at their inability to even count the teeming Irish accurately. "In a place like Boston it is exceedingly difficult to trace out the parentage and history of the foreign poor," they reported. "There are so many John Sullivans, Jerry Daileys, and William O'Briens, who are all made in the same mold." (Among the arrivals in 1847 was a young Irish farmer who left County Wexford with his wife and three children and landed in Boston on November 14. The immigrant's name was Patrick Kennedy and one of his many great-grandsons was to become the first Catholic president of the United States, John Fitzgerald Kennedy.)

The Irish immigrants were alien in every sense. Native Bostonians rejected their Catholicism, to be sure, but more than that, the thousands of poor, unskilled, famine-weary immigrants threatened the very social structure of Boston, defined by the wealthy urban Protestant aristocrats that Oliver Wendell Holmes had labeled Brahmins. As historian Thomas O'Connor pointed out, this made life for the Boston Irish uniquely difficult. Irish immigrants who traveled to Chicago, St. Louis, and other new cities of the West had the advantage of growing up with their cities. Those who settled in New York and Philadelphia lived among social, economic, and ethnic groups that were more diverse in their origins and more receptive in their attitudes. In Boston, the Irish confronted a homogeneous and solid social class that dominated the city's political and civic life. Dealing harshly with an Irish underclass was their way of fiercely clinging to power.

Influential Bostonians and a hostile press had little tolerance for the Irish newcomers. Thoreau initially believed the Irish were foolish, superstitious, and shiftless. The Reverend Theodore Parker, although a leading light in the abolitionist movement, found the Irish to be "idle, thriftless, poor, intemperate, and barbarian," more like a group of "wild bison" than human beings. Horrified Bostonians read of two stillborn infants found buried in a rubbish heap, placed there by Irish parents ignorant of American burial laws. They read of an increase in public drunkenness, assaults, and larceny, concentrated in Irish neighborhoods. The *Advertiser* expressed particular alarm over the increase in juvenile crime; most was committed by the children of Irish immigrants, the paper charged, "who imported their vile propensities and habits from across the water" and who were now passing them on to their "wretched offspring."

When the Irish were not portrayed in the press as drunken criminals, they were depicted as tragic souls or objects of morbid curiosity. The 1849 story about a young Irish laborer, John Scanlan, who was "killed instantly" and whose body was "mangled shockingly and cut in two" after he fell from a gravel train and slipped beneath its wheels, was illustrative of the macabre reportage of events involving the Irish; so too was an article that same year of a talented Massachusetts General Hospital doctor who "took from the stomach of an Irish girl...a tape worm forty-one feet and eleven inches in length."

And of course religious prejudice dogged the Irish. Papers warned of undue international influence, particularly from the papacy, and a surge of popery and "Romanism" in Boston. The *Boston Courier* warned its readers that politically active Catholics of foreign birth would vote "precisely as their spiritual guides shall dictate." The paper had blamed the election of James K. Polk in 1844 on the influence of Catholic priests who were part of a "well-connected scheme" among the Catholic powers in Europe to bring the United States "under subjection to the Holy See." Once members of the Know-Nothing Party took office in the mid-1850s, they put forth a program of "Temperance, Liberty, and Protestantism" for Massachusetts, which was, in the words of one House member, ready to eliminate "Rome, Rum, and Robbery." The new legislature made the reading of the Protestant Bible (King James Version) compulsory in all public schools, and several bills were passed to stop Catholics from burying their dead in public cemeteries.

In fact, it wasn't until 1859 that Boston officials allowed patients in Boston City Hospital to be attended to by a clergyman of their choosing; Catholic priests were finally allowed to visit patients, many of them Irish, who had formerly been denied this dignity.

Subject to such widespread contempt and hostility, the Irish crowded into ethnic enclaves whose squalor further appalled native Bostonians.

"The mason who finishes the cornice of the palace returns at night perchance to a hut not so good as a wigwam," Thoreau wrote. Dark tenements, rickety sheds, and filthy shanties were the deplorable places that the Irish called home. Indeed, the new arrivals built makeshift housing on any available plot of land. Before Paul Revere's house in the North End was restored, it was a tenement house, surrounded by other shabby tenements. By 1850, the North End averaged thirty-seven immigrants per dwelling, and in some houses in the Fort Hill neighborhood there were up to one hundred inhabitants in buildings of three to five stories. And the Irish didn't just live aboveground. In his classic work *Boston's Immigrants*, Oscar Handlin described the dank, rat-infested cellars without which the Irish population pouring into Boston could not have been housed. Often flooded during high tide, the North End cellars provided living quarters for thousands of Irish immigrants; one cellar eighteen feet square and five feet high housed eighteen persons, and the normal number of occupants ranged from five to fifteen. In the 1855 Census of Boston, Dr. Joseph Curtis rued the high death rates in the North and West ends, but asserted that they were unsurprising to anyone who "will take the trouble to visit the abodes, many of them cellars, and nearly all crowded with a dying mass of human beings."

The Irish press, too, portrayed the misery of their countrymen in Boston. One correspondent who visited Boston in August of 1850 described the plight of the city's fifty thousand Irish immigrants. "They live together almost as thick as bees," he wrote. "The most of them are miserably clad, scarce enough of filthy rags to hide their nakedness.

They fight, and howl, and scratch, and bawl, like so many whelps in a jungle; and roll in the dirt of the streets as if it were fun, and the only thing worth living for."

In 1849 Boston was the site of an outbreak of cholera, and because of their congested and unsanitary living conditions, the Irish not only suffered the worst, but they were vilified for contributing to the near epidemic—particularly when the first death, on June 3, was an Irishman (as was the last, on September 30). More than seven hundred Bostonians died in the summer of 1849, and 80 percent of those were foreigners; perhaps three-quarters of those foreigners were recently arrived Irish immigrants, according to an 1850 report of the Sanitary Commission of Massachusetts, authored by statistician Lemuel Shattuck.

As a result of the cholera deaths, the city's Committee of Internal Health investigated the Irish quarter of Boston and made this report: "Your Committee were witnesses of scenes too painful to be forgotten and yet too disgusting to be related here...the whole district is a perfect hive of human beings...huddled together like brutes, without regard to age or sex or sense of decency; sometimes wife and husband, brothers and sisters, in the same bed." Thus, the committee concluded, "self-respect, forethought, all the high and noble virtues soon die out, and sullen indifference and despair or disorder, intemperance and utter degradation reign supreme." Mayor John Bigelow later complained that the Irish immigrants were living in "filth and wretchedness," crowded together in "foul and confined apartments."

What Bigelow did not comment on was the toll these living conditions took on the Irish themselves. During this period, for example, 60 percent of Irish immigrant children did not live past the age of five.

While native Bostonians could largely avoid the Irish slums, the poverty of Irish immigrants was everywhere on display in the city. Many Irish began begging in the streets the day they landed in Boston, and officials warned that the Irish made up the bulk of Boston's pauper rolls and were fast becoming a burden to taxpayers and a strain on city resources. Sending money and aid to starving Irish in Ireland was one thing; it was quite another for city taxpayers to support thousands of unskilled, uneducated, undernourished, ill-equipped peasants— Roman Catholic peasants at that—whose presence was so jarringly

out of place in Boston. In addition to the "destitution and wretchedness of these armies" of Irish immigrants, the Massachusetts Senate
reported in 1848, what was impossible to overlook was "their ignorance, and total inability, even when in perfect health, to adapt themselves to the requirements of society here." The Irish crowded into
the city, the report asserted, and refused to venture into neighboring
towns because food, shelter, and monetary aid in such liberal doses
was unavailable outside of Boston. Thus, they clung to the inner city
"with a tenacity commensurate with their moral debasement, want of
self-respect, and abject and needy circumstances." Or, as Oscar Handlin wrote more bluntly, the Irish became "a massive lump in the community, undigested and undigestible."

Lemuel Shattuck's report on sanitary conditions provided the
statistical foundation that supported Bostonians' anecdotal experience and fanned the alarmist rhetoric of city officials. In 1849, more
than seventy-seven hundred people were listed as paupers in Boston,
nearly 60 percent of them foreigners, and most of those Irish; that
compared to only twenty-seven hundred paupers ten years earlier, an
increase of 268 percent. Boston had spent nearly three-quarters of a
million dollars on their care. In addition, the city had spent an annual
average of $350,000 on its public schools, and half of that was for
educating the children of foreign parents, "most of whom contribute
little or nothing to the public expenses, in taxation or otherwise. And
in many cases, the admission of great numbers of these children ex-
cludes the children of American parents." Moreover, 90 percent of the
"truant and vagabond" children between the ages of six and sixteen
years were foreigners, who, "from neglect and bad habits were unfit to
enter the public schools."

The crime statistics told a similarly distressing story: Shattuck reported that more than three-quarters of all the arrests by the night
watch and police in Boston between 1845 and 1850 were foreigners,
and nearly two-thirds of those committed to the house of correction
in Boston were foreigners; in both cases, nearly all the foreigners were
Irish. "The increase of crime has been very great during the last eight
years, but it has been almost entirely the foreign population," Shattuck asserted.

The Massachusetts Senate report of 1848 pointed out that during a single day in police court in June of the previous year, "there
were sixteen cases, and the parties were not only all foreigners, but all

Irishmen." The state's appropriation of one hundred thousand dollars for an additional prison in Boston "would have been unnecessary were it not for the great increase in foreign criminals." And the Senate blamed the behavior of the Irish for their increasing admittance into the State Lunatic Hospital, another costly burden to Massachusetts taxpayers: "The want of forethought in [the Irish] to save their earnings for the day of sickness; the indulgence of their appetites for stimulating drinks; and their strong love for their native land...are the fruitful causes of insanity among them." While the Senate "deplored" the misfortunes the Irish encountered and "sympathized with their sufferings," Massachusetts lawmakers felt it was the "imperative duty of those who are selected to guard the public interest."

In short, Shattuck added in 1850, the Irish issue presented Boston with one of the most "momentous, profound, and difficult social problems ever presented to us for solution." The "startling and sickening" situation, he said, has "appalled and astounded every man in whose veins course any puritan blood, as he looks to the events of the past, or forward to the hopes of the future."

When Charles Dickens visited Boston in 1842, he might have had the Irish in mind when he told guests at a dinner in his honor: "Virtue shows quite as well in rags and patches as she does in fine linen...she goes barefoot as well as shod...she dwells rather oftener in alleys and by-ways than she does in courts and palaces." He urged Bostonians to "lay [your] hands upon some of these rejected ones whom the world has too long forgotten" and to understand that "these creatures have the same elements and capacities of goodness as yourselves."

But Dickens's message went unheeded during the height of Irish immigration to Boston.

Thousands of Boston Irish, who had witnessed such devastation in their own country—who saw it transformed from a nation of bucolic splendor to a blight-infested isle of death—arrived in their adopted city to find not succor but prejudice, not welcome but suspicion and contempt. Boston's closed Yankee society, its deep anti-Catholicism, its intellectualism—all of these were completely foreign to, and conspired against, the bedraggled Irish who stepped weakly off the coffin ships and sought refuge among her narrow streets. Beginning in earnest with the ransacking and torching destruction of the Ursuline

Convent in Charlestown in 1834, the Athens of America, one of the most progressive and educated locales in the New World (or the Old World, for that matter), rejected the Irish with an unprecedented, unrelenting, white-hot vitriol that rocked the newcomers and left them dispirited and disillusioned.

But not broken.

Boston's Irish had survived the destruction wrought by the famine, they had survived the deadly Atlantic passage, and they would survive—and eventually thrive—in Boston by virtue of their resilience, faith, family bonds, and perseverance that kept them alive during the darkest of times. They battled poverty, illness, ridicule, humiliation, hatred, and religious and ethnic discrimination in Boston. When seeking jobs, the men read the "Positively No Irish Need Apply" signs at warehouses, workshops, hotels, factory gates, fishing boats, and restaurants; women saw the same restriction in the classified ads seeking domestic help to care for children. A typical example: "WANTED—A good, reliable woman to take the care of a boy two years old, in a small family in Brookline. Good wages and permanent situation given. No washing or ironing will be required, but good recommendations as to character and capacity demanded. Positively no Irish need apply."

Still, desperation begets determination and the Irish took any work they could find: cleaning stables, unloading ships, digging trenches, laying foundations; eventually traveling to Lynn to work in the shoe factories, to Lowell and Lawrence to operate looms in the textile mills and build the dams that powered the factories, or to the western part of the state to man the farms. Some went to New York to dig canals and Pennsylvania to mine coal, but the vast majority remained in Boston and Massachusetts and built the roads and laid the track for the network of railroads that the city celebrated at the 1851 Railroad Jubilee. It was dangerous and exhausting work; many Irish were killed in accidents, crushed by falling embankments that had not been properly braced, buried under cave-ins, or maimed or killed by powder blasts. Historian Carl Wittke recounted the popular saying that there was "an Irishman buried under every tie" along railroad lines. Later, it was mainly the Irish who laid the ties and track that formed Boston's horse-railroad system.

And between 1846 and 1848, it was nearly three thousand Irish laborers who dug the trenches and built the fifteen-mile-long aqueduct that brought Boston its first municipal supply of fresh water, from Long Pond (later renamed Lake Cochituate) in Natick and Framingham. The aqueduct ran to a hilltop reservoir in neighboring Brookline, which held up to 100 million gallons of water, enough to supply the city for two weeks if lake service were ever interrupted. From there, the reservoir fed two smaller reservoirs, and then more than sixty miles of cast-iron pipes that workers, mostly Irish, had laid beneath every inhabited street, according to environmental historian Michael Rawson. Boston became one of the first cities with a municipal freshwater supply—there would be no more need to exclusively draw water from wells or collect rainwater in tanks or cans—and Irish laborers provided the sinew to make it possible. When nearly three hundred thousand people from across the state gathered for a Boston parade in October 1848 to celebrate the achievement, thousands of Irish were in attendance. When a demonstration was held on Boston Common and a column of water "burst forth from the fountain to a height of some seventy-five feet," thousands of Irishmen were among those cheering. The municipal water project had provided the first, steady, long-term income to Irish immigrants who arrived after 1845.

Irish women persevered outside of the home, too, in the mills and the garment industry, and, despite the entrenched bigotry of the larger community, eventually as domestics for wealthy families on Beacon Hill, cooking, maintaining homes, and yes, caring for children.

Slowly, steadily, the Irish made economic progress in Boston. Barney McGinniskin's appointment in 1851 was symbolic of those strides, but progress was not entirely linear; there were setbacks. When the anti-immigrant, anti-Catholic Know-Nothing Party took control of the Massachusetts state government in 1854, McGinniskin was fired, and Boston was again without an Irish police officer. But he had paved the way. The continued upward mobility of the Irish, coupled with their bravery on behalf of the Union during the Civil War—more than 10,000 Boston Irish were part of the 144,000 Irish who fought for the North—did finally change things in Boston. By 1871, there were forty-five Irish police officers; by the end of that decade, there were one hundred.

In other ways, too, the Irish were changing Boston. In September of 1867, just two years after the Civil War came to an end, a crowd estimated at between twenty thousand and twenty-five thousand gathered at a building site in Boston's South End to watch Bishop John

Joseph Williams lay the cornerstone for a massive new cathedral at the corner of Washington and Malden streets. Williams went first to the place where the church's main altar would be, "sprinkling the ground with holy water and praying over the spot," historian James O'Toole wrote. "It took imagination to see the huge building that would rise on the spot, but Williams had that vision and asked others to see it too." John Francis Maguire wrote in 1868: "The vastness of its dimensions typifies the progress of Catholicity in Massachusetts." It was remarkable that such a structure could rise in Boston, "the stronghold of the Puritan...Boston, whose leading citizens, had they met a Catholic in the street, they would have crossed to the other side, such was their horror of, or such their aversion to, one of that detested creed."

When it opened eight years later, the massive Cathedral of the Holy Cross, with its great tower rising three hundred feet, was a testament to the changing religious face of Boston—the rise of Catholicism that had occurred primarily because of the influx and influence of the Irish.

For the remainder of the nineteenth century, the Irish reshaped Boston. By 1880, more than seventy thousand Irish lived in the city, accounting for a full 20 percent of Boston's population. In 1882 Patrick Collins was the first Irish-born person elected to Congress from Boston; and the first Irish-born mayor of Boston, Hugh O'Brien, took the oath of office on January 5, 1885 (Collins would succeed him as mayor in 1902, winning election by the largest majority in the city's history). What Barney McGinniskin had begun in 1851 finally paid dividends for the Irish thirty years afterward.

By the mid-1880s, a clear argument could be made that Boston's conversion was irreversible, if not complete: it was becoming both an Irish and a Catholic city.

But that was later. Well before their political success and well before they donned the mantle of power in the city—in the years preceding, during, and following the Civil War—Boston's Irish laborers played a vital role in one of the largest and most ambitious engineering and landfill projects in the history of nineteenth-century America. The contributions of the Irish were valuable, yet ironic at the same time, for it was the very arrival of thousands of Irish to Boston that finally convinced city fathers and state lawmakers to approve and undertake the massive effort.

The Irish inundation not only brought Boston to the bursting point, it chased many wealthy residents out to more desirable locations in nearby towns. If the city was to continue its growth, as well as its political and economic leadership, it needed to both expand its boundaries and create an elegant haven for its most affluent (and Protestant) citizens, the people who would ultimately fund municipal improvements and provide the capital for business investment.

Public officials needed to think big and think creatively. It was time to finally implement a concept that city fathers had discussed, in one way or another, for nearly a quarter century, an idea that carried the risks and enormous odds that accompany any grand endeavor.

It was time to fill the Back Bay.

CHAPTER 4

Filling the Back Bay

The conversion of a waste of water into a magnificent system
of streets and squares, with dwelling houses for a numerous
population, is a transformation dictated by the soundest
statesmanship and the wisest political economy.

—*Report of the Back Bay commissioners, 1856*

In May of 1858, an Irishman named William Reynolds was struck and
killed by a train transporting gravel to the massive Back Bay landfill
project. Unsurprisingly, given widespread prejudice against the Irish,
one local Yankee newspaper blamed Reynolds for his own death: "He
was warned of the approach of the train, but was angry about something and obstinately determined to punish himself by allowing the
train to run him down."

The unfortunate Reynolds was the first laborer to die during the
Back Bay project, but he would certainly not be the last; five or six
(the record is unclear) Irish workers perished in the first year alone of
the endeavor, performing dangerous tasks with few safety measures in
place. But overall, the Back Bay project benefited Irish workers enormously, providing regular paychecks for thousands of laborers for
years. If the two-year Boston aqueduct project offered the Irish a taste
of consistent employment, the three-decade undertaking in the Back
Bay provided them—and unskilled workers of all backgrounds—with
incomes that a decade earlier would have seemed unimaginable.

To resort to the feeble nomenclature that labels the Back Bay effort a "landfill project" diminishes both its magnitude and its impact. On a national level, it was unparalleled in the boldness of its scope, unprecedented in the sweep of its innovation—technological, financial, and breadth of design—and unrivaled in the audacity of its vision. It would take thirty years to complete, eliminate a polluted eyesore, and essentially double the inhabitable size of an overcrowded Boston. Perhaps most important, and the greatest impetus for the project's relentless momentum, it would create a prestigious urban neighborhood that convinced the affluent and influential business elite to remain in a city that, in the decade leading up to the project, found itself overwhelmed by an increasingly omnipresent immigrant class.

Filling the Back Bay, if undertaken in the best of times, would be a testament to the city's confidence; but beginning work on the herculean effort in 1858, in the throes of the previous year's financial depression and in the midst of sectional strife that portended civil war, bordered on outright hubris.

It was, however, understandable hubris. The Back Bay seemed the logical next step for a city that believed it could accomplish anything, mainly because, in so many instances prior to 1858, it had.

As 1851 drew to a close and Bostonians prepared for Christmas, residents watched in awe as the world's first electric fire-alarm system—or more accurately, a "fire alarm telegraph"—neared completion. Created by inventors William Francis Channing and Moses Farmer, the breakthrough municipal telegraph system would bring firefighters to the exact location of a fire. Up until then, firefighters were often bedeviled by the imprecise methods of pinpointing fires; yet getting to the scene as quickly as possible was the best way to prevent a conflagration. In most cities, Boston included, church bells pealed, or citizens shook wooden rattles or simply shouted for help when fire broke out; volunteer firefighters would rush toward the general direction of the noise and a fire foreman leading the charge might use a speaking trumpet to "bark out directions," according to fire historian Stephanie Schorow. (Schorow also points out that, eventually, trumpets became symbols of firefighting and a silver trumpet was often a fitting reward for a deserving firefighter; even today, the number of trumpet emblems on a badge signifies a firefighter's rank.)

Channing, the son of prominent Boston Unitarian minister William Ellery Channing, horrified his father when he eschewed an interest in religion as a boy and instead focused on mechanics, inventions, and how things worked. "Dr. Channing could engage his attention only by reading about the visible universe, voyages of discovery, etc…the history of mechanical discovery and physical experimenting were also his delight," wrote Elizabeth Palmer Peabody of young William, pointing out that at age nine, he was fascinated by his toy steam engine.

In 1844, at age twenty-four, William Francis Channing, along with the rest of the nation, became enthralled with the news of the successful transmission of Samuel Morse's first telegraph message on May 24. When Morse, sitting in the chambers of the United States Supreme Court in Washington, D.C., tapped out the message, "What Hath God Wrought" and his associate received it forty miles away in Baltimore and sent the message back almost instantly, the world changed forever. Channing saw untold and expanded promise for "telegraphy."

On June 3, 1845, he published a short, but remarkably visionary, article that appeared on page two of the *Boston Advertiser* titled "Morse's Telegraph for Fire Alarms." He described a central location linked by double wires to fire stations and fire bells throughout the city, "passing over the tops of houses, and returning again to complete its circuit, to the place where it started." Telegraph keys would allow fire stations to communicate with the central office and with other fire stations. Most important, "the agent would be enabled by pressing a single key with his finger at certain intervals to ring out an alarm, defining the position of the fire, simultaneously on every church bell in the city." Such a system was a by-product of Morse's breakthrough invention "to which public attention has not as yet been directed."

By 1851, Channing's dream was nearing a reality. Boston officials had warmed to the idea (Mayor Josiah Quincy called for a fire-alarm system in his 1848 inaugural address), and Moses Farmer's technological skills transformed Channing's vision into a workable system. In March, Channing made a lengthy and detailed presentation of the fire-alarm telegraph to Boston city officials ("The Application of the Electric Telegraph to Signalizing Alarms of Fire"), and the city allocated ten thousand dollars to establish the system.

By December of that year, forty-nine miles of wire had been stretched across the city, "diving under the arms of the sea which separate its main portion from South and East Boston," the *Boston Daily*

Atlas noted. Telegraph lines were strung from buildings or poles "like spider webs over a cow pasture on a June morning," reported the daily *Commonwealth*. "This arrangement is one of the wonders of the age, involving in it one of the deepest mysteries of the universe, and the more it is studied, the more mysterious it becomes." Also in December, the first of forty cast-iron signal boxes was placed on Hancock Street.

The system was completed in early 1852, and at noon on April 28, the first electric fire alarm in the world was rung for a fire from what is now Box 1212 on Causeway Street. "The system, the perfect success of which is now certain," noted the *Commonwealth*, "will stand forth as one of the finest achievements of scientific skill, and a source of just pride to Boston." Channing and Farmer had done it—and so had Boston—and their success was a model for emulation. As the *Scientific American* noted to its national readership: "It is hoped that every city in our Union; yes, every one in the world, will, at no distant day, have Fire Alarm Telegraphs."

Stephanie Schorow notes that Channing and Farmer's remarkable invention has been enhanced by computers, improved electronics, and radio communications, but its operating principles remain essentially the same as those envisioned by both men. Today, more than 1,350 fire boxes dot Boston's streets; another 1,300 master boxes are in public and private buildings. Firefighters often know from memory the location of every box in their district.

And perhaps the greatest testament to the engineering soundness of Channing and Farmer, indeed to Boston itself, is this declaration by Schorow in 2003: "In more than 150 years of operation, the fire alarm system has never once broken down."

Still other achievements contributed to the assurance that Boston's Back Bay project was eminently doable.

Boston and Massachusetts had, since colonial times, viewed themselves collectively as an educational stalwart. By the 1850s, Harvard College was one cornerstone; the influence of a highly literate, prolific, and persuasive clergy another; the breadth and reach of some of the world's finest writers, authors, publishers, and magazines a third; the contributions of a myriad of private libraries, museums, and historical societies a fourth.

But in 1852 Massachusetts revolutionized education by moving its availability beyond the affluent and the influential. Legislators amended a compulsory-education law, passed two years earlier, and became the first state in the nation to require formal education at least three months of the year for all children between the ages of eight and fourteen. The initial law exempted children who worked "at any regular and lawful occupation" from attending school; the critical change in the 1852 amendment was the elimination of the work provision. The state's educational tradition was one reason for the stronger law. Another was the dramatic increase in the children of Irish immigrants who had flooded Boston's streets; despite the expense of educating so many poor children, state lawmakers believed that the perpetuation of an illiterate underclass would be more costly in the long run. It stood to reason that the children of the Irish poor would be more likely to drop out of school at a young age to work if an "occupation option" were available.

And adhering to the educational principle that "public instruction never stops," Boston launched the first publicly supported, free municipal library in the United States, and the first to allow the borrowing of books and materials. The Boston Public Library, incorporated in 1848, opened its doors in the Adams Schoolhouse on Mason Street in March of 1854, bolstered by a fifty-thousand-dollar donation by financier Joshua Bates in October of 1852 (Bates would ultimately double that contribution). A "former poor boy with no money to spend and no place to go, not being able to pay for a light or fire in my own room [and] unable to pay for books," Bates stipulated that the library be a building the city would be proud of, and that it contain a reading room big enough to accommodate more than one hundred people. And, Bates mandated, "it shall be perfectly free to all, with no other restrictions than may be necessary for the preservation of books." The Boston Library Trustees agreed, reporting in July of 1852 that they considered a large public library "of the utmost importance as the means of completing our system of public education." With the confidence that marked Boston's emergence in the 1850s, the trustees asserted that the library "*can* be done...there can be no doubt; and if it can be done *anywhere*, it can be done *here*, in Boston; for no population of 150,000 souls...was ever before so well fitted to become a reading, self cultivating population as the population of our own city is at this moment." (Emphasis in original.)

By 1858, the library had outgrown Mason Street. On New Year's Day of that year, a municipal procession of officials, academics, military regiments, and a marching band wound through the city and celebrated the opening of a new library building on the corner of Boylston and Tremont streets, arriving "just as the clock of Park Street Church struck four," author Walther Muir Whitehill reported. In just five years, the number of volumes had increased from just under ten thousand to more than seventy thousand; the number of pamphlets from under one thousand to nearly eighteen thousand. "Joshua Bates's generosity had created one of the major libraries in the country," Whitehill noted. In 1895, after the Back Bay was filled, the library moved to its current Copley Square location.

With Boston thundering forward, exerting its influence across the spectrum of human achievement, it's no wonder that Oliver Wendell Holmes wrote in the debut of the *Atlantic Monthly* magazine in 1857: "The Boston State-House is the hub of the solar system."

Now, with its attention turned to the Back Bay, the Hub would tackle a daunting task that would test its national-leadership credentials.

Predictably, perhaps, it was Boston's oddly shaped physical footprint, coupled with the desires of its wealthy residents, that led to the vision—and the reality—of an exclusive neighborhood in the Back Bay.

At the beginning of the nineteenth century, the city was basically an island connected to the mainland at the independent town of Roxbury by a narrow, low-lying neck with room for only a single road (which is now Washington Street); this tiny peninsula of 750 acres held about twenty-five thousand people in 1800. A large tidal marsh lay behind the town, west of the Boston Common, and eventually, the Public Garden, between the Neck and the Charles River. This "Back Bay" separated Boston from Cambridge, Brookline, Brighton, and Roxbury.

In 1821 the one-and-a-half-mile Mill Dam (now buried under present-day Beacon Street, from Arlington Street to Kenmore Square) was constructed by the Boston and Roxbury Mill Corporation to separate the bay from the Charles River. According to authors William Newman and Wilfred Holton, a series of sluices and floodgates, working with the tide, provided water power for the company's mills in Watertown, Dorchester Lower Mills, and the Neponset River, part of Boston's early growth as a manufacturing center. Wagon and rail traffic eventually traveled atop the dam, and homes were built on and alongside it, and the mill company received permission from the city to fill some mudflats along its dam on the Charles River side. As part of its sophisticated system of powering mills through the management of tidewater power, the company also built a cross dam through the Back Bay—connecting Gravelly Point in the Fenway area with the Mill Dam at about the area where Massachusetts Avenue runs today from Boylston Street to Beacon Street. The cross dam created a smaller "Full Basin" west of Gravelly Point and a larger "Receiving Basin," which included all of the area that is now considered part of the Back Bay neighborhood.

As Newman and Holton explain, the area encompassed by the Receiving Basin lay between today's Charles Street and Massachusetts Avenue from east to west (later, the easterly border became Arlington Street after the Public Garden was designed and built), and between the Charles River and just short of Washington Street from north to south.

To maximize the fall of water through waterwheels in the mills, the Receiving Basin was kept as empty as possible by draining water into the Charles River at every low tide. The basin became polluted quickly since sewers continued to drain into the area and, because of the dam system, tides no longer washed it out twice daily. In the 1830s two railroad lines were built across the Back Bay on low embankments and trestle bridges that extended over the mudflat. These lines further reduced water flow in the Receiving Basin, which further increased pollution.

It was the prodigious proposal to fill and populate the Receiving Basin that is most commonly referred to as the Back Bay landfill project.

By 1849, as Boston's population exploded and the Receiving Basin pollution grew worse, a City Council–commissioned report described the dire condition of the Back Bay. "[It is] one of nuisance, offensive and injurious to the large and increasing population residing upon it...The Back Bay at this hour is nothing less than a great cesspool, into which is daily deposited all the filth of a large and constantly increasing population." Trash and refuse were thrown into the bay

Figure 2. View of the Back Bay from the State House in the late 1850s, before substantial work had begun on the massive nineteenth-century landfill project. The Mill Dam (which would become Beacon Street) crosses the bay at center. The near shoreline forming a reverse L with the Mill Dam is the site of present-day Arlington Street. *(Photo courtesy of the Boston Public Library, Print Department)*

from the Mill Dam, and wharf rats scurried in, out, and across the seawall. In colorful and evocative language, the council report confirmed what Boston residents knew well: "Every west wind sends its [the Back Bay's] pestilential exhalations across the entire city…[and] a greenish scum, many yards wide, stretches along the shores of the basin…while the surface of the water beyond is seen bubbling like a cauldron, with the noxious gases that are exploding from the corrupting mass below."

The state senate appointed a special commission to further study the problem, and in 1852 the three-member group proposed filling the nearly six-hundred-acre Receiving Basin, and laying out a neighborhood consisting of "building lots, streets, squares, and ponds. Such a configuration would "secure upon the premises a healthy and thrifty population and business, and by inherent and permanent causes, forever to prevent this territory from becoming the abode of filth and disease."

And, while Boston would be indisputably the biggest beneficiary of the project, the commissioners recommended that the Commonwealth of Massachusetts oversee the entire scope of work—landfill, sale of lots, design of the new neighborhood—to ensure that the improvements would be completed "in the most certain and thorough manner."

Environmental concerns (though not referred to as such in the nineteenth century) convinced city and state officials that the Back Bay had to be filled, but it was a form of demographic alarmism that truly drove the project.

By 1850, Boston's population approached 137,000 people, compared with 98,000 just a decade earlier, transforming Boston from merely a densely populated community to an overcrowded one, as historian Oscar Handlin has pointed out. Most of the increase was due to Irish immigrants, whose settlement habits and poverty created Boston's worst slum neighborhoods. Simultaneously, Boston's burgeoning mercantile status meant that commercial and retail buildings were replacing housing for wealthy families in the downtown area. Squeezed by a mass of impoverished Irish on one side and a shortage of quality housing downtown, Boston's high-income professionals and businesspeople—almost all of whom were Protestant and made their livings in the core city—were beginning to look to nearby suburbs to call home.

Boston officials were worried enough to commission Dr. Jesse Chickering to prepare a special report on population growth and immigration trends, and while Chickering did not specifically mention filling the Back Bay, he stressed the need to keep native-born residents in the city to prevent the "foreign class" from dominating Boston. (Chickering estimated that, by 1850, some two thousand men had left Boston for California, lured by what he termed "that golden expedition," the gold rush.) Chickering also estimated that twenty thousand people were commuting to Boston by train each day in 1850. "This emerging suburban movement of high-income Protestant families threatened to increase rapidly the relative population of Irish Catholic immigrants," authors Newman and Holton note. "It is clear that

Chickering feared this trend would continue and he felt that Boston's character would change for the worse."

The influential, albeit short-lived, reign of the anti-immigrant Know-Nothings in Massachusetts in the mid-1850s—those responsible for the firing of Barney McGinniskin from the Boston police force—also strengthened the state government's desire to retain wealthy Protestants in the capital city, stressing the allure of the Back Bay. The pristine streets, broad, tree-lined avenues, and attractive parks, plus zoning restrictions that would keep the price of house lots high, would create an elite neighborhood whose status would continue uninterrupted for decades to come. Calling the Back Bay a "useless and unsightly waste," and noting "a palpable lack of room for dwelling houses in and near the city of Boston," the Back Bay commissioners declared in their comprehensive 1856 report: "The conversion of a waste of water into a magnificent system of streets and squares, with dwelling houses for a numerous population, is a transformation dictated by the soundest statesmanship and the wisest political economy."

With a fetid Back Bay stoking fears of disease, and a swelling population overwhelming the city's livable space, with thousands of poor Irish encroaching—physically and psychologically—on the dominance of wealthy Protestants, Boston and Massachusetts had bedrock reasons to move ahead with a new and exclusive Back Bay neighborhood.

All that remained was to design it, finance it, and build it.

Even if the first two elements were wildly successful (and they would be), questions would linger on the third until workers moved enough earth, hauled enough gravel, laid enough streets, sunk enough pilings, planted enough trees, and built enough homes for Bostonians to finally witness the emergence of a diamond arising from the muck, embodying all of their city's grand plans and ambitions.

"In the centre of the remaining space," Boston architect Arthur Gilman wrote to the Back Bay commissioners in November of 1856, "a broad avenue is contemplated, similar in its effect to that of the Champs Elysees in Paris or the Unter den Linden in Berlin." After several years of fits and starts, proposals and counterproposals, commissioners chose a design mostly credited to Gilman, then thirty-five, though he had assistance from landscape gardeners and other architects.

Born in Newburyport, Massachusetts, Gilman attended the prestigious Governor Dummer Academy and spent three years at Washington (now Trinity) College in Hartford, Connecticut, before traveling across Europe and then opening an office in Boston in the early 1840s. He achieved public prominence with an article in the *North American Review* in 1844 in which he strongly condemned classical revival architecture. In 1859, once the Back Bay project was under way, he would become partners with another prominent Boston architect, Gridley J. F. Bryant. Gilman would also become the architect of the magnificent Arlington Street Church, one of the Back Bay's anchor structures, erected between 1859 and 1861 on the corner of present-day Boylston and Arlington streets, across from the Public Garden; and Boston's new city hall on School Street (today's Old City Hall), built between 1862 and 1865.

After the Civil War, Gilman would move to New York and achieve additional public accolades for his work, but it was Boston's Back Bay that was his crowning achievement. After a three-way settlement on land rights (known as the Tripartite Indenture) was signed in 1856 by the Commonwealth of Massachusetts, the City of Boston, and the Boston Water Power Company, which cleared the last legal hurdles for the project, the Back Bay commissioners moved quickly on Gilman's vision.

First, his plan called for four additional avenues parallel with the Mill Dam (today's Beacon Street) running east to west from the Public Garden, the most southerly of these being an extension of Boylston Street, which would be 127 feet wide. The avenue adjacent to Boylston Street (today's Newbury Street) would be 104 feet wide, as would the avenue adjacent to the Mill Dam (today's Marlborough Street). Running through the neighborhood's middle would be the project's jewel, a grand avenue more than 200 feet wide and a mile and a half long, linking Boston with Brookline, with a pedestrian park in its center extending the full length of the avenue and rows of trees planted along the roadway. "Several names have been suggested for this broad artery, connecting city with country," the *Daily Advertiser* of December 10, 1856, pointed out. "That which seems to us most appropriate is 'Commonwealth Avenue'... This avenue will be superior in its attractiveness to anything of the kind elsewhere. [It] will perma-

nently connect the Common and the Public Garden with the beautiful country of Roxbury and Brookline."

This urban-rural linkage, the paper noted, would benefit Boston
and its residents from both a health and convenience perspective. If
Bostonians viewed the Back Bay neighborhood as a "sort of continua-
tion of the Common in a westerly direction," then the strong possibility existed that "a reservoir of pure air may always be supplied from
the ample sources of health and freshness outside the city limits." And
consider that Boston residents "may readily pass from city to country
under the shade of trees."

The Back Bay commissioners also pointed out that Commonwealth
Avenue's central space "will be ample for walks and seats secure from
the interference of carriages." Moreover, the commissioners reported
with the soaring rhetoric typical of Boston's backers in the 1850s:
"It is believed that an ornamental avenue of this character...with
stately dwelling houses upon each side, connecting the public parks
in the centre of a busy city with the attractive and quiet...country in
the neighborhood, is a thing not possible of construction elsewhere
in the world."

Connecting the east–west avenues, according to Gilman's plan,
would be a series of cross streets running from the Mill Dam/Beacon
Street to Boylston Street, and in some cases, beyond Boylston into
Boston's South End. These would begin with the construction of a
new thoroughfare adjacent to the Public Garden (Arlington Street).
The remaining cross streets, anywhere from sixty to eighty feet wide,
would create an organized grid that would define the neighborhood;
these would become Boston's so-called alphabet streets, and eventually would be named after English lords (Berkeley, Clarendon, Dart-
mouth, Exeter, Fairfield, Gloucester, and Hereford).

Including the streets, the commissioners set aside more than 40
percent of the Back Bay neighborhood for "public purposes"—parks,
gardens, squares, sidewalks—believing strongly (and ultimately, correctly) that this would increase the value of private house lots, thus
reserving the exclusivity of the neighborhood for the appropriate
economic class. With Commonwealth Avenue as its focal point, the
design of the neighborhood into rectangular blocks served a dual
purpose for the "Protestant elite," according to authors Newman and
Holton; it set them off "from a commercial city that had a tangle of
curved streets, with the Common and Public Garden acting as an

effective barrier," separating them from Boston's impoverished immigrants, and "they remained close enough to the downtown to exercise control."

The Back Bay project would make Boston different from urban centers across the country in the 1850s, many of whose upper classes were fleeing to more fashionable outlying locations. Once it was completed, the new Back Bay neighborhood would make wealthy Bostonians proud to remain in the city center.

With the elegant and sweeping design of the neighborhood in place, the commissioners next hammered out a financing plan for the project that can only be described as a fiscal tour de force. Breathtaking in its simplicity and success, the Back Bay funding mechanism would come to serve as a model for large-scale public-private partnerships.

When the legislature authorized the creation of the Back Bay, lawmakers provided no working start-up capital to accomplish the project. Until land sales began, and the Commonwealth began to profit from the endeavor, not a dime would be taken from the state treasury (except to cover incidental administrative costs of the commission itself).

The commissioners faced a dilemma: what contractor would take on the project without an initial investment to buy equipment and assemble a workforce?

Undaunted, the commission secured start-up funds by selling as yet unfilled plots to private individuals, who in turn profited handsomely from their investments. Then, they struck an arrangement with contractors Norman Munson and George Goss, whereby both men took their pay in house lots. Essentially, the contractors worked on consignment for approximately a quarter of the land they created. For example, in 1858, in the first year of filling, some 260,000 square feet went to Goss and Munson, valued at $305,000 (or $1.17 per square foot), according to a report of the Massachusetts House of Representatives. "This was treated as a cash payment to the contractors equaling their charges for the work," authors Newman and Holton wrote. "The contractors then began filling their land as fast as they could to pay expenses and to make a profit."

While this presented some issues—for example, the state was competing with Munson and Goss to sell land—the funding operation worked astoundingly well. When enough money had flowed into the state treasury after a few years, the commissioners began to pay the contractors in cash or mortgages rather than land, which left the state more land to sell. And, land sales were strictly regulated by the State Commission to keep sale prices high—adding to state coffers—and to attract wealthy buyers as the filling of land proceeded.

The commission sold segments of the filled land at irregular intervals to keep prices up; in years when demand was low, no land was sold at all. Prices varied widely through the life of the project, but generally increased as the neighborhood became well established, reaching a high of $4.53 per square foot in 1884. The most expensive building lot, at the northwest corner of Commonwealth Avenue and Dartmouth Street, sold for $6.55 per square foot, and became the site of the Ames-Webster Mansion, built for Congressman Frederick Ames in 1872. "The highest average sale prices were obtained for house lots on the north side of Commonwealth Avenue," Holton and Newman pointed out, "because they shared the unique advantage in the winter of having bright sunlight streaming through the front windows on all floors."

The commissioners' assiduous attention to real estate prices and land management, all the while maintaining their focus on the overall aesthetics of the neighborhood and the city—they resisted a Boston City Council request to sell a portion of the Public Garden for development, and to put a road through the Public Garden—enabled the state to orchestrate this massive development without advancing any of its own funds.

Rather, money flowed into state coffers relatively quickly. By September of 1859, less than eighteen months after work began, the state treasury had realized nearly $193,000 from Back Bay land sales, according to the eighth annual commissioners' report. At the October 1860 auction, the state realized more than a quarter-million dollars in land sales. By 1869, the figure soared to a total of $830,000 from sales (in cash and notes), plus interest that the state would receive on mortgages. Even more extraordinary, state lawmakers agreed to divide the money from Back Bay land sales in half; 50 percent would pay for administration and general fund expenses, and 50 percent would benefit an educational and cultural fund. The latter amount would be split between the Commonwealth's school budget fund and numerous other educational institutions. In 1861, for example, $50,000 was donated to the state's education budget, and $50,000 more was split among Tufts College, Amherst College, Williams College, Wesleyan Academy at Wilbraham, the Agassiz Museum at Harvard, and the Museum of Comparative Zoology. The education and cultural institutions differed during the years, but land speculators "paid their indirect tribute to the cause of education," one account pointed out.

Most remarkably—almost unbelievably by modern standards— as authors Barbara Moore and Gail Weesner estimated, the Back Bay venture would ultimately realize a $3.5 million *profit* for the Commonwealth after all expenses were paid, almost half of which was contributed to the education fund.

Now that the ingenious financing structure was in place, Goss and Munson, two determined, experienced New England contractors, could begin the actual work on the daunting project. It was the spring of 1858.

For nearly the next two years, they would set a blistering pace.

Their perseverance notwithstanding, Goss and Munson benefited just as much from the fortuitous timing of the Back Bay project.

In this case, it was two Boston technological breakthroughs that not only expedited the Back Bay landfill project, but made it possible in the first place: the growth of the locomotive and the railroads, and the production of the steam shovel. Without both, the Back Bay plans would have remained on the drawing board for years to come.

By the 1850s, the former gravel pits on Beacon Hill were covered with elegant homes. The nearest sources of clean sand and gravel were several miles outside the city, and the distance and scope of the project made it prohibitive for horse-drawn wagons to transport the fill. "The problem was how to excavate and transport large quantities of sand and gravel to the Back Bay quickly and economically," Newman and Holton accurately assessed.

The steam shovel was invented in the Boston area by William Smith Otis, who received a patent on his invention in 1839. His cousin, Oliver Chapman, continued to work on the new machine after Otis's death, and early in the 1850s, Chapman approached Boston heavy-machine builder John Souther about improving the steam shovel, especially by strengthening some weak parts that continued to break down. Together, Chapman and Souther improved the machine,

increasing its weight to ten tons so it could excavate hard and compact materials. In the late 1850s, just in time for the Back Bay, Souther
began active production on the "Chapman Steamshovel" at his Globe
Locomotive Works in South Boston. The improved steam shovel required only two men, one engineer and one helper, to operate the
crane, according to Newman and Holton. They added: "It consumed
about eight hundred pounds of coal in ten hours and accomplished as
much work in one day as could be done by fifty to sixty laborers."

At the same time, Munson and Goss built a nine-mile railway to
a gravel quarry in West Needham, and employed hundreds of men
to work on the project. The combination of the steam shovel and the
locomotive-powered gravel train allowed railroad men to dump up
to eight hundred carloads of gravel into the Back Bay every work day.
Tons of gravel were transported from the hills of Needham and Newton by rail ("dirt cars," as they were called), on trains with thirty-five
cars each, making twenty-five trips in twenty-four hours, night and
day, for years. Souther's steam shovel was used to dredge the marshes
of the Back Bay and literally strip-mine the hills of Needham to provide enough fill. Hundreds of spectators traveled to Needham each
day to watch the steam shovel bite into mounds of dirt and gravel,
and load fill onto rail cars, a never-before-seen automated process
that signaled the changes that were taking place in Boston. As the
May 21, 1859, issue of *Ballou's Pictorial* described: "One hundred and
forty-five dirt cars, with eighty men, including engineers and brake-
men and all, are employed, night and day, in loading and transporting
the gravel…these trains are continually on the road, and one arrives
at the Back Bay every forty-five minutes."

Later, when the Needham gravel pits had been stripped, the contractors hauled gravel from Canton, Dedham, Hyde Park, and West-
wood.

The schedule and the work itself were grueling. Workers fought
through the brutal heat of summer, the damp New England springs,
and the dirt, grit, and grime of all seasons to adhere to the relentless
timetable; Goss and Munson got paid only when they sold lots and
they sold lots only after they were filled. The state, too, desired rapid
progress to realize its profit.

The pace and the nature of the work made it dangerous, too.
Workers were killed or injured when they were thrown from or fell
off trains, or crushed during the coupling and decoupling of cars, a

dangerous maneuver that often occurred while the train was moving because of scheduling demands. "A man only lived long enough for one mistake," author Richard Reinhardt glumly noted. In addition, most locomotives did not have brakes before 1875; gears allowed engineers to slow down the train and to stop it by throwing the drive wheels into reverse while the locomotive was still moving forward. Nor were there brakes on the gravel cars. Some locomotive tenders had friction brakes, but they were not sufficient to stop a train quickly, and they were notoriously inconsistent and unsmooth in their stopping motion, often causing the tender to buck and jerk from side to side. "If an obstruction on the track or a break in the rail was observed from the train, it was an automatic signal for the engine crew to jump off and try to save themselves," Holton and Newman pointed out. The *Boston Daily Traveler* reported in April of 1859 that Irishman John McGee, a tender brakeman on a Back Bay gravel train, was "thrown from the train while applying the brakes, by a sudden giving way of a road, run over, and horribly mangled. When reached he was dead. He was forty years of age…and leaves a wife and four children." The previous summer, weeks after work began, the *Boston Herald* had written about another Irish worker, Patrick Regan, who fractured his skull and later died when he jumped from a moving gravel train onto a newly filled section of Back Bay land. "He was a stranger in Boston and was thirty-eight years of age," the *Herald* noted.

Among the press and the public, the magnitude and unique nature of the project generated alternating feelings of fascination and consternation. One newspaper account described the discovery of an elephant's tooth some twenty feet below the surface at the excavation site in Needham, "and from the nature of the material in which it was embedded, must have been washed up by an old ocean ages ago." On the other hand, before building construction took place, sections of the expanding land section of the city resembled a dusty desert "or a waffle of mud-filled depressions, depending on the season and weather conditions," according to Newman and Holton. Sand and gravel dried out completely during very dry weather, and wind sweeping across the Charles River created severe dust storms that blanketed the Public Garden, the Common, and the rest of the old city. The choking clouds of dust "have doubtless done more injury than three times the expense of a good coating of grass would have cost," the *Boston Sunday Evening Gazette* lamented in April of 1860.

Nonetheless, despite the deaths, the difficulties, and the dust storms, work continued. Goss and Munson had great success early, and after Goss suffered a nervous breakdown in 1859 due to the pressure of the project (he left Boston to recuperate and never returned), Munson carried on by himself, and later, with new partners. His crews filled the bay, leveled the land surface for building construction, graded the streets, constructed the drainage and sewer systems, built the neighborhood parks, and laid the carriageways that adjoined the main avenues. By the end of 1859, everything east of present day Berkeley Street was filled; the land reached Clarendon Street by the end of 1860, Exeter Street by 1870, and the Receiving Basin portion of the Back Bay was complete by about 1886. Landfill reached the Fenway area by 1890 and the project was fully completed by 1894.

But Boston recognized early that the Back Bay project was something special. "The enterprise is no longer an experiment," the *Boston Daily Advertiser* editorialized on January 18, 1860. "It has long since passed the stage at which it could be derided as a visionary speculation. It will surely go faster or slower, but it will not be permitted to cease."

And very much according to plan, wealthy Bostonians, as well as those from other cities, bought land and built homes in the Back Bay. "The promises of the past have been fulfilled, and we cannot believe that those who now purchase will experience any disappointment," the *Boston Daily Advertiser* exulted in October of 1860. David Stewart of New York built a home at 152 Beacon Street for his daughter, Isabella, who married John Lowell Gardner Jr. on April 10, 1860. The Gardners moved into the house in 1862, and Isabella began assembling works of art that would one day grace the museum that bears her name. During the February 1863 land-sale auction, where one report said the "bidding [was] more spirited than at any recent sale," wool manufacturing magnate E. R. Mudge (his grandfather signed the Massachusetts constitution) purchased five lots on the north side of Commonwealth Avenue and three lots on Clarendon Street. At the same auction, Boston businessman Charles Francis purchased nine lots. In 1871 Thomas F. Cushing, a member of one of Boston's wealthiest families (he summered in Newport), built a magnificent brick house in the French tradition at 163 Marlborough Street.

It's little wonder that when Oliver Wendell Holmes Sr. vacated his Beacon Hill residence in 1870 to move to 296 Beacon Street in Back Bay, he labeled his abandonment of the old house a case of "justifiable domicide."

In addition to residences, key educational, religious, and cultural institutions heightened the allure of the Back Bay. Newman and Holton point out that, by the mid-1890s, Back Bay was home to the Massachusetts Institute of Technology (Boylston and Clarendon), the Museum of Natural History (Boylston and Berkeley), Harvard Medical School (Boylston and Exeter), the Museum of Fine Arts (Copley Square at the time), and the new Boston Public Library in Copley Square. Protestant churches whose congregations included the city's most prominent families were scattered throughout the district—Arlington Street Church, Trinity Church, The First Church, First Baptist, Church of the Covenant. (By design, the closest Catholic Church "was tucked outside the southwest corner of the area, near Massachusetts Avenue, among stables and other service buildings.")

The combination of stately homes, broad, tree-lined streets, and some of the city's most respectable cultural organizations made the new Back Bay irresistible to Boston's elite and one of the most fashionable urban neighborhood in the country.

And the very method of home construction became the subject of conversation among the wealthy and their friends. Most every structure (at least before the high-rises began to dot the neighborhood in the twentieth century) was supported by untreated wood piles driven into the ground through the landfill sediment to reach firmer layers of sand, gravel, and blue clay. The upper ends of the piles, which were spruce tree trunks measuring about twelve inches in diameter and between twenty and forty feet long, were cut off below the water table to prevent rotting (exposure to air would produce mildew and fungi and expose the wood to insects such as termites). Workers dug trenches below the average level of high tide under each building foundation and the piles were driven in them. According to Holton and Newman, the average row house was supported by 270 piles under the foundation walls, spaced eighteen inches to three feet apart. The mathematics are astounding. With 270 piles under a house and between thirty-six and forty-two houses in each block (assuming there is no church or other institution), the total number of piles per block ranged from ninety-seven hundred to more than

Figure 3. The jewel of the Back Bay was Commonwealth Avenue, shown here in the late 1870s, a broad thoroughfare more than two hundred feet wide and a mile and a half long, with a pedestrian park in its center extending the full length of the avenue and rows of trees planted along the roadway. (*Photo courtesy of the Boston Public Library, Print Department*)

eleven thousand. With more than eighteen blocks in the state's portion of the Back Bay alone, approximately two hundred thousand tree trunks supported the residential buildings in the newly created neighborhood.

Larger buildings required more piles, of course. Trinity Church in Copley Square is supported by more than forty-five hundred piles under its foundation, primarily to bear the weight of its ninety-five-hundred-ton central tower. To support the massive Arlington Street Church tower on the corner of Arlington and Boylston, the church's building committee reported that workers "rammed in concrete" between thousands of wood piles to form a solid bed upon which granite blocks were laid, each block resting on two piles. "A solid pyramid of granite blocks cemented together to form a single mass and weighing more than a thousand tons was then erected to seat the tower," the report points out.

Local newspaper reports reassured doubters that the pile-driving approach was safe and provided "permanent" support. "[Some] have to be reminded that...piles are driven until unyielding clay is reached," the *Daily Advertiser* wrote in an 1862 editorial expressing exasperation at the skeptics. "Here is a foundation as immovable as the solid rock...the structure [will] have a firmer foundation—one less liable to change from accidental causes—than one laid upon natural land."

To call the Back Bay building construction "innovative" hardly seems adequate. "Consider the large, dense inverted 'forest' of spruce trees buried in the ground below the Back Bay neighborhood," Holton and Newman write in wonderment. Or as a mid-1890s report pointed out about filling the Back Bay: "Whole forests from the State of Maine...[had] been put to service in...furnishing pilings and solid foundations." For its day—more accurately, for a period of nearly forty years—the construction of Back Bay homes, churches, and other buildings represented an exquisite engineering marvel, yet another Boston achievement whose impact stretched far beyond her borders.

Without doubt, the Back Bay signaled a new era in Boston's history: the magnificent new neighborhood served as a testament to the city's wealth and influence in so many areas. Even the aura and physicality of the Back Bay—with its broad and almost serene tree-lined streets and avenues, its orderly and unified grid layout, the solidity and dignified stateliness of its homes—stood in marked contrast to the rest of the city, in which loud, dirty, narrow, immigrant-crammed, tenement-lined, horse-railroad-congested, serpentine streets wound circuitously and often chaotically through the old "Boston Neck." These were streets laid out two hundred years earlier, when Boston was in its infancy, a fledgling community struggling to survive and just learning how to get things done. Even with all of its elitism, segregationist, and anti-Catholic overtones, the brilliant success of the Back Bay project—from design to financing to fill to building construction—was emblematic of how far Boston had come.

Meanwhile, as the 1860s approached, even as the Back Bay work proceeded apace, as land was filled, bought, sold, and resold, as piles were driven and foundations constructed for fine homes and grand churches, Bostonians remained aware of larger forces at play around the country, forces with the potential to disrupt their lives in a way far more explosive than Back Bay gravel trains or dust storms.

In December of 1859, the collective eyes of Boston, and the nation, looked to Virginia.

John Brown was dead.

Now the question remained: could the Union survive?

CHAPTER 5

The Gallows Glorious

Today Virginia has murdered John Brown;
tonight we have witnessed his resurrection.

—*William Lloyd Garrison, 1859*

FRIDAY, DECEMBER 2, 1859. Four thousand Boston abolitionists and antislavery advocates jammed the Tremont Temple, while a crush of three thousand more thronged the streets outside. Moments before the official program began, a young man unfurled a banner from the gallery that read, "He dies by the mandate of the Slave Power, yet 'still lives' by virtue of heroic deeds." The boisterous crowd erupted in shouting and applause that set the tone for the evening, author Henry Mayer recounted.

All of them had gathered to pay tribute to abolitionist John Brown, who had been hanged earlier in the day in Charles Town, Virginia, on charges of conspiracy to incite a slave insurrection, treason against the State of Virginia, and first degree murder, all related to his unsuccessful October raid on the federal arsenal at Harpers Ferry. His goal: obtain weapons, free slaves, and ignite a slave uprising that would reverberate across the land. Instead, his capture, his trial, and this morning's execution established him as a martyr to abolitionists and anathema to slave owners. "At fifteen minutes past eleven, the trap fell," read one account of his hanging. "A slight grasping of the hands and twitching of the muscles was visible, and then all was quiet."

But most cities and towns around America did not know quiet

in the aftermath of Brown's death. Instead, citizens gathered in great numbers to praise or curse him, to deify his memory as a courageous, forthright liberator and a passionate defender of human dignity and freedom, or to further pillory his already stained reputation as a violent, arrogant, even insane crusader who resorted to murder without provocation. Since his slaughter of unarmed proslavery men in Kansas in retaliation for the South's illegal and forceful attempts to disrupt fair elections in the frontier territory, Brown's incendiary rhetoric and radical actions had galvanized abolitionists, frightened Northern moderates, and infuriated the South.

Harpers Ferry further inflamed those passions.

Tonight, in Boston, it was longtime abolitionists William Lloyd Garrison and Lydia Maria Child who decorated the platform and positioned placards and banners around the auditorium. No black crepe or funeral drapes—this was not to be a night of mourning, but of unconditional and unrestrained celebration of Brown's life's work. "They made instead a lectern centerpiece of Brown's portrait supported by a cross and wreathed in evergreen and amaranth," Henry Mayer noted.

Soaring oratory filled the temple. Speakers read poems and recited prayers. Militant fugitive slave John Sella Martin brought the audience to its feet by charging that America had delivered up "the Barabbas of Slavery" and crucified the "John Brown of Freedom." Garrison continued the martyr drumbeat that would keep Brown's memory alive for months: "Today Virginia has murdered John Brown; tonight we have witnessed his resurrection." Now that Brown was dead, Garrison urged the crowd to offer its "sympathies, prayers, and noblest exertions" to the "four million John Browns" who served in bondage as Southern slaves.

Boston's leading abolitionists were inextricably linked with Brown, and their voices rose in his defense, amplified by a religious fervor. Thomas Wentworth Higginson and Theodore Parker were members of the "Secret Six" who helped finance the Harpers Ferry raid. They continued to back Brown and defend the raid even when previous supporters began to desert him after the violence at the arsenal (even Frederick Douglass, fearful of capture, had fled to Canada after Brown's arrest). Higginson called the raid "the most formidable insurrection that has ever occurred," and dared the federal government to indict him as a coconspirator. After the raid, Ralph Waldo Emerson called John Brown "the new saint…awaiting his martyrdom, and who, if he shall suffer, will make the gallows glorious like the cross." The "gallows glorious" phrase was published in major newspapers North and South—to hosannas of praise and howls of protest—and, according to Brown biographer David Reynolds, was the most polarizing statement made about the abolitionist; its impact rivaled the phrase Emerson had coined about the battle of Lexington to start the American Revolution—the "shot heard 'round the world." Henry David Thoreau pronounced Brown "a crucified hero," and Henry Wadsworth Longfellow wrote in his diary on the day of Brown's execution: "This will be a great day in our history, the date of a new Revolution, quite as much needed as the old one."

As 1859 came to a close, and in the months that followed, John Brown's name remained in the news and abolitionists kept his memory alive by decrying what they saw as more aggressive proslavery statements from the South. Boston abolitionists, who had filled Tremont Temple in 1851 to call for the freeing of Thomas Sims and filled it again in December of 1859 to pay homage to John Brown, continued to lead their northern counterparts. "John Brown failed for the hour, but success will grow out of the rashness of his act," Garrison wrote in the December 31 issue of the *Liberator*. "His name will echo in every hovel in the arctic midnight confines of slavery, and the motive of his action will illuminate every heart like the blaze of a million beacons."

While abolitionists honored Brown's memory, they also anticipated the turning of the calendar: a presidential election loomed in 1860. In the past decade, Boston had blossomed into one of America's most influential and important cities, its national cachet and gravitas bolstered by the resonance of its abolitionist movement, the growth of its commerce and transportation, the explosion of its population, the innovativeness of its technology, the sparkling grandeur of its new Back Bay neighborhood.

Would Boston's success continue?

Abolitionists and most everyone else knew that the answer to that question, and so much more, would depend on the results of the upcoming presidential election. A watershed moment was approaching for the nation; John Brown's raid, arrest, trial, and execution had deepened the intensity of the darkest clouds that had been gathering since the Fugitive Slave Law of 1850.

The 1860 election had the potential to shake the country to its very foundation. It would determine not only Boston's future, not only the future of slavery, but—in one of the few things North and South agreed upon—the fate of the Union itself.

PART TWO

A City Transformed

1860–1875

Old Boston vanishes and a new Boston seems sprung
from the waters of the Bay.

—The Boston Daily Advertiser, *June 1869, promoting
the city's hosting of the Great Peace Jubilee*

CHAPTER 6

No Turning Back

There must be no yielding on our part. We are on the eve of great events.

—Senator Charles Sumner in a letter to
Henry Wadsworth Longfellow, December 3, 1860

APRIL 5, 1860. New England poet laureate Henry Wadsworth Longfellow and his good friend George Sumner—Senator Charles Sumner's brother—gingerly mounted the creaking stairs inside the tower of the Old North Church in Boston's North End. Bells chimed and dozens of pigeons fluttered and squawked as the two friends climbed higher and approached the steeple. Longfellow was well aware of the historical significance of the church, of the story of two other men who, in the dead of night eighty-five years earlier, had climbed these same 154 stairs, plus a rickety ladder, while a third accomplice stood guard at the church door. Theirs was a daring, dramatic, and dangerous mission, part of the first successful and organized subversive actions in the improbable chain of events that would lead to American independence. "From this tower were hung the lanterns as a signal that the British troops had left Boston for Concord," Longfellow would write in his diary upon returning home.

More important, at this crucial moment in the nation's history, his words would lay the foundation for the elevation of Paul Revere to a national hero and icon, and assure that the story of his valor in 1775 would serve as an example to all Union loyalists as they dealt with the crisis America faced in 1860.

Longfellow's visit to Old North Church was part of an excursion

George Sumner suggested when the two friends dined together at Longfellow's Cambridge home the previous evening. A mutual acquaintance (whose name is lost to history) served as a guide to the neighborhood Longfellow characterized as the "Little Britain" of Boston, though the historic section of the city had changed dramatically since Longfellow and Charles Sumner had escorted Charles Dickens there in 1842. Yes, the North End still dripped with the glory of Boston's Revolutionary spirit, but now it also teemed with thousands of Irish immigrants who had settled amid its narrow streets and within its dilapidated tenements. On this trip, Longfellow and George Sumner had first visited the Copp's Hill Burial Ground to see the tomb of Puritan clergyman Cotton Mather, then walked down the hill to Old North, "which looks like a parish church in London," Longfellow asserted.

The next day, April 6, Longfellow began work on "Paul Revere's Ride," a poem that would eventually capture the public's imagination by creating a stirring and mythic patriotic hero whose exploits would inspire the North to remain steadfast and courageous in her defense of the Union should the impending crisis explode into civil war. Two weeks later, Longfellow was still hard at work on the poem that would become one of the most memorized works by students in American schools for more than a century. On April 19, 1860, his diary entry read: "I wrote a few lines of 'Paul Revere's Ride,' this being the day of that achievement."

Perhaps on the anniversary of Revere's ride, Longfellow penned the poem's opening stanza, among the most recognizable lines in the American canon:

> Listen my children, and you shall hear,
> Of the midnight ride of Paul Revere,
> On the eighteenth of April, in Seventy-five;
> Hardly a man is now alive
> Who remembers that famous day and year.

Longfellow's opening lines tell us a great deal of the poet's intent; by invoking children, he implicitly defined the Revere story as one that adults must pass on to the next generation. His inclusion of the exact date of Revere's achievement is of critical importance too. "The message is clear," poet and critic Dana Gioia wrote years later. "Paul Revere's achievements were of such singular importance that we must learn the date by heart and teach it to posterity." The fact that "hardly a man is now alive" who remembers Revere's ride personally is another reason for the audience to preserve its memory.

But it is Longfellow's final lines, ones that are not so well remembered, that summarize the larger themes and purposes of the poem:

> For, borne on the night-wind of the Past,
> Through all our history, to the last,
> In the hour of darkness and peril and need,
> The people will waken and listen to hear
> The hurrying hoof-beats of that steed,
> And the midnight message of Paul Revere.

Longfellow painted Revere's actions in 1775 as heroic at a time when the yet-to-be American nation needed heroes to even dream about a future independent of British control. Now, the nation faced a new peril, and, in the words of historian David Hackett Fischer, Longfellow had issued a "call to arms for a new American generation."

"Paul Revere's Ride" was first published in the December 18, 1860, edition of the *Boston Transcript*, a little more than one month after Abraham Lincoln had been elected the nation's sixteenth president without the support of a single Southern state, and just two days before South Carolina became the first state to secede from the Union.

But it was the poem's publication in the January 1861 issue of the *Atlantic Monthly* that conveyed Revere's deeds to a widespread audience, one that transformed Revere from a fairly well-known Boston silversmith and folk hero to a national celebrity—at least in the North—whose actions were worthy of emulation eighty-five years later and whose cause was as noble as the present challenge of preserving the Union. The poem "had an extraordinary impact," David Hackett Fischer wrote in his historical account of Revere's ride. "The insistent beat of Longfellow's meter reverberated through the North like a drum roll." Like Stowe's *Uncle Tom's Cabin* eight years earlier, "Paul Revere's Ride," in Fischer's words, "instantly captured the imagination of the reading public." Not only did the poem issue a call to arms, "it was also an argument from Paul Revere's example that one man alone could make a difference."

"Paul Revere's Ride" might have done all of these things, but what the poem did *not* do was accurately depict the events of April 18, 1775. In between his evocative opening stanza and the emotional sweep of his closing lines, Longfellow took enormous liberties with the facts; or as Fischer bluntly writes, "the poem was grossly, systematically, and deliberately inaccurate." Despite Longfellow's overall knowledge of history, his visit to the Old North Church, and his climb to the bell tower, "Paul Revere's Ride" contains a series of glaring falsehoods that, interwoven with myth, have become ingrained as historical facts. For example, Paul Revere did not merely receive the lantern signals from the Old North Church, as the poem states, he helped send them; he did not row alone across the Charles River to await the signals, but was transported by others; he never reached Concord as the poem romantically intones ("It was two by the village clock, / When he came to the bridge in Concord town"), but was captured by British regulars in nearby Lincoln; Revere was not the solitary rider that night as Longfellow asserts, but one of dozens, perhaps as many as sixty, who fanned the countryside warning of the advance of the British troops.

The alteration of facts to create a patriotic myth was, of course, Longfellow's intent, regardless of the veracity of some of the details he includes in the poem (Revere's friend "startled the pigeons from their perch…masses and moving shapes of shade" as he climbed the church tower to hang the lanterns, the same bird species Longfellow encountered on his climb.). He was not interested in historical precision, but for his own interpretive purposes, he "invented an image of Paul Revere as a solitary hero who acted alone in history," Fischer points out. Despite efforts by historians through the years to correct the impressions Longfellow's poem left with the American public, "the scholars never managed to catch up with Longfellow's galloping hero." Longfellow biographer Charles Calhoun wrote: "Despite every well-intentioned effort to correct it historically, Revere's story is for all practical purposes the one Longfellow created for him." Even most contemporaneous New England historians responded with indignation to Longfellow's poem. In 1868 Lexington town historian Charles Hudson wrote angrily: "We have heard of poetic license, but have always understood this to be confined to modes of expression and regions of the imagination, and should not extend to historic facts…when poets pervert matters of history…they should be restrained, as Revere was in his midnight ride."

Yet his protests and those of his fellow antiquarians fell upon deaf ears. Inaccuracies aside, the general theme of Longfellow's poem *did* reflect historical reality—Revere's actions (and those of his associates) required great stealth and courage; he (and they) risked freedom and life to carry out the mission; Revere recognized that the cause he (and others) rode for was far greater than himself and carried grave implications for the future of his homeland. All of these components could be applied to the crisis the nation faced in late 1860 and early 1861. "The genius of Longfellow's poem was to link this powerful theme [of a solitary American hero] to a patriotic purpose," Fischer points out. "Paul Revere entered the pantheon of patriotic heroes as an historical loner of the sort that Americans love to celebrate. It [Longfellow's poem] stamped its image of Paul Revere as an historical loner indelibly upon the national memory."

Longfellow's intentions were overtly political when he published "Paul Revere's Ride." A longtime antislavery voice and Unionist, he set his goal to build public resolve to fight slavery and protect the Union, which was on the verge of disintegration. "Lincoln is elected," he proclaimed in his journal entry of December 3, 1860. "This is a great victory; one can hardly overate [sic] its importance. It is the redemption of the country. Freedom is triumphant."

By 1861, Longfellow had achieved worldwide fame, and in America he was a household name. In 1857 he calculated that he had sold more than fifty thousand copies of *The Song of Hiawatha*, more than forty-three thousand copies of *Voices of the Night*, and thirty-five thousand copies of *Evangeline*. As popular as Dickens by the late 1850s, Longfellow sold twenty-five thousand copies of *The Courtship of Miles Standish* within the first two months of its publication, plus another ten thousand copies on the first day it appeared in London, according to biographer Charles Calhoun. On the brink of civil war, his voice was clear, strong, and persuasive—"Paul Revere's Ride" was his reminder to Americans of the courage their ancestors displayed to form the Union, and the courage they would need to save it.

Published across the North just three months before the Confederate attack on Fort Sumter, the poem's message could not have been timelier.

JUNE 4, 1860. Exactly two months after Longfellow and George Sumner dined together and planned their North End visit, U.S. Senator Charles Sumner of Massachusetts rose from his chair at the stroke of noon in the Senate chamber to deliver his first speech in more than four years. The occasion was the debate over the admittance of Kansas to the Union as a state. The title of the speech, "The Barbarism of Slavery," was vintage Sumner, who, despite the beating he endured in 1856, his painful convalescence, and his lengthy absence from the Senate, remained vociferous about his hatred of slavery, the slave owners who profited from it, and the Southern economic system that perpetuated it.

Washington, D.C., was abuzz over Sumner's speech. He had returned to the Senate six months earlier after an absence of three and a half years, but had eased into his duties due to his doctor's concern about overexertion. More specifically, since leaving Europe in late 1859, he had struggled to find his equilibrium, both physically and politically. From his long and disagreeable transatlantic voyage ("Out of its 16 days I was sea-sick 12; so that I was most happy to touch the firm earth," he wrote), to his arrival in Washington ("This is a barbarous place. The slave-masters seem to me more than ever *barbarians*—in manner, conversation, speeches, conduct, principles, life."), Sumner felt out of sorts. He believed his health was still precarious and his role in the Republican Party just as uncertain. "During his absence, Republican leaders seemed to have become more concerned with respectability than with human rights," Sumner biographer David Donald asserted. They felt confident of the antislavery vote in the 1860 election, and were adopting a more moderate position on slavery to attract Whigs and Know-Nothings. They went out of their way to condemn John Brown and worried that William Seward, a leading candidate for the Republican nomination for president, was too radical for some. In Sumner's words, "men representing the great middle states declared that their voters were not far enough advanced in the Anti-Slavery cause to sustain him."

Where did that leave Sumner?

"Nobody writes to me now & I feel solitary enough here," he fretted to Samuel Gridley Howe in late April of 1860. "I feel also the little faith of our own men in the true principles of our cause." He was disappointed when the Republican convention, held in Chicago, bypassed Seward and nominated little-known Illinois attorney Abraham Lincoln on May 16. To Seward he wrote: "My personal feelings have been so much disturbed by the result … that I cannot yet appreciate it as a public act."

Still, he acknowledged that Lincoln "is a good honest Anti-Slavery man," and while he has "very little acquaintance with Govt.," Sumner conceded: "We think he will be the next President." Two weeks after Lincoln's nomination, with the Kansas statehood issue before the Senate, Sumner felt compelled to speak after four years of silence.

Curiosity abounded in the nation's capital. Would Sumner have the physical strength to engage in one of his patented lengthy and impassioned orations? Would he mention the savage beating inflicted on him in 1856 and his difficult recovery? Would he moderate his public position on slavery? Would he be speaking for himself or for Lincoln and the Republican Party? How would the South respond?

Even his loyal friends were fearful of the combative mind-set he had continued to express since returning to Washington. Howe and Longfellow thought he was "too full of fight" and warned him "against saying a word not qualified by beneficence and charity." Another friend cautioned: "You have floored those dirty fellows [Southern slave owners] and I would not stop to piss on them while they are down." Sumner had given a hint of his feelings about these appeals when he wrote to Howe back in January: "When crime and criminals are thrust before us they are to be met by all the energies that God has given us by argument, sarcasm, scorn and denunciation. The whole arsenal of God is ours and I will not renounce one of the weapons—not one!"

As he began speaking in the Senate chamber on June 4, it was clear that Sumner would unleash his full rhetorical arsenal. When it came to the subject of slavery, the twin political pillars of conciliation and compromise were simply foreign notions to him; he had never backed down or wavered and he would not start now.

He answered one of the questions quickly: how much emphasis would he give the Brooks assault? "I have no personal griefs to utter...I have no personal wrongs to avenge; only a barbarous nature could attempt to wield that vengeance which belongs to the Lord," he began quietly. In the only reference he made to the recent deaths of Preston Brooks, his assailant, and Andrew Butler, the object of his scorn in his 1856 speech, he said: "The years have intervened and the tombs that have been opened since I [last] spoke have their voices too...Besides, what am I—what is any man...compared with the Question before us?"

Then, without further preliminary, Sumner launched into a searing indictment of slavery and slave owners, a thirty-five-thousand-word polemic unsparing in the forcefulness of its content and tone, virtually every sentence and paragraph wielded as a cudgel, clubbing into submission the South's proslavery arguments. The crime against Kansas, an enraged Sumner reminded his audience, was an "exuberance of wickedness, detestable in itself," but it became "tenfold more detestable when its origin is traced to the madness of Slavery." He spent half his oration refuting Southern senators' claims that slavery was a beneficent institution, arguing that a slave society was no civilization at all. "Barbarous in origin; barbarous in its law; barbarous in all its pretensions; barbarous in consequences; barbarous in spirit; barbarous where it shows itself," Sumner roared. Then, framing the argument that filled the second half of his speech, he declared: "Slavery must breed Barbarians."

His language, at once stinging and eloquent, roiled the chamber with a rancorous turbulence that had long been missing while his chair remained vacant. He summoned all the passion of the powerful Massachusetts abolitionist movement, of which he served as standard-bearer and champion on the national level. It was as if he knew this was a speech for the ages; at the least, a clarion call to the new Republican Party of Abraham Lincoln to stand up and be counted. Invoking religious themes in a way he had never done, Sumner referred to slavery as "nothing less than a huge insurrection against the eternal law of God, involving...the denial of all human rights, and also the denial of that Divine Law in which God himself is manifest—thus being practically the grossest lie and the grossest Atheism."

Between freedom and slavery, Sumner informed his colleagues and those in the gallery, there is an "essential incompatibility. If you are for the one, you can not be for the other; and just in proportion to the embrace of Slavery is the divorce from Civilization." The barbarism of slavery appeared in both the character of slavery, and—in a theme that he had heretofore only alluded to—in the character of *slave owners.*

He mocked the laws that regulated slavery, pointing out that a Southern Negro might be "marked like a hog, branded like a mule, yoked like an ox, maimed like a cur, and constantly beaten like a brute; all according to the law."

How, Sumner thundered, could any man equate slavery with civilization?

His arguments transcended the moral; the practical consequences of slavery, too, were debilitating to a society. In relentless statistical detail—a shift from his lyrical emotional rhetoric—Sumner compared the populations of the North and South. He found that slavery had stunted progress in the South, "in population, values of all kinds, manufactures, commerce, railroads, canals, charities, the post office, colleges, professional schools, academies, public schools, newspapers, periodicals, books, authorship, [and] inventions." He could not resist ridiculing South Carolina, pointing out that a smaller percentage of her white population than of Massachusetts free Negroes attended school.

Even more shocking, Sumner concluded, was the impact of slavery upon slave owners. Slavery was "founded on violence, intimidation...brutal and vulgar pretensions...*to compel the labor of fellow-men without wages.*" (Sumner's emphasis.) How could one expect civilized leaders—indeed, civilized men—to emerge from such a society? It was no wonder that "the bludgeon, the revolver, and the bowie-knife" were the constant companions of the slave owners.

By the time a drained and weary Sumner concluded his speech, virtually all of his Senate colleagues, Northerners and Southerners, were present in the chamber. They all bore witness to a simple fact: during his absence, the outspoken senator from Massachusetts had lost neither his antislavery fire nor his ability to infuriate his opponents. Preempting an anticipated rebuttal defending slavery, Sumner scolded a hypothetical Southern senator: "Say, sir, in your madness, that you own the sun, the stars, the moon; but do not say that you own a man, endowed with a soul that shall live immortal, when sun and moon and stars have passed away."

When Sumner finished, disgusted South Carolina senator James Chesnut rose and spoke only briefly: "After ranging over Europe, crawling through the back doors to whine at the feet of British aristocracy, craving pity, and reaping a rich harvest of contempt, this slanderer of states and men has reappeared in the Senate." Explaining why Southern senators had listened quietly to Sumner's scathing speech, Chesnut said he had hoped the Massachusetts senator, "after the punishment he had received for his insolence," would have learned propriety and manners. Yet, that clearly had not occurred; Sumner had made his reappearance in the Senate none the wiser nor better for his experience.

Unflappable, Sumner replied that he planned to print Chesnut's remarks in an appendix to his speech to ensure the record was complete, and to illustrate the barbarism he had just described. Back in Boston, a gleeful William Lloyd Garrison wrote: "To the Senator of South Carolina, nothing could be more felicitous than the retort of Mr. Sumner."

Sumner himself was pleased with his speech, quickly sending a copy on June 8 to Abraham Lincoln with a note that read in part: "It is my earnest hope that what I said may help our great cause, by vivifying its principles, & by inspiring good men every where to join in their support." (Lincoln replied a week later from Springfield, Illinois, thanking Sumner for his note. He had yet to read the speech, he explained, "but I anticipate both pleasure and instruction from it.")

But the Massachusetts senator's explosive words generated fresh fury in the South. Southerners could barely restrain themselves after hearing the speech, which, according to one newspaper report, "was regarded as being more offensive than the one which created such a sensation before," and "but for prudential considerations, it might have been attended with similar results." A New Orleans paper labeled Sumner a "pestilent knave and low demagogue, who, from the meanest of motives, is trying to create sectional hatred in the country." Some Southerners could not let Sumner's latest volley of insults stand. Four nights after the speech, a drunken Virginian forced his way into Sumner's chambers and threatened that his friends would cut the senator's "d——d throat before the next night," according to several accounts. Sumner replied that his room was no place for the conversation and ordered him out. He initially refused, but finally left after he threatened Sumner "in the most violent and bloody terms." In his view, the threats against him only buttressed his argument about the lowly character of slave owners.

Yet, if Sumner's speech elicited raw hatred from his enemies, it also drew initial criticism from his friends. At best, his oration received a tepid response even from Republican quarters in the North, many of whom sought to distance the party from its controversial senator. Things had changed since 1856, when the brutal assault on Sumner provided the incentive and ammunition for the meteoric growth of the Republican Party. With Lincoln's nomination, and a real chance at the presidency, most Republicans feared that Sumner's remarks would alienate moderate voters. In the words of Iowa senator James W. Grimes, Sumner's speech "sounded harsh, vindictive, and slightly brutal…His speech has done the Republicans no good." Even Massachusetts Republicans responded tepidly. The *Boston Advertiser* credited Sumner for the "careful and patient" crafting of the speech, but wondered if the occasion of debating Kansas statehood "called for such a display of power, whether the object of attack needed such ponderous blows."

Though he deeply resented the criticism from fellow antislavery voices, Sumner remained undeterred. "*That* speech," he declared, "will yet be adopted by the Republican party." For weeks after Congress adjourned, biographer David Donald reported, he remained in "sweltering Washington" franking thousands of copies of the speech for distribution all over the country. Some of his personal abolitionist friends also helped spread word of the speech; in Boston, Samuel Gridley Howe distributed copies and Garrison reprinted it in the *Liberator*, calling it "dignified and bold…and [with] a noble purpose." On the evening of June 18, black worshippers at the Joy Street Church paid tribute to Sumner's speech, praising its eloquence and honesty.

As the summer progressed, Sumner's efforts to publicize his speech began to pay dividends. Again, as in 1856, members of the general public became his earliest and strongest allies. Hundreds of letters poured in from antislavery Northerners (the Sumner correspondence contains about 450 letters that arrived in the month after his speech), virtually all supportive of the senator, a groundswell that buoyed his spirits and reinforced his resoluteness. "Behind you," wrote a Pittsburgh man, "stand a million of your fellow-citizens in whose hearts your speech finds an echo." Sumner recognized the populist appeal of his speech and his bedrock antislavery position, and wore the beleaguered maverick's mantle with pride. The letters were "full of feeling & gratitude," Sumner wrote in late July, "& all expressing interest in my position."

During late summer and fall, Sumner addressed one Republican rally after another, according to David Donald, telling voters the choice in November was between Northern civilization and Southern barbarism, between the ideas of John Quincy Adams and John C. Calhoun, between the *Mayflower* and the first slave-ship, "with its fetters, its chains, its bludgeons, and its whips…choose ye, fellow-citizens between the two."

—m—

"I do not doubt the result," Sumner wrote on September 3, 1860, of the upcoming November election. "Lincoln will be chosen. Then, however, will commence a new class of perils & anxieties…idealist as I am, I shall prepare myself in advance for many disappointments."

But he could not have been disappointed in the profound influence he exerted on the slavery debate in the crucial summer of 1860. His was the strongest, the clearest, the most unyielding antislavery voice that rang through the nation's capital and across the country since taking leave from the Senate four years earlier. The 1856 caning silenced him for a time, perhaps nearly killed him, but it failed to change him, his position, or his approach. Without question, the ideas he promulgated, the arguments he crafted, the language he employed, formed the basis not only for the strong antislavery platform eventually adopted by the Republican Party, but for the antislavery fervor that spread throughout the North in the days leading up to Lincoln's election. Where others sought compromise, he remained steadfast regardless of the consequences (though many argued that civil war would be the inevitable result of his—and other abolitionists'—unwillingness to consider a more moderate position). His combination of inspired oratory, unshakeable conviction, and tenacity inspired those who agreed with him, swayed the fence-sitters, and, eventually, even converted some naysayers.

Charles Sumner, whose attitudes on slavery had taken root, grown, and finally, flourished, among Boston's most outspoken and impassioned abolitionists, transplanted those ideas and that passion across a nation—with remarkable success.

He was well aware of the consequences of this success; Southern states threatened secession and, if that happened, war could not be far behind. Sumner detested violence and feared this prospect. "Much as I desire the extinction of slavery, I do not wish to see it go down in blood," he wrote.

Still, as 1860 drew to a close, even as the war threat loomed, Sumner was loath to compromise on what he considered the most important issue of his time. To Longfellow he wrote on December 3: "There must be no yielding on our part. We are on the eve of great events."

DECEMBER 3, 1860. Frederick Douglass felt someone grab him by the hair and mockingly shout, "Wool won't save him." With the help of several other ruffians, the man hurled the onetime slave onto a pile of chairs that antiabolitionists had heaped upon the stage. Struggling to his feet, Douglass attempted to elbow his way to the podium to speak, shouting angrily at his assailants, "I know your masters. I have served the same masters as yourselves!"

It was the one-year anniversary of John Brown's death, and the commemorative gathering organized by black and white abolitionists at Boston's Tremont Temple had deteriorated into a donnybrook of mob violence. Antiabolitionist Unionists ("mainly Irish hired by commercial interests," according to the *Boston Evening Transcript*), wealthy businessmen (Amos Lawrence was one), and State Street merchants crowded into the temple, too, anxious to let the South and the nation know that abolitionists alone did not represent the views of the city.

Reaching the podium, Douglass informed the raucous audience that a clerk in the front row had just called him a "nigger." He retorted: "If I were a slave-driver and got hold of that man for five minutes, I would let more light through his skin than ever got there before!" Fresh fistfights broke out and the verbal slugfest continued for another hour before police arrived and began clearing antislavery advocates from the hall. Douglass was thrown down the main staircase. The pandemonium continued amid cries from Unionists to "put them out, all out" and "blow them up," referring to the more than one hundred black abolitionists and their white counterparts in the meeting hall.

Like much of the country, Boston had been on edge since Abraham Lincoln's election in November and the threatened Southern response. Lincoln had made clear his immovable support for the Union and his opposition to slavery's extension: "Let there be no compromise" on the issue, he wrote. "The instant you do, all our labor is lost."

Without the sustenance that could only come through slavery's extension, the South recognized that it was only a matter of time before the peculiar institution, and the way of life it supported, would wither and die. Less than three weeks after Lincoln's election as the nation's sixteenth president, Governor John J. Pettus of Mississippi declared to his state legislature: "Our deliverance from this great danger, in my opinion, is to be found in the reserved right of the States to withdraw from injury and oppression." Indeed, Pettus argued, secession was the only way to avoid the blight of "Black Republicans and free negro morals"—elements that would transform Mississippi into a "cess pool of vice, crime, and infamy." Four days later, on November 30, the legislature authorized Governor Pettus to appoint secession commissioners to every slave state. Alabama followed with commissioners of its own. In the midst of the Tremont Temple melee, the South Carolina legislature was hammering out secession plans; two weeks later the state's two United States senators resigned their seats, and the state legislature prepared to arm a defense force of ten thousand men.

In an analogy Bostonians recognized well, the *Charleston Mercury* proclaimed: "The tea has been thrown overboard; the revolution of 1860 has been initiated."

While Boston's abolitionists had enjoyed growing support, Lincoln's election and the resulting Southern action frightened Boston merchants and Unionists, and drove home the possibility that the Union would not survive. Six years earlier, the Anthony Burns case evoked sympathy for the abolitionist cause in their opposition to the Fugitive Slave Law. But secession, the dissolution of the Union, was something else entirely. Those who earned their livelihood—and in some cases, made their fortunes—from factories, mills, textiles, shipping, and other industries that depended on Southern cotton and other crops, used the Tremont Temple riot of December 3, and subsequent events, to send their own message. They circulated handbills for a "Union meeting" at Faneuil Hall on December 8, calling upon all those who "honor and cherish the Constitution" to attend. The building was packed with prosperous businesspeople and conservative political leaders, again eager to show that many in Boston and Massachusetts disdained the radical abolitionist agenda.

Back and forth it went in the waning weeks of 1860. Rallies and counterrallies often turned to violence. Antiabolitionists threatened to burn the black Baptist church on Joy Street, and Wendell Phillips had to seek police protection from a mob that followed him home after he delivered a speech at the Music Hall. "The storm seems to howl more fearfully than ever," wrote abolitionist Maria West Chapman, "but it is a comfort to have it raging where the North can see and understand." Distinguished orator Edward Everett, a onetime Massachusetts governor, president of Harvard College, secretary of state, and U.S. senator, blamed the Republicans and their abolitionist supporters for exploiting the John Brown affair and pushing the country to the brink of a "final catastrophe." More than twenty thousand Massachusetts Unionists signed a petition favoring a compromise on slavery and slavery extension and delivered it to Congress. Charles Sumner dismissed it as "all wind."

The press took a stand, too. The *Boston Advertiser* scolded abolitionists for their meeting commemorating John Brown's execution, claiming, like Everett, that they exploited the historic date. "They knew the record of their meeting would be eagerly snatched up and spread throughout the country," the paper said, "and that this record would be taken as representing the feelings of a large party in the city." Not surprisingly, Garrison's *Liberator* took the opposite view, calling the Unionists' actions at Tremont Temple "another dastardly attempt to suppress freedom of speech."

Coming as they did following Charles Sumner's "The Barbarism of Slavery" speech and Abraham Lincoln's election to the presidency, the Boston abolitionist meetings during December of 1860—which were publicized around the country—placed the city of Boston and the state of Massachusetts squarely in the crosshairs of the slaveholding South. Boston abolitionists embodied the worst qualities the South railed against as it contemplated secession: radicalism, federalism, elitism, and, perhaps most repulsive considering the number of Bostonians who had become rich though the factories and textile mills that were fueled by Southern cotton, blatant and craven hypocrisy. With sectional tensions at a fever pitch, Boston's national influence, so strong during the tumultuous 1850s, now resonated with particular fervor in the South. The region's profound concerns about the threats to its way of life were reflected most starkly in the actions of Boston's abolitionists; the December protests offered a preview of what the South believed would be its plight under a Lincoln administration. Antiabolitionist protests by business leaders and conservatives proved to be too little, too late to salvage Boston's reputation among Southern secessionists, and thus unpersuasive in preserving the Union.

More than any other city in the nation, Boston embodied what the Southern states most feared and despised as they prepared to sever their ties with the United States of America.

On December 20, 1860, South Carolina became the first state to secede from the Union. Meeting in Charleston, secession-convention delegates submitted the ordinance to dissolve the Union shortly after

1:00 p.m., and by 1:30, all 169 members had voted yes. Church bells pealed and business activity ceased in celebration. "Men rushed joyously about, whooping and shouting," historian Maury Klein wrote, "rending the air with cheers, waving palmetto flags and blue cockades that were the secessionist badge." One celebrant proclaimed: "The greatest enthusiasm pervades our entire community. We feel we have done right, and are prepared to defend our act."

In January of 1861, five more Southern states followed: Mississippi, Florida, Alabama, Georgia, and Louisiana. Texas voted to secede on February 1. While the president-elect was constructing his cabinet, "the country was falling to pieces," Lincoln biographer David Donald asserted. Lincoln himself, on the advice of bodyguard Allan Pinkerton, who feared an attempt on the president-elect's life, slipped into Washington incognito aboard a secret overnight train.

On March 4, in his inaugural address, Lincoln tried to reassure the South that "their property, and their peace, and their personal security" would not be jeopardized by a Republican administration, but he also warned: "No State, upon its own mere motion, can lawfully get out of the Union—that *resolves* and *ordinances* to that effect are legally void…and acts of violence…against the authority of the United States, are insurrectionary or revolutionary, according to circumstances." He was hopeful, though, that the country could settle its differences without violence, emphasizing that the North and South were "friends, not enemies…though passion may have strained, it must not break our bonds of affection." In his memorable close, Lincoln predicted that the "mystic chords of memory…will yet swell to the chorus of the Union, when again touched, as they surely will be, by the better angels of our nature."

But fate decided otherwise. On April 1, Major Robert Anderson, who commanded the federal garrison at Fort Sumter in Charleston Harbor, South Carolina, sent word to Washington that his troops required provisions by April 15 or would have to be withdrawn. The request "occasions some anxiety to the President," Secretary of War Simon Cameron replied to Anderson on April 4. If Lincoln did not resupply Sumter, he would be publicly acknowledging that the Confederate states had indeed broken from the Union, and in a sense, legitimize their secession. If he did send supplies, South Carolina would view the move as an act of aggression, which would precipitate its retaliation and a civil war. Lincoln thought hard about his decision and labored under tremendous strain. "The pressure was so great that Mary Lincoln reported that he 'keeled over' and had to be put to bed with one of his rare migraine headaches," David Donald wrote. Finally, he reached a decision: he would send provisions to Fort Sumter.

On April 9, days after the Fort Sumter supply ships had departed, William Appleton, a wealthy Boston businessman, U.S. congressman, and a close friend of Amos Lawrence's, departed from New York Harbor aboard the steamer *Nashville*. At age seventy-five, Appleton wrote that he was heading South for "reasons of health," but some of his Whig friends suspected that he was trying to broker a last-minute compromise for peace. On Thursday evening, April 11, the *Nashville* lay just outside of Charleston Harbor, "waiting for the rise of the tide that we might cross the Bar," Appleton wrote.

On Friday morning, April 12, 1861, around four o'clock, Appleton and the other *Nashville* passengers were awakened by the sound of ear-splitting cannon fire. They rushed to the railings and saw Fort Sumter under attack. "The interest and excitement was great," Appleton wrote. "Every flash we could see; then the smoke; then followed the report; the bomb shells we saw ascend & would anxiously watch whether they fell in Fort Sumter." Appleton recorded in his diary that the shelling continued Friday "without any long cessation from either party; at one time we thought most of the men in the Fort must be destroyed by fire, but again they shew they were alive by commencing again their works." Finally, he reported, the firing stopped on Saturday afternoon, though Appleton's ship was "compelled to remain outside the Bar until Sunday morning." Upon arriving in the city of Charleston and finding "no one killed," Appleton said he felt "emotions of gratitude in my breast that I have seldom or never before felt."

He also knew the magnitude of what he had seen. Appleton found a telegraph in Charleston and transmitted word to his friends back in Boston. The two cities—Boston in the North and Charleston in the South—had for years served as the unofficial seats of power for their respective regions, defining the polar opposite forces battling within the stormy vortex over slavery, sectionalism, and social order. Boston and Charleston, which adopted extremist and immovable positions on either side of the spectrum, exerted enormous pressure on the center. How appropriate, then, that a Bostonian, visiting Charleston, was on hand to witness the cracking of that center and the beginning of what would become America's most cataclysmic event: the Civil War.

CHAPTER 7

War

I don't believe there is any North. The Seventh Regiment is a myth. Rhode Island is not known in our geography any longer. *You* are the only Northern realities.

> —*President Abraham Lincoln, speaking to the Sixth Massachusetts Volunteer Regiment, the first Union troops to arrive in an otherwise undefended Washington, D.C., with the Confederate army threatening attack, April 1861*

APRIL 22, 1861. Dawn's murky light had just begun its slant across Boston, yet the morning gloom did little to dampen the festive mood that gripped the thousands of people who jammed the city's downtown streets at 5:00 a.m. The Fifth Massachusetts Regiment, consisting of more than eight hundred troops, was heading to war, and Boston residents cheered them lustily as they marched from Faneuil Hall onto State Street, proceeded down Court, Tremont, West, and Washington streets, then onto Beach, Albany, and Oak streets, and finally to the Boston and Worcester freight-train station near South Cove (adjacent to present-day South Station).

All along the route, Bostonians roared their approval, and a huge throng gathered at the station to wish the soldiers well. Men and equipment filled nineteen railroad cars, and at ten minutes to seven the train lurched forward—amid the joyous shouts of a crowd that had swelled to several thousand and two bands playing "The Star-Spangled Banner"—beginning its conveyance of troops to Washington, D.C. "In view of the stern reality of their mission, we can see only the brave hearts and noble souls of this gallant regiment," one Boston reporter wrote of the Sixth's departure.

The Fifth Massachusetts had arrived in Boston two days earlier, on Saturday, part of a second wave of troops called out by Governor John Andrew, who was responding to President Lincoln's April 15 proclamation calling on Northern states to commit seventy-five-thousand militiamen to suppress the Southern rebellion. "I appeal to all loyal citizens to favor, facilitate, and aid this effort to maintain the honor, integrity, and the existence of our National Union, and the perpetuity of popular government," Lincoln said, "and to redress wrongs already long enough endured." Governor Andrew quickly ordered out the first wave of troops: the Third, Fourth, Sixth, and Eighth regiments from outlying towns, all of whom rendezvoused at Faneuil Hall on the morning of Tuesday, April 16. These soldiers, too, were greeted by huge crowds of people, who braved a violent and soaking rainstorm—which prevented a full-dress assembly on Boston Common—to cheer on the military men. As the Sixth Regiment marched from Faneuil Hall along State Street to the nearby armory where it would spend the night, the corps was greeted "with loud cheers from the immense throng that lined the street," waving flags and handkerchiefs, according to one report, "and on passing up Washington Street, every window and door thronged with both males and females of all ages, who kept up a continuous exhibition of enthusiasm."

One day later, on the evening of Thursday, April 17, the Sixth Massachusetts left Boston by train en route to Washington, under the command of Colonel Edward Jones, the first unit to respond to President Lincoln's call, the first Northern unit to go to war. Earlier that day, at a State House ceremony attended by thousands of Bostonians, Colonel Jones had accepted the regimental colors from the governor's hands with the pledge, "So help me God, I will never desert it." As part of the same ceremony, Jones's four-hundred-man regiment adopted his twelve-year-old daughter, Lizzie, as "Child of the Regiment." Governor Andrew, addressing the men, urged them to act worthy of the "glorious tradition of the state they represented." He added: "I thank you from the bottom of my heart for this noble response to the call of the State and your country."

With the departure of the Sixth, Massachusetts had become the first state to commit troops to war on behalf of the Union, much as its militias had been first in the field to fight for independence sixty-six years earlier. "The spirit of '76 is alive," one newspaper proclaimed; "these are the sons of Concord," boasted another.

Indeed, it was just days after the attack on Fort Sumter and Boston already stood on a firm battle footing, her citizens flush with war fever. One city newspaper reported that "news from the South has aroused the enthusiasm of our citizens and military men, who will respond with alacrity to the call of the National Government." Boston crackled with activity. American flags were draped from buildings, hoisted up flagpoles, and ceremoniously unfurled from storefronts; the Jordan Marsh store hired a band to accompany its display of the Stars and Stripes. The merchants of Franklin Street raised the flag on a 140-foot-high pole directly in front of the office of William Lloyd Garrison's *Liberator*, the U.S. flag waved atop the Custom House, and miniature flags decorated the interior of Faneuil Hall. Bands played throughout Boston's downtown and cheering crowds gathered as troops arrived from all parts of the state.

The governor's and adjutant-general's offices at the State House were jammed with men seeking commissions to command regiments or volunteering their services to fight for the Union. Among them was a group of 150 young Boston men who gathered unofficially and marched to the State House with drum and fife, playing "Yankee Doodle" and bearing the American flag. A peddler outside the State House approached a colonel, who told him he should enlist to help the cause. "I have no uniform," the peddler replied. "That can easily be arranged," the colonel replied. The peddler emptied the contents of his bag, followed the colonel into the State House, enlisted, and was provided with a cap and overcoat to take his place with a regiment, where he was "received with loud cheers," according to one report.

From all quarters, Bostonians rushed to support the call to war. Supplies flowed into the city, as factories and armories excitedly responded to Governor Andrew's order. During the afternoon and evening of April 16, as the first troops arrived, military overcoats and blankets were distributed to the men. The Commonwealth's stockpile of thirty-five hundred muskets (with twenty-five hundred additional expected each day from the Springfield armory), five hundred thousand cartridges, and "an abundance of ammunition" were transported to Boston. Boston banks offered money to Governor Andrew to fund the war effort: one hundred thousand dollars from Suffolk Bank;

fifty thousand dollars each from Webster Bank, C. P. Hovey & Co., and the Lowell Institute for Savings; smaller amounts from several others. Railroad executives offered to transport troops at no charge. Telegraph operators gave preference to troops transmitting messages to loved ones. Many business owners agreed to continue to pay their employees' salaries if they enlisted, with the money going each week to their families until they returned from battle (one paid an enlistee six months' salary in advance). Affluent citizens from outlying towns contributed to the families of volunteer militiamen who were leaving for places like Washington, D.C., or Fort Monroe, Virginia. Average Bostonians distributed water and oranges to troops mustering at Faneuil Hall or the State House, or awaiting deployment at the railroad stations or the docks.

"The enthusiasm...shows that our people are not only in earnest but united, and the spirit displayed...cannot fail to send a thrill of encouragement among the loyal people of the whole land," proclaimed one editorial. One letter writer from Kansas, who was visiting Boston, echoed the sentiment: "I have witnessed during my visit here some of the noblest manifestations of true patriot spirit I have ever known."

And Boston *was* united in its support for war; an uneasy coalition of its differing points of view, perhaps, but this fight was greater than any differences between its citizens: between abolitionists and merchants, who had been at loggerheads over the slavery issue for the years leading up to hostilities; between Irish immigrants and free blacks, who competed for many of the same jobs; or between abolitionists and the Irish, who deeply resented the antislavery movement's focus on the plight of African Americans while virtually ignoring the hardships and discrimination faced by Irish immigrants. None of these differences mattered now. Words flowed from pen and pulpit, from street corner and boardroom, exhorting the Union cause.

Abolitionists, who normally deplored bloodshed, nonetheless saw the war as a chance to abolish slavery forever. If it put an end to "that execrable system," Garrison said, it would be "more glorious in history" than the American Revolution. Henry Ward Beecher, in his sermon on April 21, challenged his congregation: "We must draw the lines...Let every man take sides one way or the other; let every man show his hand; we want no middle men, no shufflers; all must now stand each for himself on this great question. He who is not with us and for us is against us."

The Irish had become steadfast Unionists and viewed the war as an opportunity to express their unconditional support for their adopted country; they enlisted and volunteered by the thousands. The *Pilot*, the Irish Catholic newspaper, assured the city that "the Irish adopted citizens are true, to a man, to the Constitution," and would fight bravely to preserve the Union. Even while deploring abolitionist tactics and editorializing that the South had suffered at the hands of Northern fanatics, the *Pilot* insisted that nothing could justify secession and civil war.

Boston merchants, Democrats, and old-line Whigs, while also sympathetic to some Southern concerns, believed nothing was greater than supporting and defending the Union. Without peace and a unified country, commerce, production, and capital were all threatened. The *Boston Post*, the city's leading Democratic newspaper, urged readers in an editorial to "stand by the flag." Added staunch Massachusetts Democrat Caleb Cushing: "Whatever may have been our antecedents, there is no uncertainty as to the duty of every citizen of the United States. Party now is but the dust in the balance, the foam on the wave in comparison with Union and liberty."

And, unsurprisingly, Boston's free black community unalterably and unabashedly trumpeted its support for war. "The colored people want to fight," the *Boston Investigator* reported. "[They] are in a high state of excitement, and express their readiness to volunteer whenever permitted to do so." Black leaders in Boston met with Governor Andrew at the State House, pleading with him to form colored troop companies and dispatch them southward forthwith; "placed in the slave States, [they] would soon have an army of thousands of slaves at their backs."

Thus, Massachusetts and Boston—which at once had come to define the North's most radical and uncompromising abolitionists, her most prosperous merchants and businessmen, her most literate and activist black population, and her changing demographic face—spoke with one voice as the Civil War began: unwavering and ebullient support for the Union.

All of these groups spoke with passion, and in some cases, anger—emotions that would intensify when word spread of a deadly civilian mob attack upon the men of the Sixth Massachusetts in Baltimore as they marched toward Washington, D.C.

They were the first casualties of the Civil War.

—m—

By the time members of the Fifth Regiment arrived in Boston to great fanfare on April 22, they were prepared to avenge their brethren in the Sixth, who had shed the war's first blood hundreds of miles to the South, much as troops from Lexington had done to begin the American Revolution. That the Baltimore attack on the Sixth Regiment occurred on April 19, the anniversary of the battles of Lexington and Concord, reinforced the feeling of patriotic righteousness in the attitudes of most Northerners, further fueling their outrage and intensifying their calls for vengeance.

The Sixth's journey southward began triumphantly. On the morning of April 18, they arrived to a tremendous welcome in New York City, and an even bigger reception as they marched smartly down Broadway from the train station to the Hudson Ferry—thousands waved flags, banners, and handkerchiefs honoring the volunteers from Massachusetts. New York's George Templeton Strong acknowledged the "immense crowd; immense cheering" in his diary, and recorded his own emotions: "My eyes filled with tears, and I was half choked in sympathy with the contagious excitement. God be praised for the unity of feeling here! If it only lasts, we are safe." On the same day as the Sixth Massachusetts's historic march through Manhattan, New York greeted the returning *Baltic* as it steamed into the harbor, carrying Major Anderson and his troops from Fort Sumter. "The coincidence was a sign, people said," historian Nelson Lankford wrote. "Surely the Massachusetts volunteers would avenge brave Anderson's surrender."

The next day, Friday, April 19, 1861, shortly after 10:00 a.m., the Sixth Massachusetts arrived in Baltimore, where a dramatically different kind of reception awaited them.

Colonel Jones had warned the men that they could face hostilities. Maryland was a border state, whose loyalties would be divided throughout the war. "One moment Southern sympathizers would be singing 'Dixie' or tearing down the Stars and Stripes," Thomas O'Connor wrote. "The next moment Union sympathizers would be singing the 'Star Spangled Banner' or burning Rebel banners in the streets." Colonel Jones informed his volunteer troops: "You will undoubtedly be insulted, abused, and perhaps, assaulted, to which you must pay no attention whatever."

But Jones's warning could not have prepared the Sixth for what awaited them in Baltimore.

Since different rail companies owned and managed track, there was no through-route from Philadelphia to Washington, D.C.; the troops had to switch trains in Baltimore for the final leg of their journey. The Sixth Regiment would arrive at Baltimore's President Street station and travel in horse-drawn railroad carriages for a mile along Pratt Street to the Camden Street station, where they would transfer to the train to the nation's capital. Despite the presence of a "large and angry crowd" that greeted the Sixth Regiment and surrounded their horse-cars, the first seven companies made it safely to Camden Street station.

But for several remaining companies, about two hundred men, the situation turned ugly. The large crowd became a mob, several thousand strong, surging toward the horsecars and blocking their passage. Members of the Sixth exited the cars and began marching hurriedly along Pratt Street, bearing a white flag, even as the crowd pressed against them, hurling insults and epithets. The crowd tore up the horsecar tracks and placed large anchors, dragged from the nearby docks, in the middle of Pratt Street to prevent more troops from passing. Suddenly, the mob began pelting the soldiers with bricks, rocks, cobblestones, and paving stones, and brandishing knives and revolvers. Gunshots rang out from the crowd and one soldier was killed; others were hit and wounded. The Sixth's officers finally ordered their men to return fire, and they killed several civilians. A Baltimore judge who witnessed the melee wrote the next day that "the soldiers bore the pelting of the pitiless mob for a long time under a full trot" before returning fire. Southern partisans swore that the soldiers fired first, without provocation.

Baltimore mayor George William Brown, who had been at the Camden Street station to supervise the transferring of the Sixth to the Washington, D.C., train, received word of the Pratt Street riot and raced toward the scene. When he arrived at the Pratt Street bridge, he plunged into the crowd, urging those assembled to cease their hostilities, while several of them shouted, "Here comes the mayor." Brown wrote later that he "shook hands" with the officer in command, "then placed myself by his side and marched with him...doing what I could by my presence and personal efforts to allay the tumult." But Brown's efforts were to no avail: "The mob grew bolder and the attack more violent," he wrote. "Various persons were killed or wounded on both sides. The troops had some time previously begun to fire in self-defense, and the firing, as the attack increased in violence, became more general." The mayor feared for his own life as the violence escalated: "At last, when I found that my presence was of no use, either in preventing the contest or saving lives, I left the head of the column."

As Brown moved to safety, Police Marshal George Kane and about fifty officers arrived, pushed the mass back, formed a line across the street between the troop's rear guard and the angry citizenry, drew their revolvers, and formed a bulwark to protect the Sixth Massachusetts, enabling the soldiers to reach the Camden Street station to continue their journey to the nation's capital. "The movement...was perfectly successful and gallantly performed," Mayor Brown reported later. "But for the timely arrival of Marshal Kane with his force...the bloodshed would have been great."

At the train station, as members of the Sixth Massachusetts boarded, Colonel Jones ordered the blinds lowered to "avoid eye contact with the locals," Nelson Lankford wrote, as a huge crowd surrounded the station. "Only with great difficulty was Jones able to prevent his men from jumping off the cars and avenging their fallen comrades." As Baltimore residents continued to throw stones at the railroad cars before they departed, some troops fired back, and killed Robert Davis, a popular Irish-born dry goods merchant. Colonel Jones said later that he regretted the shooting of Davis, but "the men were infuriated beyond control."

As it was, four soldiers and twelve civilians were killed in what would become known as the Pratt Street Riot. Dozens more were wounded in an incident that, in the words of one local paper, was over before "most of the citizens even within three or four square of the place knew anything of it." But both Northern and Southern sympathizers and supporters recognized the gravity of the clash in Baltimore.

"The first blood of the American Civil War to be shed in anger had been spilled," Lankford wrote. "The mute tongues of the dead on Pratt Street would not lack for surrogates on both sides crying out for vengeance."

Outraged and indignant Bostonians became even more united, if possible, behind President Lincoln and Governor Andrew when news spread that their boys had been fired upon by hostile rebels. Across the state, residents, newspapers, politicians, and clergymen focused on the historic date of the attack, drawing parallels between the action against the Sixth Regiment and the "shot heard 'round the world" that opened the American Revolution. (Nor was the date lost on Southern newspapers. The *New Orleans Picayune* of April 21 proclaimed: "It reads like a rehearsal of the Past—another battle of Lexington—another immolation of life for the purposes of another war upon Freedom.") One Boston newspaper deplored the "wanton attack" on the Sixth, and declared: "The most experienced soldiers could not have behaved better under the circumstances…the Sixth can never be called to encounter any more terrible ordeal than that which they have already so gallantly and successfully endured." The Boston Board of Aldermen unanimously appropriated one hundred thousand dollars for war purposes, and the City of Roxbury added twenty thousand dollars. Any vestige of empathy for the South, any hope that war could be avoided, was obliterated with the news from Baltimore.

For his part, Governor Andrew wrote to Baltimore mayor Brown urging him to "cause our Massachusetts soldiers dead…to be immediately laid out, preserved with ice, and tenderly sent forward by express [train] to me. All expenses will be paid by this Commonwealth." Brown apologized to Andrew for the mob violence against the Sixth, saying he "deplored" the events in his city, but he called the riot inevitable. "Our people viewed the passage of armed troops to another State through the streets as an invasion of our soil and could not be restrained," he wrote to Andrew. Indeed, to prevent more Northern troops from marching through Baltimore and provoking "severe fight and bloodshed," Brown ordered the burning of railroad bridges north of his city, cutting off both Baltimore and Washington, D.C., from the North. "This act," Brown said, was undertaken to preserve his city, "but with no purpose of hostility to the Federal Government."

Nevertheless, Brown's astonishing reaction, which incensed the North and panicked the capital, also had the practical effect of preventing the Baltimore mayor from complying with Governor Andrew's request to return the bodies of the Sixth Regiment's dead. "All communication between this city and Philadelphia by railroad, and with Boston by steamers, [has] ceased," Brown wrote to Andrew. As such, Baltimore would place the bodies in "cemented coffins" and provide "proper funeral ceremonies in mausoleums" until (and if) transportation was resumed between Maryland and the North. Brown also thanked Andrew for his offer, but said Baltimore "would claim it as her right to pay all expenses incurred."

An angry and perplexed Andrew replied in his return letter to Brown: "I am overwhelmed that a peaceful march of American citizens over the highway to the defense of our common Capital should be deemed aggressive by Baltimorians [sic]. Through New York the march was triumphal."

Andrew wasn't the only one angry. Militiamen and merchants alike, who were stunned by the Pratt Street Riot, demanded revenge and full support for the war effort. Those feelings reached a fever pitch when word arrived from Richmond that thousands of Virginians participated in a torchlight celebration of secession and the heroic acts of "the gallant Baltimoreans." As the Fifth Regiment mustered in Boston, their officers were anxious to begin moving them southward by rail and ship, but they were not fully provisioned as yet. An order was issued that some of the regiment should move out immediately and the rest would follow when supplies arrived. "But when the case was stated to the men, they voted unanimously to live on crackers and water rather than the regiment should be divided," one newspaper reported. "The order was immediately revoked." One militia commander stood on a balcony overlooking State Street and told a cheering crowd: "Let us show the world that the patriotism of '61 is not less than that of the heroes of '76." Businessman and carriage maker Edward Riddle, who transformed his warehouse into a place where volunteers could assemble packages of supplies for the troops, addressed the same crowd, reminded them that Massachusetts had answered the president's call and rapidly mustered four thousand troops "to uphold the flag of the Union as their fathers did in the former Revolution." Bostonians let out a deafening roar when Riddle added: "That flag will never be taken from them, except over their dead bodies."

Across the city, young men rushed to enlist, the wealthy contributed funds, women signed up to aid the wounded. Governor Andrew, heartened by the response, pledged that he would always remember "that great week in April when Massachusetts rose up at the sound of the cannonade of Sumter, and her Militia brigade, springing to arms, appeared on Boston Common."

—⚉—

The Sixth Massachusetts Regiment arrived in Washington, D.C., none too soon. They were the first armed volunteers to come to protect the nation's capital, whose residents justifiably feared that the sudden secession of Virginia and the burning of the Maryland bridges would leave the city defenseless if the rebels attacked. Desperation gripped Washington, evidenced by the bold headline in the *Evening Star:* "NO TRAINS—NO TELEGRAPH—NO ANYTHING." It was only the Sixth—bedraggled, exhausted, unnerved by their experience in Baltimore—that stood between the Southern forces and the possible destruction of the nation's capital. "The men who had paraded through the streets of Boston only a few days earlier were now the only Union regiment on hand that could have met a Confederate attack upon the capital during its six days of complete isolation," Thomas O'Connor wrote.

Weary members of the Sixth Regiment made their way to the Senate chamber, where they found some warmth and rest in anticipation of the uncertainty that lay ahead. There, they were greeted by an unexpected visitor. President Abraham Lincoln told the troops that he appreciated their gesture more than words could express, that he was inspired by the role that Massachusetts would once again play in fighting for the nation's freedom. "I don't believe there is any North," an uneasy Lincoln told the Sixth. "The Seventh Regiment is a myth. Rhode Island is not known in our geography any longer. *You* are the only Northern realities."

But the Confederates did not come, and on April 25, the Seventh New York did arrive, followed by the First Rhode Island, and, to the delight of the Sixth, the Fifth and Eighth Massachusetts regiments. Some arrived by steamer, others by rail after the Massachusetts troops repaired the tracks leading into Maryland. Washington was reinforced and saved—and Boston and Massachusetts once again set the example for the rest of the nation.

As troops rolled into Washington and mobilized across Pennsylvania, Ohio, Illinois, and other Northern states, it was yet another Massachusetts activist who captured the mood of those who supported the Union and whose opinions had solidified since the events at Fort Sumter, and then in Baltimore, Washington, and Richmond. "The whole country is intensely hot with the conflagration of civil war, on a scale such as, perhaps, the world has never seen," William Lloyd Garrison wrote in the *Liberator* on April 26, 1861. "Those who

have stood by the South…are now many of them the loudest in denunciation of their recent allies, and the fiercest to meet them on the
battlefield!"

In this case Garrison's characteristically hyperbolic account accurately described the support for war that was sweeping the North:
"The change in Northern feeling…is total, wonderful, indescribable…So mighty and irresistible is the popular feeling, that nothing
can stand before it."

JANUARY 1, 1863. As the eleven o'clock hour struck at Boston's
Tremont Temple, tension built among the thousands assembled there.
Only sixty minutes from midnight on New Year's Day, and still no official word that President Lincoln had issued his promised Emancipation Proclamation. Boston had been celebrating for the entire day;
church bells rang throughout the city and jubilee celebrations were
held, as blacks and whites joined together to mark the beginning of a
new era in the country's history.

Frederick Douglass had addressed the Tremont Temple crowd
earlier; in his speech he thanked God that he was alive to see the
beginning of the end of slavery. While he knew that Lincoln's proclamation would not have the immediate effect of liberating the slaves,
Douglass had no doubt of its ultimate weight and historic significance, since it finally put the full power of the United States government on the right side of the struggle between "beautiful right and
ugly wrong." As the day turned into evening, the crowd at the Tremont Temple grew and attorney Edward Atkinson excited the throng
when he held up an exhibit of Sea Island cotton and declared it the
first-ever crop raised in South Carolina by free labor. By unleashing
the economic potential of the freed slaves, this one plantation owner
"will be able to pay a surplus of $400,000 above all expenses into
the United States treasury." In response, Douglass declared that since
its founding, the American nation "was fighting with one hand—the
black hand—tied behind them. The time was coming when that hand
was to be untied."

But precisely when, on this first day of 1863, would that time
arrive?

—⚏—

Anxious citizens wondered aloud whether Lincoln would keep his promise. While Douglass led the meeting at the Tremont Temple, Boston's literary and social elite packed the nearby Music Hall: Emerson, Longfellow, Whittier, Charles Eliot Norton, Harriet Beecher Stowe—all awaited the long-sought news from the nation's capital.

In fact, Lincoln had signed the document shortly after noon earlier that day, after greeting guests in a lengthy New Year's Day reception line at the White House. "I never, in my life, felt more certain that I was doing right, than I do in signing this paper," President Lincoln remarked to his aides. But, he added, his arm was so stiff and numb from three hours of shaking hands that he was unsure he could control his pen. "Now, this signature is one that will be closely examined," the president said, "and if they find my hand trembled, they will say 'he had some compunctions.' But, any way, it is going to be done!" Then, President Lincoln grasped the implement and, in the words of biographer David Herbert Donald, "slowly and carefully wrote his name at the end of the proclamation."

Messengers had been stationed at Boston's telegraph office since early evening, charged with bringing word to the Tremont Temple and Music Hall rallies that Lincoln had signed the proclamation. "We…waited on each speaker, keeping our eye on the door, and no proclamation," Douglass recounted later. "And I said, 'We won't go home till morning.'"

Then suddenly, shortly after eleven o'clock, Judge Thomas Russell, who had gone to the telegraph office himself for news from the capital, burst through the Tremont Temple's front doors, shouting to the crowd, clutching the Emancipation Proclamation text in hand, along with the notification that Lincoln had signed it. "Hats, muffs, cushions, overcoats, and even umbrellas were thrown heavenward, and dancing and stamping became general all over the hall," one reporter recounted. Crowd members shouted "God Bless Abraham Lincoln," "Glory to God," and "Bully for Old Abe" as the cheering reached a crescendo. "The colored people seemed to be crazy with joy," a journalist noted. Frederick Douglass wrote later: "I never saw Joy before. Men, women, young and old were up; hats and bonnets were in the air."

Abolitionist Charles W. Slack ascended the rostrum and asked for order. The crowd quickly complied, and Slack read the words of the historic text: "That on the 1st day of January, in the year of our Lord, 1863, all persons held as slaves, within any State or designated part of a State, the people whereof shall then be in rebellion against the United States, shall be then, thenceforth, and forever free."

Slack was interrupted with thunderous applause, waited for the noise to subside, and continued: "And the executive government of the United States, including the military and naval authority thereof, will recognize and maintain the freedom of such persons..."

More sustained applause.

"And will do no act or acts to repress such persons or any of them in any effort they may make for their actual freedom."

And again, the audience erupted with cheers.

When Slack finished, Frederick Douglass led the singing of the psalm "This Is the Day of Jubilee," the meeting concluded, and the ecstatic crowd spilled onto Tremont Street, many of them heading for Boston's leading black church, the Twelfth Baptist, which the Reverend Leonard Grimes had helped build, shouting and singing "Glory Hallelujah," and "Blow Ye, the Trumpet Blow," and praise for President Lincoln. Frederick Douglass recalled: "We got up such a state of enthusiasm that almost anything seemed witty—and entirely appropriate to the glorious occasion."

Meanwhile, at the Music Hall, Ralph Waldo Emerson addressed the crowd after the proclamation was read, after the crowd roared its approval for Lincoln and abolitionist William Lloyd Garrison. Emerson read "The Boston Hymn" with feeling and dignity, a song of liberty and justice:

> Today unbind the captive,
> So only are ye unbound;
> Lift up a people from the dust,
> Trump of their rescue, sound!
>
> Up! And the dusky race
> That sat in darkness long—
> By swift their feet as antelopes
> And as behemoth strong.

Emerson asserted that the historic moment was vindication for Boston's history of antislavery activity, despite its vilification by the South and more moderate Northerners.

For the Bostonians who celebrated that night, into the wee hours of January 2, Lincoln's Emancipation Proclamation—as toothless as it was unless and until the North won the war—was far more than a presidential order. It was a document that bordered on the sacred, one considered and accepted with near-biblical reverence, one unimagined a decade earlier when abolitionists were considered fringe radicals and Northern acquiescence to Southern slave owners was seen as essential for commerce to thrive.

No longer. The men and women who filled Boston's streets on the morning of January 2 fully recognized the power and potential of the Emancipation Proclamation's content and they fully concurred with the conclusion reached by the *Boston Daily Advertiser* later that day:

"No instrument of more momentous import has ever been published since the Declaration of American Independence challenged the attention of the world, and this proclamation affects the welfare of as large a number of human beings as did that."

The paper's editorialist conceded that the *Advertiser* was not among those who believed that the "mere dash" of Lincoln's pen "secures freedom to the full…[or] that it straightaway crushes the rebellion and ends the war." Still, once the proclamation "passed from the field of controversial policy to the domain of an actual fact," it provided the North with advantages. It cleared the way for colored troops to fight in the federal army and deprived the South of this resource. Politically, it all but removed serious disputes among those who supported the United States government and those who questioned Lincoln's opposition to slavery.

But perhaps the proclamation's greatest value was more symbolic in nature, the *Advertiser* argued. After nearly two years of war, Lincoln's words meant that the North, at long last, "shall now have thoroughly on our side the immense support which springs from the cordial sympathy of the moral sense of the whole world." And that moral sense, it was believed, would endure.

Of Lincoln's January 1, 1863, signing, Massachusetts senator Charles Sumner wrote: "It is done, & the act will be firm throughout time."

JANUARY 11, 1863. Days after his fellow abolitionists' euphoric celebration of the Emancipation Proclamation in Boston, Thomas Wentworth Higginson watched with awe as his entire South Carolina volunteer regiment, nearly one thousand strong, faces "black as coal" and standing tall under the branches of great oaks at Camp Saxton, near Beaufort, raised their right hands and pledged themselves "to be faithful to those still in bondage." Higginson, irrepressible Boston abolitionist, a man who had declared war on slavery years before armed hostilities broke out between North and South, was once again at the center of a controversy. He had taken command of the North's first colored combat unit, and the way his men performed in battle would go a long way in determining which side prevailed in the Civil War.

Higginson, who entered the army in late August of 1862 and was commissioned a captain, had raised a traditional company of all-white volunteers in Massachusetts and was training them at a camp near Worcester, Massachusetts, when he received the stunning request to assume command of a regiment of colored troops, the First Regiment of South Carolina Volunteers.

Higginson had heard rumors of Union efforts to organize former slaves and free blacks. Union troops had seized the Sea Islands off the coast of South Carolina, where slaves labored on large plantations producing rice and cotton. As the Yankees approached, plantation owners fled their homes, carrying what belongings they could, and most abandoned their slaves. Thousands of slaves were on hand to greet the Union soldiers and sailors, and after the North occupied the islands, runaways from the mainland also found their way to the islands. By late 1862, more than eighteen thousand black men, women, and children were harbored on the Union-held territory in the Deep South. The question, as one historian put it, was "what to do with these anomalous, masterless slaves, an issue unprecedented in American history."

At once an idealist and a pragmatist, Higginson recognized the monumental importance of his new task: "As many persons have said, the first man who organizes & commands a successful black regiment will perform the most important service in the history of the War."

Tactically, strategically, symbolically—so much was riding on the efforts of Higginson's South Carolina volunteers. They were training for a mission whose goal was to transform the South, and whose by-product would likely hasten the war's conclusion. Within months of Higginson assuming command, the plan was for his men to steam southward along the Atlantic coast to Florida, turn up the St. John's River, and seize the town of Jacksonville. The bold incursion into Confederate territory was not designed as a mere raid, as historian Stephen Ash pointed out. Rather, its intent was to establish a permanent post in Florida's interior, "to serve as a beacon of freedom, a haven for black fugitives, and a firebrand of liberty that would help ignite the destruction of Southern slavery from within."

Even more than that, the performance of the South Carolina volunteers would largely determine whether the notion of arming black troops would be taken seriously. If Higginson's men failed, the reputation of black troops in the North would be seriously undermined, their capabilities forever suspect. If the South Carolina volunteers succeeded, however, they would establish the credibility of black troops as a fighting force—and if then recruited in large numbers, could provide the North with an enormous advantage in an increasingly bloody war of attrition.

The eyes of a nation—two nations, actually, for the Confederate States of America was watching, too—would be fixed hard upon them.

For three weeks inside Florida during March of 1863, Higginson's troops performed superbly in wartime conditions: they fortified Jacksonville, fought side by side with white Union troops sent in as reinforcements, seized rebel provisions, and freed slaves. White Floridians feared them, but Higginson had given strict and repeated orders not to harm civilians and his men complied. "My men have behaved perfectly well here, though many were owned here & do not love the people as you may suppose," he wrote from Jacksonville on March 13.

But inexplicably and mysteriously, just as the South Carolina troops believed they could deliver a fatal blow to slavery in Florida—and perhaps the rest of the South—the regiment was ordered to evacuate Florida. Union general David Hunter terminated the expedition and recalled Higginson's troops. Higginson and his men were distraught. "Just as our defenses are complete and all in order for the transfer of part of our forces up river to other points, we are ordered away," he lamented.

Hunter never made known his reasons for ordering the evacuation. Some speculated that he needed additional troops for the assault on Charleston, though Higginson noted to friends that the Charleston campaign had been planned well before the Jacksonville mission. Others surmised that Hunter felt the South Carolina volunteers had proven themselves with their accomplishments in Florida and that they should be withdrawn before a black soldier mistakenly injured or killed a white civilian, thus undoing the stellar reputation Higginson's men had built. Still others considered General Hunter mentally unstable.

Still, the mission's lofty goals set a standard that could not be minimized. "The…expedition of 1863…stands as unique in the annals of the Civil War and perhaps in the annals of all military history," historian Stephen Ash wrote years later. "Conceived and commanded by radical abolitionists in uniform, in a shining moment of optimism inspired by the Emancipation Proclamation, it was intended first and foremost to ignite the destruction of slavery within the world's most powerful slaveholding society, and to establish and defend a homeland for the freed people." While those goals were not achieved, the progress Higginson's men made played a pivotal role in the outcome of the Civil War: the South Carolinians demonstrated that black troops could fight, that they possessed the bravery and the discipline to perform under fire. "Colors that will not run are what are chiefly wanted in an army," quipped one editorial. The newspaper then captured the essence of what Higginson's men had accomplished: "In choosing horses for military service, we have never heard it urged that white horses are better than black ones. Why, then, in a question of fighting, should we refuse black men and confine ourselves to white men?"

Massachusetts Governor John Andrew had been asking himself the exact same question and reached the same conclusion. Shortly after President Lincoln signed the Emancipation Proclamation, Andrew traveled to Washington and got permission to enlist volunteer troops that "may include persons of African descent, organized into special corps." Historian Thomas O'Connor noted that Andrew raised five thousand dollars in private money to place advertisements in newspapers throughout the North for a new black regiment, to be called the Fifty-fourth Massachusetts. Realizing that the Fifty-fourth would be the first of its kind in the North, Andrew was well aware that its success or failure would go far "to elevate or depress the estimation in which the character of the Colored American will be held throughout the world." He wanted young officers, "gentlemen of the highest tone and honor" to command this regiment, and settled on Robert Gould Shaw, then a captain with the

Second Massachusetts Infantry, to lead the new regiment as a colonel.

Shaw arrived in Boston in mid-February of 1863 to assume his duties, and he—along with the rest of the North—watched with great interest as Higginson's South Carolina troops performed courageously in Florida.

By May 14, the Fifty-fourth Regiment was fully staffed, more than one thousand men strong; in fact, so many black men were pouring into the Commonwealth to volunteer that Shaw and Governor Andrew decided to organize a second regiment, the Fifty-fifth. On May 18, Governor Andrew formally presented the Massachusetts colors to Colonel Shaw and said to the regiment: "I stand or fall as a man and a magistrate with the rise and fall in history of the Fifty-Fourth Massachusetts Regiment." This was an opportunity, as he presented Colonel Shaw with the colors, "for a whole race of men."

Four days later, at 9:00 a.m., with thousands of cheering Bostonians lining the streets, a marching band led Shaw and his proud regiment up Boylston Street, around Boston Common, onto Tremont Street, up to the State House, and onto the Common parade ground where Governor Andrew and his staff reviewed the troops. At noon, the regiment marched down State Street to Battery Wharf and boarded the *De Molay*, which would take the troops to their destiny, and their glory, in South Carolina.

On July 18, 1863, just two weeks after the Union's hard-fought victory at Gettysburg and the nearly concurrent fall of the Confederate's Mississippi River stronghold of Vicksburg following a ghastly six-week siege by Ulysses S. Grant, the Fifty-fourth Massachusetts took part in the assault upon Charleston, which was heavily fortified by islands. Their specific mission was to capture Fort Wagner on Morris Island from rebel troops. At dusk, Shaw led his men on a daring charge across a third-of-a-mile of open beach, facing blistering cannon and rifle fire from the heavily fortified batteries. The Fifty-fourth kept charging and men kept falling under the relentless Confederate guns, the sand stained red from the blood of the Massachusetts regiment. For nearly two hours, the Fifty-fourth continued its attack, finding whatever cover it could by digging into the sand dunes approaching the fort, losing men at an astonishing rate. Shaw was killed just as he reached the fort's parapet. Finally, with a third of its officers and nearly half of its enlisted men either killed or badly wounded, the federal troops pulled back from the beach.

For their doomed but courageous assault, for their valor and tenacity under fire, the men of the Fifty-fourth Massachusetts earned the title of heroes from the people of Massachusetts. Colonel Shaw achieved near reverential status for taking his place at the head of his regiment during the company's assault, for leading his troops by example, and for making the ultimate sacrifice. Ralph Waldo Emerson memorialized the fallen soldiers in his 121-line poem, "Voluntaries," offering an especially fitting eulogy to Shaw and his men with these lines:

> So nigh is grandeur to our dust,
>   So near is God to man,
> When Duty whispers low, *Thou must,*
>   The youth replies, *I can.*

William Lloyd Garrison's son, George, a second lieutenant with the all-black Fifty-fifth Massachusetts, expressed his desire to avenge the Fifty-fourth when his men arrived in Charleston. "The fall of that city," his father said after getting word of the Fifty-fourth's defeat, "will give more satisfaction to the entire North than that of any other place, not excepting Richmond."

Thomas Wentworth Higginson's South Carolina volunteers and the heralded bravery of the Fifty-fourth Massachusetts altered the course of the Civil War. Along with the Emancipation Proclamation, they helped spur an estimated 1 million slaves to escape to the North and add thousands of fresh troops to the ranks of the war-weary Union armies in the final two-plus years of the war. At one point during the latter part of the war, the Union army ranks included 180,000 black troops, more than the total number of Confederate combat troops, according to historian Jay Winik.

And arming black troops was more than a necessity for helping the Union achieve victory, Higginson declared—it was a necessity for blacks to achieve their full and unbounded freedom. White men were less likely to attach a second-class citizen label to blacks who had faced terror and death during combat, and performed valiantly. "'Till the blacks were armed, there was no guaranty of their freedom," Higginson wrote several years later. "It was their demeanor under arms that shamed the nation into recognizing them as men."

Still, not everyone in Boston approved of recruiting and arming black troops. Much of the Irish Catholic community, which had also sent thousands of sons to fight for the Union cause, resisted it or expressed outright hostility. For Boston's Irish, this elevated status of blacks was the latest example of what they perceived as outright nativist prejudice toward Irish immigrants, and an insulting diminishment of their own status.

Boston's Irish had also fought bravely and earned a reputation as fierce warriors in regiments such as the Ninth Massachusetts and the Twenty-eighth and Twenty-ninth Massachusetts; they had taken heavy losses at Antietam in September 1862, at Fredericksburg in December of that year, in the bloody battle of Chancellorsville in May of 1863, and at Gettysburg in July. The list of dead and wounded took its toll in Irish communities. What had begun as a war that the Irish enthusiastically supported as a means of displaying loyalty and patriotism on behalf of their adopted homeland had become, thanks to heavy casualties and perceived policy injustices, a source of deep bitterness. "The Irish spirit for the war is dead! Absolutely dead!" wailed the *Boston Pilot* on learning of the Irish casualties at Chancellorsville. "There are a great many Irish yet. But our fighters are dead. Their desperate valor led them, not to victory, but extinction...How bitter to Ireland has been this rebellion!"

And for their sacrifice, the Irish felt they were not lauded but belittled, and even deliberately antagonized, by military leaders and the Lincoln administration. After the heavy casualties at Antietam, most Irish troops and community leaders were furious when Lincoln announced the Emancipation Proclamation in the fall of 1862. "Irishmen envisioned millions of former slaves rushing North to take unskilled labor opportunities from them," military historian Susannah Ural Bruce wrote. The *Boston Pilot* declared that the proclamation was "violently opposed to the constitution," and warned that abolitionist extremism could ultimately hurt the Union's war effort. "The suppression of abolitionism is necessary to save the Union," the paper editorialized. The *Pilot* and other Irish newspapers were calling for an armistice and a negotiated peace in the fall of 1862 as the only way to stop both the bloodshed and what many Irish saw as the hypocrisy of abolitionists, who were willing to sacrifice Irish troops without adopting Irish social issues as part of their cause.

And if the Irish (who were mostly Democrats) weren't upset

enough about the war, the Lincoln administration exacerbated the situation when the president relieved General George B. McClellan of his command of the Army of the Potomac in November of 1862.

Republicans and military personnel applauded the move as the only way to lift the inertia that had dogged the army under McClellan's leadership and stalled the North's "On to Richmond" goal. But among Irish troops, the decision to remove McClellan was devastating. They were loyal to McClellan, whom they saw as thoughtful rather than reckless, and protective of their lives rather than willing to simply sacrifice them as fodder by ordering them to charge repeatedly into lethal and relentless cannon fire. McClellan's removal was evidence of Lincoln's ineptness, the *Pilot* said, in calling upon Boston Irish to oppose him: "At one time we did support Lincoln, but then he had the full promise of constitutionalism about him. He has changed and so have we. It is now every man's duty to disagree with him."

First were the terrible Irish losses at Antietam and Fredericksburg. These were followed by the controversial Emancipation Proclamation, the decision to relieve McClellan, the arming of black troops, and rumors of a future federal draft. "For increasing numbers of Irishmen, the war's cost and its goals were creating a nation they would not wish to call home," Susannah Bruce wrote years later. As 1863 began, as the cracks grew wider in the foundation of Irish support for the war, one Irish soldier captured the mood of his countrymen: "All is dark, and lonesome, and sorrow hangs as a shroud over us all."

Further, Irish enlisted men, officers, and community leaders resented what they saw as disrespect and a lack of gratitude from Republicans for their sacrifice. In fact, the Irish saw the Emancipation Proclamation not only as an unconstitutional overstepping to protect the rights of blacks while the government blatantly ignored the plight of the Irish, but as a gesture that would strengthen the resolve of the Confederates to fight to the bitter end, thereby causing thousands of *additional* Irish casualties. Instead of recognizing that the means for ending the war was to "withdraw its causes," the *Pilot* blamed Lincoln for having "deliberately increased it" with the Emancipation Proclamation. Further, the president's decision to recruit black soldiers was not seen by the Irish as a means to reduce their own burden, but as a largely symbolic policy that would antagonize Irish soldiers even more. "The feelings against nigars is intensely strong in this army, as is plainly to be seen wherever and whenever they meet them," wrote Peter Welsh of the Twenty-eighth Regiment to his wife in Boston. "They are looked upon as the principal cause of this war, and this feeling is especially strong in the Irish regiments."

Irish women, too, were not shy about expressing their resentment toward the war. Mothers and wives of Boston Irish troops complained bitterly of the sacrifices their sons and husbands had made and the financial strains their families faced with their main breadwinners away at distant battlefields. The records of the all-Irish Ninth Regiment contain letters from women lobbying for pay raises and promotions for their men. One North End Irish woman appealed to Governor Andrew for money to help pay for burying her son, who died after serving two terms in the army. "The temporary loss of male income hit immigrant and working-class families hard," wrote historian Judith Ann Giesberg. "By 1863 letters from home often complained of wartime inflation and rising prices." Growing government demand, for example, doubled the price of staples like beef, coffee, sugar, eggs, and bread between 1861 and 1863; coal, wood, and clothing prices also spiked dramatically. "Irish working-class women were experts at managing the meager resources of their families," Giesberg noted, "but even so, they could only scrape by for so long without funds from their husbands, sons, or fathers."

All of this Irish bitterness culminated in mid-July of 1863 with the draft riots, first and most violently in New York City. There, during five days of terror, many Irish Americans protested the newly imposed draft, emancipation, the Republican administration, and the war. "Bloody rioting swept the city," historian Thomas O'Connor wrote. "Telegraph lines were cut, buildings destroyed, property looted, and innocent African Americans brutally murdered." Order was not restored in New York until U.S. army troops were brought up from Gettysburg to quell the rioting. Some of this violence spilled over into Boston. When two provost marshals called upon a home on Prince Street in the North End to serve a draft notice, they were set upon by a large group of irate mothers. Later, Irish men beat up several policemen—some nearly to death—and a wholesale riot broke out. The violence spread to Dock Square and Faneuil Hall marketplace, and additional police officers and army troops were called in to restore order. Despite simmering tensions between authorities and the Irish neighborhood in the ensuing days, additional violence was sporadic and limited, though the City of Boston reported expending thirty thousand dollars to put down the July 14 riot.

After their early enthusiasm, Irish resentment continued throughout the rest of the war. Irish enlistments thinned during 1864 and 1865, and most Irish supported former General McClellan in his failed bid for president against Lincoln in the election of 1864. While many Americans saw the declining support for the Union cause as a betrayal, most Irish Americans considered it an act of loyalty by remaining faithful to their fellow Irishmen. "A sense of responsibility to their heritage and families in Ireland and America had inspired Irishmen to wear Union blue," wrote Susannah Bruce, "and it was these same dual loyalties that led to their eventual opposition to that cause."

The Civil War had an enormous impact on Boston abolitionists and its burgeoning Irish population, and thus on the city itself.

For abolitionists, General Robert E. Lee's surrender to his counterpart, Ulysses S. Grant, at Appomattox Courthouse in Virginia on April 9, 1865, was vindication for years of marginalization, at best, and revilement most often, especially in the fifteen years since the Fugitive Slave Law went into effect. The defeat of the Confederacy wiped away the bitterness of the Thomas Sims and the Anthony Burns affairs, of the Charles Sumner caning, and of John Brown's execution. John Wilkes Booth's assassination of President Lincoln on April 14 made the sixteenth president abolitionism's final and greatest martyr. From the day Lincoln had issued the Emancipation Proclamation, William Lloyd Garrison declared, the president had grown in "grace and knowledge" and had understood "that he was to be an instrument in the hand of God to bring about great and glorious ends."

Without a doubt, Boston abolitionists had begun, and continued undeterred for decades, the monumental task that Lincoln and the Civil War had finished: expunging slavery from the United States.

Just a few weeks after Lincoln's funeral, Garrison attended the last meeting of the American Anti-Slavery Society in New York City. He had already announced that he would cease publication of the *Liberator* at the end of 1865, confident that the Thirteenth Amendment would be fully ratified "in time to make his newspaper's thirty-five volumes a complete record of antislavery agitation," biographer Henry Mayer noted. Along with his fellow Boston abolitionists, an exhausted Garrison, who had pledged himself to the abolition of slavery in 1829 and had published his first issue of the *Liberator* in 1831, had achieved the seemingly insurmountable goal they had longed for. "He [Garrison] had instigated a revolution, that, at the outset of his career, had seemed a social and political impossibility," Mayer wrote.

Garrison got his wish—the Thirteenth Amendment outlawing slavery in the United States was ratified on December 6, 1865, and went into effect on December 18. In his paper's last of an astonishing eighteen hundred issues, datelined December 29, 1865, Garrison expressed pride that his journal had covered "the historic period of the great struggle." He insisted that no other newspaper in the country had done more than his to advocate the equality of human rights.

Harriet Beecher Stowe mourned the passing of the *Liberator* as a "staunch and faithful friend," but others were more upbeat; one minister noted that the paper had disappeared in the light of its own victory. From Tennessee, one army officer asked for a copy of the final issue "as a relic…that our tale is true." Without such proof, he said, future generations would never believe "that there was once such a thing as slavery."

Charles Sumner joined his name to a list of those demanding an even sturdier testament to the truth. In October of 1865, he placed an ad in the *Boston Daily Advertiser* calling for the construction of a memorial to the Massachusetts Fifty-Fourth Regiment near the State House. Such a monument and a location would enable everyone, "but especially legislators of Massachusetts—by daily sight of the symbolic statue, be gratefully led to constant support for the cause for which [they] had died."

The war also changed in profound ways the status and influence of Boston's growing Irish population. Unlike the abolitionist movement, whose embers would extinguish naturally, the heat of Irish assimilation and progress now intensified.

When the April 10 edition of the *Boston Daily Advertiser* proclaimed "PEACE!" in a bold page 1 headline, Boston's Irish community rejoiced as enthusiastically as any other, perhaps more so due to the proportionally large number of sons it had sent, and lost, to war. "It was one of the greatest days Boston ever saw, and was like a dozen 'Fourths of July' concentrated in one day," the paper added, and

Boston's Irish residents were among the thousands who flocked to impromptu celebrations across the city.

And too, when the mood in Boston suddenly darkened upon the news of Lincoln's assassination, when word arrived, as one newspaper put it, "like a thunderbolt from a clear sky," the Irish mourned along with the rest of the city, despite their disillusionment with Lincoln's policies. On the day of Lincoln's funeral, April 19, the anniversary of the battle of Lexington and Concord and of the Sixth Massachusetts Regiment's struggle in Baltimore to come to Washington's defense, Irish Catholics were among those who attended special services at churches across Boston. More than ever, the Irish believed what Peter Welsh had written to his wife from an encampment in Virginia in 1863: "This is my country as much as the man that was born on the soil. And so it is with every man who comes to this country and becomes a citizen."

Unmistakably, the opposition of the Irish to Lincoln's wartime decisions—relieving McClellan, issuing the Emancipation Proclamation, allowing black troops to serve in the Union army—hurt them politically, as it did all Democrats, for many years. After Lincoln's assassination, the sixteenth president attained an almost Christ-like status, and those who opposed him were scorned. "For years to come, the Irish would be punished for [their opposition to Lincoln] and for their loyalty to the Democratic Party," Susannah Bruce pointed out, "which would so commonly be associated by Republicans with the Confederacy, violence, and treason." While Irish immigrant Patrick Collins was elected as a state representative from South Boston in 1867, and a year later formed the Young Men's Democratic Club to enlist Irish Catholics in the Democratic Party, the Irish political ascendancy would not take hold until well into the 1870s.

Nonetheless, at ground level, many Bostonians saluted the bravery of the Irish troops and sympathized with the losses the Irish regiments had suffered. Their political views notwithstanding, they were now perceived by others as true Americans, not merely foreigners living on American soil.

Economically, too, the war transformed the fate and future of the Irish in Boston. Soldiers received bonuses upon their return from the battlefields and those who did not serve had worked hard for four years in armories and arsenals, foundries and factories, to produce equipment for the war effort, and in textile mills and garment shops to clothe the troops. This economic progress continued and expanded after the war, as the Back Bay landfill project continued and provided steady and relatively prosperous employment for Boston's Irish; and as word of this upward mobility crossed the Atlantic, still more Irish made their way to Boston.

The Irish, once almost exclusively crammed into dilapidated tenement neighborhoods like the North End and West End, soon began to move out into the neighborhoods of South Boston, Charlestown, and East Boston, and even further into the independent towns of Roxbury, Dorchester, and West Roxbury.

As Irish contributions to the Civil War were measured in the years after the conflict, and as Irish fortunes improved, so did nativist attitudes toward the Irish.

The progress his people were making in Boston was not lost on Peter Welsh, who wrote to his wife: "It is our duty to do our share for the common wellfare [sic], not only of the present generation but of future generations."

CHAPTER 8

Peace, Expansion, Perseverance

For half a century, [Boston] has carted gravel into the bay,
making land for streets and warehouses to the serious damage
of her harbor. What she most needs at the present time is room.

—*Massachusetts Senate report on Boston's*
impending annexation of Roxbury, May 1867

DECEMBER 2, 1867. Charles Dickens ascended the platform in the Tremont Temple amid vociferous applause and wild cheering from the hundreds of people who had each paid two dollars to hear the British novelist read from his latest work. Many audience members had stayed in line all night when tickets were put on sale, bringing mattresses, food, and drink to make their wait more comfortable. "Dickens has arrived for his readings," Henry James Jr. had written ten days earlier when the famed author's ship landed in Boston. "It is impossible to get tickets." On this evening, literary giants such as Ralph Waldo Emerson and Henry Wadsworth Longfellow (with whom Dickens had shared Thanksgiving dinner) were among those who had procured tickets to attend their friend's long-anticipated reading.

It had been twenty-five years since Dickens's last visit to Boston, and the fifty-five-year-old author was battling health issues as he began his speaking tour of the United States. Still, he climbed the platform at Tremont Temple "with a brisk step, almost on the run," according to one newspaper report, and, in the words of another, still had "the air and port of a young man—his step firm and free, his bearing erect and assured."

Clutching his book in one hand, Dickens bowed to the audience, and without preamble, began reading *A Christmas Carol* for the first time in the United States. Before a large maroon backdrop, and behind a specially designed waist-high desk that included a block for supporting his elbow and a rail near the floor for him to rest his feet, Dickens read for nearly two hours, delighting his audience first with the stories of characters such as Ebenezer Scrooge, Bob Cratchit, and Tiny Tim; and later, expounding on the tales of Samuel Pickwick, Sergeant Buzfuz, and Sam Weller from *The Pickwick Papers*.

"We have never seen an audience watch the speaker more closely," a reviewer wrote breathlessly. "Great is Dickens—not much less as a reader than as a writer." The audience responded with "tempests of applause," one newspaper reported. Another concluded: "We have little doubt that he may safely be said to be the most popular author who ever wrote in any tongue." Clearly, as *Harper's Weekly* wrote after Dickens's Tremont Temple reading, Boston was "perfectly mad" for him.

Bostonians loved Charles Dickens, and in return, Dickens always referred to Boston as his American home. "[It is] a memorable and beloved spot to me...delightful...and that spirit will abide with me as long as I have sense and sentiment left." Of his first Boston trip in 1842, he had written: "The city is a beautiful one, and cannot fail, I should imagine, to impress all strangers very favourably."

But in 1867, his second trip to Boston, a full generation after his first, it is unlikely the author even recognized the place. "The last five and twenty years would seem to me but so many months, were I not sometimes reminded of their sweeping changes," Dickens wrote to Charles Sumner in late November 1867.

Indeed, Boston was a much-changed city in the late 1860s.

It was not just that the abolitionist point of view had become mainstream—a far cry from the fringes on which it operated in the early 1840s—or that Boston had played perhaps the nation's most prominent role in ending slavery (Dickens believed slavery was "foul" and wrote that he was "sickened and repelled" by the institution).

Nor was it merely Boston's dramatic population growth, booming from about ninety-three thousand inhabitants in 1842 to more than two hundred thousand in 1867, largely on the strength of immigration and industrial growth during the Civil War.

And, while Dickens was well aware of the massive Irish influx into

Boston, even the city's vastly altered demographic face and number of foreign-born residents did not fully capture the depth of its change.

Certainly all of these were important, but Dickens would also have taken notice of other major differences that continued the transformation of Boston Town into a large and highly influential city, changes that would continue long after he sailed back to London in April of 1868.

Buoyed by the strength of her influence before and during the war, by her ability to tackle difficult projects and succeed, by the sterling reputation she had developed across the country in so many areas, Boston would not rest on her laurels as the nation headed into the uncertain first few years after the South's surrender.

Instead, in social, cultural, educational, medical, and physical endeavors, she powered ahead.

"My vocation has ended," William Lloyd Garrison wrote after he published the last issue of the *Liberator*, and now he and other Boston abolitionists concentrated their attention on righting another grievous injustice by demanding the right to vote for women. Lucy Stone, Abby Kelly Foster, Louisa May Alcott, and Julia Ward Howe led the New England Suffrage Association, and were assisted by Higginson, Douglass, and Garrison (Howe had already achieved national prominence when she wrote the lyrics to "The Battle Hymn of the Republic" in 1861). The group soon enlarged itself into the American Woman Suffrage Association, and based its agitation on the abolitionists' natural rights argument: governments could not deny citizens their fundamental civil rights, whose source derived from a higher power, either God or nature, a principle clearly articulated in the "inalienable rights" language of the Declaration of Independence. Perhaps "life" could be carried on without the right to vote, but "liberty and the pursuit of happiness" would always be unacceptably curtailed.

Once the Fifteenth Amendment granting blacks (including former slaves) the right to vote was ratified in 1870—the amendment said nothing about women—the Boston women's suffrage group intensified its efforts, working in parallel with Susan B. Anthony's and Elizabeth Cady Stanton's National Woman Suffrage Association (NWSA), until the groups merged in the 1890s. The NWSA had opposed the Fifteenth Amendment unless it was accompanied immediately by a Sixteenth Amendment that would enfranchise women. "It is infinitely more important at this hour to secure the rights of 15,000,000 women, black and white, Saxon and Celt, than to bring 2,000,000 more men to the polls," Stanton wrote during the Fifteenth Amendment debate.

After the Fifteenth Amendment's passage, Thomas Wentworth Higginson argued that the same logic must be applied to the question of women's suffrage: "If the white man cannot justly represent the negro…how impossible that one sex should stand in legislation for the other sex! This is so clear that, so soon as it is stated, there is a shifting of the ground." For Higginson and the entire group, the issue of women's suffrage was an educational process, just as abolitionism had been. The justness of their cause was undebatable in their minds; it now was a matter of employing the proper combination of logic and passion to change the minds and hearts of others. To succeed, Garrison pointed out, would require "mighty work" to build more enlightened and sympathetic public opinion.

Of course, Stanton, Garrison, Higginson, and their allies would not live to see this dream realized. The Nineteenth Amendment to the Constitution, forbidding the federal government or states from denying citizens the right to vote "on account of sex," would finally be ratified on August 18, 1920, well over a half century after the Boston abolitionists had turned their full energies and persuasiveness to their greatest post–Civil War cause.

Though women's suffrage would not require a war to become a reality, educating the public on the issue took even longer than the abolitionists' organized three-decade effort to end the scourge of slavery.

The long battle for women's voting rights notwithstanding, Boston made much more rapid progress both during and after the war on other educational matters, efforts that enhanced its stature and reflected its growth and changing demography.

In September of 1864, Boston bishop John Bernard Fitzpatrick saw his dream realized for a "college in the city," where the sons of poor immigrants, mostly Irish, could receive a good Catholic education. Boston College opened on Harrison Avenue and St. James Street in the South End (just a few blocks from where construction would begin on Boston's new cathedral in 1867) under the auspices of the Society of Jesus, led by its first president, the Reverend John

Bapst, SJ, and its first dean of studies, Rev. Robert Fulton, SJ. Its first class consisted of only twenty-two students—whose parents scraped together the thirty dollars for tuition—enrolled in a seven-year combined secondary school and college program, of whom Fulton wrote dourly: "Many came gratuitously, and only one had talent."

Nonetheless, the opening of the Jesuit schools (Boston College High School and Boston College, which initially shared the South End quarters) represented a profound advancement for Irish and Catholics in Boston, and had been a long time coming. When John Fitzpatrick became bishop in 1846, he requested that a Jesuit become pastor of St. Mary's Church in the North End; his request was granted when Rev. John McElroy, SJ, who had been the first United States Army chaplain during the Mexican War, arrived in Boston in 1847 to begin his duties at St. Mary's. Bishop Fitzpatrick confided in McElroy his desire for a Catholic school in Boston, a goal that seemed unattainable as the two clergymen ministered to the suffering of Boston's Irish during the worst of the post-famine years.

But McElroy persevered and spent years raising funds, acquiring property, and securing permissions—and on April 1, 1863, after approvals by the Massachusetts legislature, Governor John Andrew signed the charter of Boston College. The first meeting of the college's trustees was held on July 6, mere days after hundreds of Boston Irish-Catholic troops had fought and perished at the battle of Gettysburg.

War also raged as Boston and Massachusetts were establishing another unique institution of higher learning, with plans to locate it in the newly filled prestigious Back Bay neighborhood. Initially, educator and scientist William Barton Rogers authored a long proposal to the Massachusetts legislature suggesting that land in the Back Bay should be used as the site of an elaborate complex of educational institutions. Lawmakers rejected the plan as simultaneously too grandiose and too vague, but Rogers, with assistance from a supportive Governor Andrew, pressed on for a school dedicated to scientific, industrial, and artistic education.

Indeed, Rogers's passion for education and for Massachusetts was laced throughout his plan. "In New England, and especially in our own Commonwealth, the time has arrived [that] calls for the most earnest cooperation of intelligent culture with industrial pursuits," he wrote. In fact, Rogers said, while all of New England had experienced industrial growth, the "concentration of these interests" centered on

Boston, "rendering the capital of the State an eligible site for such an undertaking."

Rogers wrote that Boston's growth and success to this point was the result of the city's "superior intelligence which has inspired our enterprise and guided our activity."

But Boston could not continue to rely alone on serendipitous progress and good fortune to compete with other world-class cities. To provide for the "intelligent guidance of enterprise and labor," to prosper in an era when "material prosperity and intellectual advancement are felt to be inseparably associated," the city required a rigorous industrial and scientific institution of higher learning. The community, Rogers argued, would provide hearty support for an enterprise that would advance the industrial and educational interests of the Commonwealth. Persuaded by Rogers's arguments, the legislature eventually approved an amended bill for a scaled-down institute consisting of three components: a Society of Arts, a School of Industrial Science, and a Museum of Arts.

On April 10, 1861, just two days before the Civil War began with the attack on Fort Sumter, the Massachusetts Institute of Technology was incorporated. The school's charter called for it to aid "the advancement, development, and practical application of science in connection with the arts, agriculture, manufactures and commerce."

MIT's officers spent the war years organizing the institution, and the first students did not matriculate until after the war ended in 1865. The school opened its temporary quarters at the Mercantile Library Building in downtown Boston before moving in 1866 to a Back Bay location near Clarendon Street between Newbury and Boylston streets (near the present site of the Boston Public Library). MIT's first class graduated thirteen students in 1868.

While Rogers's proposed Museum of Arts was never established, MIT would quickly develop a reputation as one of the world's finest scientific and industrial institutions. It continued to make its home in the prestigious Back Bay until 1916, when—in a symbolic loss to Boston—board members voted to move the institute across the Charles River to Cambridge.

The founding of Boston College and MIT, the growth of its immigrant population, and the continued development of both the Back Bay and South End neighborhoods, propelled Boston's progress during the last half of the 1860s in the spheres of education and medicine, culminating in a slew of foundings in 1869: the Horace Mann School for Deaf-Mutes; the establishment by five Catholic women of St. Elizabeth's Hospital to meet the needs of sick immigrant women who were unable to afford more expensive hospitals; and the opening of Children's Hospital by Dr. Francis Henry Brown, a twenty-bed facility in the South End dedicated to caring predominately for Irish immigrant children who had contracted infectious diseases or suffered traumatic injuries. Boston's Children's Hospital was founded fourteen years after the first such hospital in the United States, the Children's Hospital of Philadelphia; prior to these institutions, children were treated along with adults in general hospitals, and often were subjected to neglect, cruelty, and even infanticide.

And in May of 1869, another college opened its doors; this one had its origins as an institution of training for Methodist clergy, and later became the Boston Theological Seminary. Ironically, when Boston University received its wider charter, empowering it to provide instruction and confer degrees for the promotion of "learning, virtue, and piety," the document banned all religious tests for faculty and students (apart from the theological school), an unusual measure for the time. Instructors would never be required to "profess any particular religious opinion," and students would never be refused admission "on account of the religious opinions which he may entertain."

As the years passed, Boston University continued its reputation of tolerance. In 1873, four years after its founding, the pronoun "he" in its documents was expanded to "he or she"—BU became the first university in the world to open all its departments to women.

Boston's postwar progress manifested itself in other dramatic ways.

Its population and commercial growth and need for expansion exceeded even the new acreage provided by the Back Bay project. Further, some Irish immigrants whose economic fortunes had improved—but who still could not afford the Back Bay—were abandoning the crowded tenements of the North End and moving into nearby suburbs, raising the demand for water, sewers, streets, and schools. As Thomas O'Connor has pointed out, Boston desperately wanted to maintain a potentially growing middle class, and the surrounding towns sought annexation to Boston so they could obtain vital municipal services their newly arrived residents demanded but the municipalities could not afford.

Would a marriage work?

SEPTEMBER 9, 1867. It would not become official until the beginning of 1868, but members of the Roxbury Friends of Annexation roared their approval each time a speaker at their outdoor rally addressed the crowd as "fellow citizens of Boston!" Residents of both communities had just voted overwhelmingly for Roxbury to become part of the City of Boston; 4,634 to 1,059 in Boston, and 1,832 to 592 in Roxbury. It was no contest; every ward in both cities voted for the union, and Roxbury—in the words of one author punning the town's new county affiliation—was "Suffolkated."

While some voices in both communities expressed skepticism over annexation (Boston objectors believed taxes would rise to support services for the new neighborhood; Roxbury naysayers decried the loss of their town's history and identity), resounding majorities in both city and town foresaw economic and quality-of-life benefits. Voters generally agreed with a joint Massachusetts Senate Committee report issued four months earlier that laid out the rationale for the imminent merger: "A dense population, crowded business and thickly packed buildings join Roxbury along the dividing line, making the two cities *one* in all the purposes of civil, social, and business life. The Committee see [sic] no good reason for continuing two separate governments over different portions of the same city."

But Boston's desire to annex Roxbury transcended cultural commonalities and political and economic opportunism. Boston's growth and progress since 1850 had helped infuse her leaders and residents with a sense of municipal entitlement, what one might call a sense of urban manifest destiny, which went to the heart of the capital city's desire to complete the agreement with her sister town.

Boston's expansion through annexation had been a topic of conversation since the early 1850s, well before Boston mayor Frederick W. Lincoln finally appointed commissioners in April of 1866 to study, in earnest, the potential of acquiring Roxbury. The Back Bay landfill and the Civil War had forestalled any real progress on the matter, but by the mid-1860s, as the commissioners pointed out, "large, additional territory will soon become a necessity for the healthful growth of Boston." Unless Boston acquired additional territory, her increasing population "will be compelled to seek residences beyond her limits...to our loss and injury."

The commissioners noted that the annexation of Roxbury would add twenty-one hundred acres of land to Boston, giving her a total of fifty-four hundred acres, and increase Boston's population by about thirty-thousand people. As for the benefits to Roxbury, in addition to city services, annexation proponents argued that the value of her real estate would soar, since the neighborhood was situated "in the direction in which Boston is most rapidly growing." House and Senate committee members closed their report with the unanimous opinion that the "benefits to Roxbury, the necessities of Boston, and the interests of the Commonwealth, sanction and require the annexation."

After the lopsided vote in favor of annexation, most Boston newspapers praised the judgment of citizens. Noting Boston's ambition to increase its influence, a New York Times columnist predicted in October of 1867 that Boston's annexation of Roxbury was only the beginning. "Boston is not satisfied with its enlarged area and yearns for more territory...having in view a consolidation of all the suburbs and neighboring municipalities," the paper reported.

The Times reporter was entirely accurate. Shortly after the Roxbury vote, Dorchester commissioners requested annexation, a move that met with vigorous resistance in the independent town. Opponents argued that Dorchester's history and traditions would be engulfed by those of Boston, while supporters argued that Dorchester's "pocketbook issues" would improve markedly, along with the town's city services, industry, and real estate market: "We have an abundance of cheap land, which will be sought after by householders of moderate means," annexation proponent William Coffin pointed out.

The Massachusetts legislature approved an act of annexation of Dorchester on June 4, 1869, submitting the proposal to voters of both communities. Boston voted more than six to one in favor, and Dorchester agreed by a small majority.

Other dominoes fell when the 1873 legislature passed separate acts annexing Charlestown, West Roxbury, Brighton, and Brookline to Boston, each dependent on the approval of the towns' voters. Boston voters approved all the annexations by wide majorities, as did voters in Charlestown and Brighton. West Roxbury voters narrowly approved the annexation (720–613), but Brookline voters rejected the measure, and in a resounding way (299–706). Charlestown, West Roxbury, and Brighton became part of Boston at the outset of 1874 and Brookline remained an independent town. The annexation movement had ended: some factions in Cambridge later sought a merger with Boston but could never gain a majority, while Hyde Park was the last town to approve a merger in 1912.

When the smoke had cleared, Boston was a vastly different city. Its population had ballooned from 180,000 in 1850 to more than 341,000 in 1875. Once a small town of some 780 acres, a postage-stamp peninsula attached by a narrow neck-like strip to the mainland, Boston now spread over almost twenty-four thousand acres, nearly thirty times its original size. "It was no longer the tight little island that had always made it so distinctive, so aloof, so parochial," Thomas O'Connor wrote. "It was something else entirely."

Boston's burgeoning physical size and population growth was accompanied by a city that at once was more progressive and more prosperous, more Irish and more Catholic, more renowned and more respected for the breakthrough and strides it had made in transportation, commerce, engineering, social causes, and education.

On the eve of the 1870s, Boston was a city with much to celebrate.

And for a week in June of 1869, with a grandness befitting its remarkable progress and enhanced stature, it did just that.

JUNE 16, 1869. More than fifty thousand spectators rose as one, cheering wildly, stomping their feet, waving flags, hats, and handkerchiefs, as President Ulysses S. Grant strode down the five-hundred-foot-long center aisle of Boston's Great Coliseum, followed by members of his cabinet. On stage, an elaborate orchestra, accompanied by the world's largest pipe organ and its biggest bass drum—twenty-five feet in circumference—played "See, the Conquering Hero Comes." Grant reached his seat, the music ended, but the crowd continued to thunder its approval. The nation's eighteenth president stood only five feet, seven inches tall, but to the adoring throng, the Civil War's Union hero, the great general who had accepted Robert E. Lee's surrender at Appomattox, possessed the bearing and status of a giant.

Grant repeatedly, and almost shyly, bowed his head in recognition of the tremendous reception, which excited the crowd even more;

for several minutes the ovation continued unabated, until finally, as Grant raised his hands pleading for quiet, the noise subsided, and the president, in a few words, expressed his pleasure and thanks for the humbling reception Boston had accorded him.

The occasion, the 1869 National Peace Jubilee, was a mammoth weeklong event featuring a standing one-thousand-piece band and a ten-thousand-member chorus, along with smaller novel acts such as the one-hundred-piece Anvil Chorus, comprised of Boston firemen who banged away with blacksmith's hammers upon anvils amid a shower of sparks; all of it played out before what the *New York Times* called, "the largest, most eager throng that ever awaited admission to an American place of entertainment."

After a decade that included four years of destructive war, three years of painful rancor over Reconstruction, and the impeachment (though not the conviction) of former president Andrew Johnson, the nation shared the sentiment Ulysses S. Grant expressed when he accepted the Republican nomination: "Let us have peace." In his March inaugural address, Grant pledged to approach issues stemming from the "great rebellion" calmly, "without prejudice, hate, or sectional pride, remembering that the greatest good to the greatest number is the object to be attained."

Boston's National Peace Jubilee was a grandiose symbol of the peace the nation craved, and judging by the overwhelming response from around the country, it exceeded all expectations. President Grant's second-day appearance was the highlight, but Bostonians had anticipated the event for weeks and had celebrated since the early-morning hours of the jubilee's opening day. They were joined by thousands of visitors who traveled by train and steamboat to reach Boston; as one newspaper described it, "a crowd of people ... mighty, innumerable, seeming as if the population of New England had been poured into our streets." By ten o'clock in the morning of day one, a swarming mass of people had congregated outside the Great Coliseum in the Back Bay, at the former site of St. James Park (near the present-day Trinity Church), listening to strains of music from the rehearsals inside, eagerly awaiting the first concert, scheduled for two o'clock.

For the previous three months, since construction began on the coliseum, also known as the Temple of Peace, the area pulsated with activity. Regiments of carpenters and craftsmen descended on the area to ply their trades, and much of Boston turned out to watch "as the great coliseum took shape like the ribs of Noah's ark," as author Rufus Jarman described it. A small city of tents and wooden shacks surrounded the construction site, with vendors offering lodging, entertainment, soft drinks and beer, notions and souvenirs. When the coliseum was completed—stunningly, only ninety days later—the colossal structure, constructed of Georgia pine, stood five hundred feet long, three hundred feet wide, one hundred feet from floor to roof ridge, and contained 144 windows. The main doorways were twenty-four feet wide, and forty-five flagpoles projected from the roof. More than seventy-five hundred pounds of paint covered the exterior with sandstone color; the interior with blue, gray, pink, and gold. Inside, giant murals of harvest fields symbolized the return of peace and plenty after wartime deprivation and scarcity. Above the stage, the arch was formed by two huge gilded angels clutching olive branches and gazing at a large scroll bearing the words, "Glory to God in the Highest; Peace on Earth, Good Will Toward Men." *The Boston Herald*, stunned by the sheer magnitude of the building, marveled at the twenty-four hundred gas jets, fed by twenty-five thousand feet of pipe, that provided the interior lighting, and, after a reporter counted the building's forty-eight water closets, he pronounced the building "completely equipped for every necessity of nature."

Shortly before the jubilee's opening, Ole Bull, the internationally renowned Norwegian violinist, agreed to serve as guest conductor, and British soprano Euphrosyne Parepa-Rosa consented to be chief soloist. Oliver Wendell Holmes wrote "A Hymn of Peace" as the festival's theme song, and finally, President Grant and his cabinet agreed to attend as honored guests. "The jubilee was now a sure-fire box-office success," Jarman noted.

Up until that point, however, even as the planning for the jubilee began, its success was in doubt. It had come to life as little more than a fragile concept, and lost momentum early.

Only the passion and tenacity of the person who conceived of the Boston celebration in the first place, America's most flamboyant musical showman (later, people would rank his contributions as a populist band leader second only to John Philip Sousa), kept the idea of the 1869 Peace Jubilee alive, and ultimately, with the help and financial backing of one of Boston's most prominent retail merchants, he assured its resounding success.

—m—

Figure 4. Regiments of carpenters and craftsmen toiled around the clock to construct the Great Coliseum that would host the Boston Peace Jubilees of 1869 and 1872. *(Photo courtesy of the Boston Public Library, Print Department)*

County Galway's Patrick S. Gilmore was born of humble origins on Christmas Day, 1829, and some admirers attributed his subsequent widespread success to the many blessings bestowed upon him by virtue of his special birth date. Tenacious yet winsome, visionary yet realistic, talented yet pragmatic, he possessed both a quick Irish wit and an ability to grasp sobering business realities. He was part musician, part conductor, part showman, and—perhaps most relevant to the success of the 1869 Peace Jubilee—he had an "ear for perfect pitch, sales as well as musical," Rufus Jarman wrote.

He started his musical career playing cornet for a town band in Ireland, and after emigrating to Boston at the height of the famine in 1848, established himself as a talented soloist and soon took over as leader of the Boston Brigade Band and the Salem Brass Band. Restless and innovative, Gilmore reshaped the look and sound of traditional military bands by adding woodwinds and orchestral arrangements to their repertoires. During the Civil War, his band accompanied the Twenty-fourth Massachusetts Regiment to the battlefront, and his wartime compositions included "When Johnny Comes Marching Home." In 1864 he went to Louisiana to organize the celebration for the governor's inauguration, for which he recruited five thousand New Orleans schoolchildren and several hundred military musicians for a concert in Lafayette Square, a prelude to the Boston Peace Jubilee.

But the road to the Boston celebration was fraught with pitfalls. When Gilmore shared his vision for the national jubilee with his own wife, he recalled her asking: "Why, are you crazy? Have you lost your senses?" The business community and potential contributors reacted similarly. When New Year's Day, 1869, arrived—just six months away from his target date—he had "not a penny in the jubilee treasury," Rufus Jarman wrote. Gilmore pressed on, sharing his plans with the press in Boston ("One of the most gigantic musical schemes in the world's history is brewing in Boston," the *Boston Herald* wrote), but many reporters were skeptical. "There is a limit to the number of voices which can sing effectively together," the *New York Tribune* warned, "a limit fixed by the laws of acoustics—and ten thousand is about ten times too many."

Despite several small contributions from hotel owners and music publishers, Gilmore was worried when, by the end of February, his concert and his coliseum were no closer to reality. One day he called on seventy businesses and obtained seventy refusals "to subscribe so much as a dollar," according to one account. Gilmore wrote that his "distress of mind at this time was indeed almost unbearable." He was "so enraptured" with his dream that he had given up "all remunerative sources of employment." He was broke. At one point, he fell ill for several days.

When March arrived, and his dream of building a coliseum still seemed a fantasy, Gilmore considered holding his jubilee outdoors, "with the blue vault of Heaven as its canopy."

But then he had a stroke of fortune that bordered on the miraculous.

Boston's leading retail businessman, Eben D. Jordan, head of Jordan, Marsh and Company, had been watching Gilmore with admiration. Jordan organized a meeting on March 13 at the New England Conservatory of Music, at which time Gilmore described his plans to the assembled business leaders, who included prominent merchants, hotel proprietors, bankers, and railroad officials. Jordan then spoke to the group, calling the jubilee a Boston idea, and, according to Sarah Lawrence's account of the meeting, appealed to the "public spirit of all good citizens in behalf of a project destined to add to the renown of the city, to give an impetus to the art of music—of which Boston always had struck, and always would strike, the key-note for America—and to increase the business of the city in every channel." Jordan told his fellow business titans that he would give five thousand dollars from his own pocket "rather than have this Jubilee fall through."

A sixty-member committee was chosen, with former Boston mayor and congressman Alexander Rice as president and Jordan as treasurer, and agreed to raise funds from local businesses to build the coliseum and help with organization of the event. They agreed to raise ninety-five thousand dollars for the coliseum (financiers would be paid back from ticket sales), and with Gilmore's help, convinced the New England Conservatory to organize choral societies from across the United States—103 vocal groups and several dozen bands eventually made it to Boston for the jubilee. Gilmore handled the correspondence with foreign bands, musicians, and vocalists, including Ole Bull and Madame Parepa Rosa. "I accept with the greatest pleasure to sing at the Peace Festival," Parepa Rosa wrote on May 11. "If good will can be of avail, in being heard, in so great a building, I shall certainly do my best to *lift up my voice and sing to my utmost power*, and try (at any rate) to achieve the feat!"

By March 27, two weeks after the first meeting, the finance committee announced that seventy-five thousand dollars had already been pledged and Eben Jordan offered to provide funds for immediate cash-flow use until collections were completed—and construction began on the Great Coliseum.

Patrick Gilmore and Boston would have their dream concert.

Thousands of people flooded the main streets of the city on opening day, while the carriageways were "packed with every sort of vehicle on the way to the Coliseum," Sarah Lawrence observed. "Fragments of infantry, cavalry, and artillery were scattered about the city, all awaiting the coming of General Grant, President of the United States, on the next day." From across the nation, people came to bask in the celebratory mood that had eluded the country for so long, to witness a world-class musical event, to catch a glimpse of President Grant. For those who had visited Boston before, the *Daily Advertiser* noted, they would witness a far different city in June of 1869. "Disreputable alleys have become broad streets; secluded courts have become noisy thoroughfares," the paper pointed out. "Old Boston vanishes and a new Boston seems sprung from the waters of the bay."

The weeklong Peace Jubilee was an overwhelming success: Patrick Gilmore's welcoming remarks on the first day, as he stood beneath red, white, and blue streamers in the balcony and amid towering columns festooned with American flags and decorative banners; the first overwhelming performance of the orchestra and full chorus that shook the building (one man, so overcome by the spectacle, rushed from the audience and telegraphed his wife: "Come immediately! Will sacrifice anything to have you here! Nothing like it in a lifetime!"); President Grant's breathtaking day-two review of fifty-five hundred troops— almost the entire militia of the Commonwealth—stretching for a mile and a half down Tremont Street; and the president's triumphal arrival at the coliseum and genuine enjoyment of the concert. (Grant, not known as a music-lover, had earlier wondered whether he would fully appreciate the event: "I know only two tunes," the president reportedly said. "One is 'Yankee Doodle' and the other one isn't.")

The National Peace Jubilee was more than an emotional success; it made money as well. Total expenses exceeded more than $280,000 (the coliseum cost $120,000), but receipts topped $290,000. Bostonians held a testimonial on behalf of Patrick Gilmore and raised another $32,000. Sarah Lawrence noted that the money was placed in a trust fund and presented to Gilmore, "whose genius, energy, and indomitable will conquered all obstacles and crowned him the Napoleon of managers and musicians."

Boston's Peace Jubilee appeared to be exactly what America needed as it closed out the 1860s. It was emotionally uplifting for a nation that had started the decade ripped apart by war and it was culturally important for a country, and city, whose dedication to the arts was still questioned by Europe. "[It] is a success," wrote the *New York Tribune's* Kate Field. "Those who went to scoff remained to praise. The Peace Jubilee is stunning." The *New York Times*, while citing the occasional unevenness of the performers, called the Peace Jubilee "one of the most remarkable successes ever accomplished in this or any country."

Gilmore would try to further capitalize on his triumphant venture by organizing an International Peace Jubilee in Boston in 1872, but it

Figure 5. More than fifty thousand spectators jammed the massive coliseum in Boston to take part in the 1869 National Peace Jubilee, a mammoth weeklong event featuring a standing one-thousand-piece band and a ten-thousand-member chorus. (*Photo courtesy of the Boston Public Library, Print Department*)

lacked the artistic and emotional panache, spontaneity, and enthusiasm of the 1869 event, and was disappointing both musically and financially. "The National Peace Jubilee was the peak of Gilmore's career," Rufus Jarman declared. "It was his shining hour, and he never touched that height again."

Patrick Gilmore died of a heart attack in 1892 while playing a series of concerts for the St. Louis Exposition. Two days later, John Philip Sousa's band gave its first concert; Sousa truly picked up where Gilmore left off. As Rufus Jarman concluded: "Gilmore left behind him a musical tradition that paved the way for the great age of American bands."

When Boston mayor Nathaniel Bradstreet Shurtleff opened the National Peace Jubilee, he noted that it was an event "instituted to commemorate the return of peace to our country, the restoration of our ancient liberties unimpaired, our national bonds of union unbroken." Those three concepts—peace, liberty, and union—were far from clichés as the 1860s ended; Bostonians held them dear and they would form the foundation upon which the city would build its future. Those three words also reflected the monumental changes that had swept the city, the nation, and the world in the past ten years.

"When '59 went out," the *Daily Advertiser* reminded its readers on the first day of 1870, "the shadow of John Brown's scaffold still lay across Virginia and the nation, our manhood was a matter of doubt, our nationality a loose partnership."

Things had changed dramatically in ten years.

"Hardly one of the questions of that time puzzles us today," the paper editorialized. We go by rail from New York to San Francisco, by steamer to the Red Sea…we may count ourselves as entering today a new period of the nineteenth century, which is so fast an age that its tens of years are as the hundreds of the slower growth of the world."

A new world lay ahead: perplexing, perhaps; different, likely; unknowable, certainly. Boston should not fear it, the *Advertiser* declared in its January 1, 1870, message, but embrace it with the verve and enthusiasm befitting a national leader. "Surely," the paper said, "we have every reason to take a new hold of our several tasks cheerfully, hopefully, with thankfulness and pride for what is past, with confidence in what is to come."

NOVEMBER 9, 1872. John Damrell, gear in hand, raced from his home at 60 Temple Street and sprinted frantically down Beacon Hill. The Boston Fire Department's chief engineer had heard the fire bells ring clearly—five blows, then a pause, then two more blows. Box 52. Every firefighter in Boston knew it as a "bad box" because of its location: in the heart of the city's commercial district, at the intersection of Summer, Lincoln, and Bedford streets. Small rusted pipes along Summer Street that limited water supply and pressure, tall buildings topped with vulnerable French-style mansard roofs, and congested narrow streets presented the ingredients for a nightmarish scenario anytime fire broke out. More serious alarms had been sent from Box 52 in the last twenty years than from Boston's other five hundred boxes.

What would tonight bring?

It was nearly 7:30 p.m. on Saturday, an unseasonably mild evening following a glorious autumn day, a cloudless night with a bright moon over Boston. But Damrell was focused on only one thing. He ran harder, and when he reached the corner of Park and Beacon streets, he heard the second alarm and spotted an orange glare in the night sky ahead of him. He pushed himself to go faster, toward the blaze, which had started in an area that was once a fashionable residential neighborhood (home to Ben Franklin, and later, Daniel Webster) and now housed the city's wholesale leather and clothing businesses, small factories, banks, retail stores, and newspaper offices. The third alarm was sounding as he approached Kensington Street—he had covered the distance from his house in eight minutes—and as he rounded the corner of Summer and Kensington, he gaped at a sight he had never seen in his quarter century as a firefighter.

A four-story granite building at 83–85 Summer Street, on the corner of Kingston Street, was engulfed in flames, its exterior walls serving to intensify the fire and turning the building into a giant furnace. Damrell noticed quickly that the heat was so ferocious that few could get within seventy-five feet of the building. Suddenly, ten- to twenty-pound chunks of flaming granite were bursting from the building, white-hot cannon shot that rained blazing sparks on the streets and spectators below. It was "as if the earth itself had broken open to reveal its molten core," author Stephanie Schorow would write years later. Damrell knew the danger his city's downtown was facing; in fact, flames were already ripping through a second building on Kingston Street, and within moments, another on Summer Street. Later, he would say that he had never encountered such an appalling blaze. "I have no language that I could describe it," he testified. "Within eight minutes from the time the alarm sounded, I was on the ground, and the building was literally consumed, on fire from the basement to the top. I don't understand it [even] today. It is a phenomenon which I cannot possibly fathom."

For now, he ordered the general alarm turned in—the dreaded "three-twelves" rang in City Hall, fire stations, the homes of engine captains, church towers, and public buildings. "For God's sake, hold the corner," Damrell shouted to the fire companies that had already arrived and were setting up operations at the corner of Devonshire and Summer streets. The brave men of Engine companies No. 4 and No. 7 and Hose Company No. 2 had assumed positions as close as possible to the deadly heat. The forty-four-year-old Boston-born Damrell watched as flames spread faster than he had ever seen a fire spread. For five years, he had been warning city fathers about the potential danger of a great fire, and had sought funding for larger water pipes and updated hydrant couplings in the downtown commercial districts; they were warnings issued even more strenuously and vehemently after the deadly and devastating Chicago fire a year earlier.

But the warnings were ignored.

Now, directing firefighters as the downtown burned, Damrell was forced to overcome yet one more obstacle. A deadly distemper epidemic had felled horses throughout the region, a disease that was not always fatal, but weakened horses to the point where they could barely stand. Damrell's fire horses, the animals that pulled his engine companies, were among those affected, and he was reluctant to use untrained healthy horses for fear they would become skittish and bolt during the chaos at fire scenes. Thus, men would have to replace horses. Just two weeks earlier, at a meeting of city officials, the department was authorized to hire five hundred human "volunteers" (in reality, they were paid one dollar per fire and twenty-five cents an hour), issue them drag ropes, and train them to haul fire equipment to the scene of blazes. There was no shortage of willing, able-bodied men, but their efforts were not nearly as efficient as the horses, nor their response as rapid, particularly when traveling a long distance. As a temporary measure, the department changed its rules so that only one steam engine (there were six in all) was required to respond on the first alarm. If any fire was above the second floor, police were to ring a second alarm immediately. As fire spread in front of him, Damrell knew that this new procedure had cost his department precious time.

The fire was raging, creating its own wind, beginning to feed on itself and spreading, the crackle of flames sounding like a steady stream of gunshots. A small boy, about twelve years old, stopped Damrell and pleaded with him to rescue his mother and father, who were trapped upstairs in a burning building. Damrell led the boy to safety, then stormed through the first-floor entrance, only to be blocked by an enormous pile of debris that clogged the stairway. "It was impossible to go further," Damrell recalled later. "I never knew whether they were [in the building] or not." Outside, Damrell heard one of his captains beg for additional water to pour on the blaze. "I would have been most happy to do it," he lamented later, "but I had not the water to give him."

With the destruction in Chicago fresh in his memory, Damrell wondered how he would overcome a limited water supply, highly flammable rooftops, crammed warehouses and garment shops and newspaper offices, utter chaos, and no horses to draw his heavy equipment. He had never beheld a sight "in this city or in any other" like he was witnessing now. Already, this blaze could be described with the one word that any firefighting professional dreaded most.

Inferno.

Boston had numerous reasons to swagger in the years leading up to the Great Fire of 1872; it was a city on the move.

Like much of the nation, it had enjoyed a postwar economic boom that saw its manufacturing, publishing, mercantile, and transportation businesses thrive. The annexation of Roxbury and Dorchester (and the coming annexation of the other towns), coupled with better horse-drawn streetcar service, enabled people who worked in the city's downtown to commute from the less-congested outer-band sections of the city that were once part of the independent towns: places like Savin Hill in Dorchester and Roxbury Highlands. With the annexations and an increase in postwar immigration, Boston's total population was approaching three hundred thousand by the early 1870s.

In the downtown area, too, Boston was flourishing. By 1872, the Back Bay landfill work had been completed to a point halfway between present-day Exeter and Fairfield streets, and nearly 2 million square feet of land had been sold. Authors William Newman and Wilfred Holton point out that, in 1871, contractor Norman Munson signed a contract with the Boston City Council for three hundred thousand dollars to construct, within two years, and grade "with good clean sand" the following new streets in Boston: "Commonwealth Avenue two-hundred feet wide from its present termination to its junction [of present day Massachusetts Avenue]; [and] Huntington Avenue one-hundred feet wide from Boylston Street to [present-day Gainsborough Street]." The ambitious and unprecedented Back Bay plan was working to near perfection. Elsewhere, too, the city was engaged in landfill work to keep pace with its commercial growth.

In the most costly improvement of its kind in any city, Boston spent more than 2 million dollars in a multiyear project to fill in water between its wharves and create Atlantic Avenue by 1870, an enterprise that provided a "broad way along the waterfront, which has proved of the greatest value to the commerce of Boston," wrote Harvard librarian Justin Winsor a decade later.

And with the land and transportation improvements, the city continued its cultural and scientific progress. Bostonians were excited about the nation's first transcontinental rail excursion in the summer of 1870 that originated in their city, the incorporation of the Museum of Fine Arts the same year (General Charles Loring became its first curator in July); the 1872 opening of the first training school for nurses in America at the New England Baptist Hospital for Women and Children (the city's first ambulance would be put into service one year later at Massachusetts General Hospital, a one-horse vehicle capable of carrying two patients and three attendants); and the founding of the *Boston Globe*, which published its first issue on March 4, 1872, adding to Boston's reputation for strong journalism and its extensive downtown newspaper row.

Adding to the city's overall stature and reputation was the 1872 publication by landscape gardener Robert Morris Copeland of *The Most Beautiful City in America: Essay and Plan for the Improvement of the City of Boston*. Copeland, who was among the handful of experts involved in the original design for New York's Central Park, proposed an integrated system of large parks linked by boulevards and an improved sewage system in the Back Bay. He examined every major neighborhood in Boston and made proposals for street construction, land acquisition, development, and then outlined how to make the functional city beautiful through the creation of a system of parks and scenic reservations. While, coincidentally, Harvard University established the Arnold Arboretum (the first in the United States) that same year, Copeland never saw his stunning plan achieve reality. He died two years after the publication of his pamphlet at the age of forty-four; and it was not until several years later, in the hands of Charles Eliot and Frederick Law Olmstead, that ideas similar to Copeland's were finally brought to reality.

The years of Boston's postwar bonhomie and progress on virtually all fronts took a turn for the worse, however, in the spring of 1872, when a smallpox epidemic broke out among the latest wave of immigrants in the North End. For the next year, Boston struggled vainly to contain and overcome the ravages of the deadly disease, even closing its public schools in May to prevent infection among children. In less than a year smallpox claimed the lives of 738 Bostonians, more than 200 in the North End neighborhood where the outbreak began.

Then came November, when, even as smallpox continued to claim lives and rend families, an explosive and white-hot conflagration rained another form of destruction upon Boston.

From the roof of the sixth-story building on Milk Street, a weary John Damrell surveyed the disaster unfolding before him. It was 10:00 p.m. on November 9, 1872, and the roaring fire had traveled three blocks to the edge of Franklin and Federal streets. The fire had spread "with a malignant restlessness," one witness later described, and had already devoured a huge block of commercial buildings in Winthrop Square. Boston's night sky was illuminated red from the leaping flames, which were just beginning to lick the wharves along Boston Harbor (the schooner *Louisa Frazer*, which was not moved to safety, was eventually destroyed by fire). Firefighters gallantly sprayed the flames as long as they could, but the water streams were weak and the men had to constantly fall back and regroup as "the narrow streets turned into block-high blow torches," Stephanie Schorow described. *Harper's Weekly* reported later, "The flames ran rapidly up Summer Street, and each street opening on to it became at once a funnel through which the fire poured with inconceivable force. Catching the fatal Mansard-roofs, it went roaring and crackling along the streets, wrapping block after block in flames. The scene was one of dreadful magnificence."

Damrell, who had smashed the front door of the building whose roof he now stood upon, surveyed the scene from a vantage point that filled him with fear and a sense of helplessness. If the fire spread to South Boston, with its sugarhouses, oil mills, and stables, "the loss would have been terrible beyond description." Not a single piece of apparatus was available to protect the area, and South Boston "would have been consumed" if the flames were allowed to reach the neighborhood.

He now considered one of the most dangerous and controversial weapons in his firefighting arsenal—the use of gunpowder to destroy buildings and create "no-spread zones" as a means to halt the fire's relentless advance. While gunpowder explosions were consid-

ered acceptable last resorts to halt the spread of out-of-control fires
(gunpowder had been used with limited success in Chicago), its un-
predictability and instability presented tremendous risks. Ill-timed
detonations could kill firefighters unable to get far enough away in
time after setting charges, and poorly planted charges could actually
act as a catalyst for the fire to spread more quickly. Less important,
but a consideration nonetheless, were lawsuits filed by property owners after their buildings were destroyed by explosions.

Damrell, a student of firefighting methods, knew all of this and was
reluctant to use gunpowder for these and other more specific reasons.

First, the buildings were mostly large warehouses "filled with merchandise from cellar to roof." An explosion might blow the roof off
and shatter the walls, but an ignitable merchandise pile would remain
and likely provide the fire with an uninterrupted path to spread along.
Second, Damrell feared, an explosion could "destroy every gas pipe in
every building and open the gas mains," resulting in a "perfect flood of
gas [that] would permeate every part of the debris, which would make
it inflammable." Finally, concussive force would "shatter every window
within four rods" of the building in which charges were placed, turning the structure into a "conduit for cinders, flames, and heated air."

But standing six stories above a burning downtown, Damrell
knew there was another side to the story. Failure to use gunpowder
could not only leave him open to castigation later, but also result in
the greatest destruction in Boston's history.

If he did not try the experiment, "citizens would never feel satisfied" that he had done everything in his power to halt the spread of
the deadly flames.

How could he live with that?

By midnight, thousands of Boston residents rimmed the fire scene and
hundreds more crowded into the flaming area itself, making it difficult
for firefighters to work. Some reports put the number of spectators
at one hundred thousand, which was almost surely an exaggeration,
since it would represent more than one-third of the city's population.
Among the spectators was Beacon Hill resident Sarah Putnam, who,
with her brother, John, decided to make their way across the Boston Common to witness the scene. "The trees on the common were
lovely, with the branches all illuminated," she wrote in her diary. The
brother and sister watched as thousands of people carted possessions

and goods from the center of the fire scene onto the Common in an attempt to salvage them. "The fire kept bursting out in awful great masses," she wrote.

The blaze was unprecedented in Bostonians' memory, and almost indescribable in its horrific intensity. "Few observers would ever forget the unholy light that turned Boston's streets as bright as day," Stephanie Schorow wrote. "A passing flock of ducks, reflecting the light, was first thought to be a meteor shower. The glow in the sky could be seen as far away as New Hampshire. Twenty-one miles away, in South Abington, a scorched $50 bill was picked up." Another chronicler called the blaze "hideous...[with] its steams of hellish flames...[it was as though] the earth had yawned, and loosed those weird, traditional denizens of its fiery depths."

John Damrell did witness scenes from hell that night, but aside from the destruction wrought by the fire itself, the worst of them were played out by humans, not supernatural beings. Many of those fleeing the fire scene with their arms laden with packages were not business owners, but citizens who had responded to merchants' initial entreaties to carry away their goods rather than watch them burn. But the gesture of generosity turned ugly when, even in the midst of conflagration and pain, greed ran rampant. A disgusted Damrell spied hundreds of Bostonians going well beyond salvaging goods and instead becoming full-fledged looters, while failing to help extinguish the fire and impeding firefighters' efforts to do so. "There were whole blocks of stores that were completely filled with the greatest number of thieves I ever saw," he testified shortly after the fire. "I never saw anything like it." The chief could not stand by idly. "I went into one building, and took my fire-hat, and beat out fifty to sixty people," he said. "The awnings were all burning, and they never touched an awning; so eager were they to plunder, that they never attempted to save property." A horrified Damrell even speculated that some looters "set fire to get an additional amount of plunder. I am not sure of it in my own mind, for I feel that some of the fires were in very strange places." One looting incident ended in tragedy for the thieves and firefighters when one wall in a Washington Street store collapsed on civilians plundering goods; when a group of Boston and Charlestown firefighters tried desperately to extricate the buried citizens, a second wall collapsed and killed the men under Damrell's command. "They lost their lives in the endeavor to save the lives of those who were in there when no legitimate business called them there," he recounted angrily.

Figure 6. Boston's Great Fire of November, 1872, ravaged the prime business section of the city (what would be today's financial district), leaving sixty-five acres of smoldering ruins, destroying 776 buildings, and incinerating merchandise and other personal property estimated at close to $7 billion in today's dollars. (*Photo courtesy of the Boston Public Library, Print Department*)

Ultimately, Damrell declared, the decision by Boston merchants to give their goods away was "one of the worst things that was ever done." It would have been better—"twenty-five times, yes, a hundred times over"—to let them burn. The decision led to behavior that was "thoroughly disgraceful, and I am sorry to say that any Boston gentleman would have resorted to it for a single moment."

By the early morning hours, with the fire still raging, Damrell's critics were furious that he had not employed gunpowder to halt or contain the rapid spread of the flames. Postmaster General William L. Burt, angry at what he deemed a disorganized approach to fighting the fire, was convinced that gunpowder explosions could halt its relentless march. "The fire was then getting so large that it required a systematic defense, a systematic resistance, and no such defense appeared to be made," he testified later.

While mail had been removed from the new post office building on Devonshire and Milk streets to the safety of Faneuil Hall, Burt said he'd "be damned" if he'd see his new building, designed to be fire-proof, consumed without taking all possible steps to save it. Burt and other prominent citizens convinced the mayor to hold an emergency meeting at City Hall to discuss the issue; a chagrined Damrell was ordered to attend though it meant he had to leave his men at the fire scene. "We must blow up buildings," Burt told the group. "The fire-men are falling back, they are losing confidence and energetic action is needed." Still reluctant to resort to risky explosions, which he believed could make matters worse, a weary Damrell finally buckled under the political pressure. "I notified him [Burt] that I was ready to receive the assistance of any gentlemen…even to the blowing up of buildings," the fire chief recalled later. "I cheerfully would receive any aid that they might offer in that direction."

And thus the explosions began. Burt oversaw the planting of charges and the destruction of an entire block of buildings between Federal and Devonshire streets. Other men destroyed a building at Congress and Water streets; still others brought down a structure at State and Congress. Damrell blew up two buildings on Milk and Batterymarch streets, with the help of one of his captains. As he lit one fuse, Damrell told his officer: "If we go up, we will go up together; but we will make a clean thing of this." They barely made it to safety before the explosion brought down the building. Explosions rocked the center city, as gunpowder charges were set across the fire scene in an attempt to slow down the blaze. Afterward, Burt insisted the use of gunpowder saved the city. "The roar of the explosions was the first sign of hope and sent a joy through the entire city," he said. One Boston diarist wrote: "At last, about 3 o'clock, some buildings were blown up and everyone rejoiced to hear the explosion for it seemed as if someone would check the flames."

But while spectators on the fire's perimeters cheered the explo-sions, firefighters inside the fire zone feared for their lives.

Gunpowder chargers were not set in any systematic fashion; sometimes they would explode and other times they would not, leaving firefighters to wonder whether a delayed charge would finally detonate and kill them as they approached the building. There were even places where the explosions fed the fire and strengthened its ferocity. And the most potentially deadly element of all was the natural gas that provided the lights to homes and businesses. Gas could only be shut off building by building—there was no central check-valve to stop the flow of gas to an entire street. Firefighters risked their lives to shut off gas in some buildings, and in others, explosions were igniting "huge gas fireballs," according to Stephanie Schorow. Postmaster Burt described one scene with a macabre sense of satisfaction: "I saw in the most intense part of the fire, huge bodies of gas; you might say 25 feet in diameter—dark, opaque masses, combined with the gases from the pile of burning merchandise—rise 200 feet in the air and explode, shooting out large lines of flame fifty to sixty feet in every direction, with an explosion that was marked as the explosion of a bomb." Damrell testified later that the mixture of natural gas and gunpowder was terrifying inside the fire scene.

By early Sunday morning, Damrell's men were begging him to stop the gunpowder experiment, and the chief ordered all explosions halted. Later, he would testify that he felt a "weakness of which I am ashamed" by succumbing to political and citizen pressure to use gunpowder. "I had no confidence in the work," he recounted. "I deprecated the use of powder, but felt the experiment must be tried…consequently, I was willing to take the responsibility, although it was against my better judgment that I acted, and I confess it."

And still the fire burned, gutting the blocks between Franklin and Milk streets by 4:00 a.m., and destroying Pearl Street. Indeed, most of the interior downtown streets resembled a war zone after intense artillery shelling; burned-out husks of buildings and the occasional misshapen wall stood amid piles of rubble.

The destruction dealt a terrible blow to Boston's publishing industry, Stephanie Schorow noted. Consumed were newspaper buildings housing the *Transcript*, the *American Union*, the *Saturday Evening Gazette*, and Boston's Catholic newspaper, the *Pilot*. Fire then devoured Trinity Church, at the corner of Summer and Hawley streets. The Reverend Phillips Brooks, Boston's Episcopal bishop (and author of the Christmas carol "O Little Town of Bethlehem") observed: "She burnt majestically. I did not know how much I liked the great gloomy old thing till I saw her windows bursting and the flames running along the old high pews."

Among the most frightening scenarios was the threat to the Old South Meeting House, one of the city's last remaining colonial structures, the building in which five thousand Bostonians gathered ninety-nine years earlier to hear Sam Adams outline a plan of defiance against the British Crown that would turn into the Boston Tea Party. Flames licked at the venerable church's door, even as crews poured streams of water on its wall and several brave firefighters climbed the roof to sweep away sparks. Even Burt resisted demands that Old South be blown up. The battle to save the church raged through the night, and when the steeple clock struck 6:00 a.m., one bystander said, "Dear old church, I'm afraid we shall never hear that bell again." But at the last moment, a steam engine from Portsmouth, New Hampshire, arrived; it had been loaded on a flatbed train with the Portsmouth fire company and taken to Boston. Fresh firefighters and equipment turned the tide; the fire was stopped at Washington Street and Old South survived.

By 2:00 p.m. Sunday, the fire was deemed under control and out-of-town men and equipment were being sent home. But, because inexplicably the city's gas mains continued to flow, at midnight Sunday a tremendous explosion again rocked the city and leveled a building on the corner of Summer and Washington streets. Finally, all the city's gas mains were turned off and for two days, Boston was plunged into darkness. "The gas has been shut off, so we have only candles & no street lamps, and it is altogether so melancholy that I should like to have a good cry," wrote Mrs. Grace Revere of Boston to her friend in Europe.

Firefighters continued to douse buildings until Monday morning, when the fire was definitely out. An exhausted Damrell, his lungs "very sore from being burned," could finally head home. Later, he would laud the efforts of his firefighting crews, testifying that "never did a body of men work more heroically or better. I have no language to express my gratitude to those men." And with the exception of the use of gunpowder, which upon reflection he would not have employed on the downtown Boston fire, Damrell said he would not have changed his tactics "in any way, shape, or manner" if he had the fire to fight all over again.

"All that I can say is, that I have the inward satisfaction of knowing that I gave to the city the best ability that I possessed with an experience of twenty-five years in the department," Damrell told a special commission investigating the fire. "I don't see how there could have been anything more done. I did my best and I don't know any place where I could have done better."

The Great Fire of 1872 ravaged the prime business sections of Boston, leaving sixty-five acres of smoldering ruins, destroying 776 buildings assessed at more than $13.5 million, and incinerating merchandise and other personal property estimated at more than $70 million (perhaps close to $7 billion in today's dollars); in all, about one-tenth of the city's assessed value. "It will be remembered as the great fire, the greatest that America has seen, with the exception of that which laid waste Chicago," Charles Carleton Coffin wrote. Thousands of people were left homeless, about twenty thousand jobless, and some twenty of the thirty-three insurance companies in Boston declared bankruptcy attempting to cover losses. Declared the *Boston Investigator*: "Our city…was the scene of one of the most destructive fires ever known here, if not, indeed, in the entire Union." The scene in the streets, "one of Boston's saddest," concluded the *Daily Advertiser*, may well appall the stoutest hearts."

If there was any consolation, it is that the fire broke out on a weekend night, meaning many of the businesses were deserted and the loss of life was minimized. Nine firefighters (from Boston, Cambridge, Charlestown, Malden, and Worcester) and one former firefighter died at the conflagration and two more succumbed later to injuries suffered in the fire. Sixteen other people, including two children, were reported killed or missing, but as several accounts pointed out, officials never determined an exact toll of the dead and injured. During his testimony, Damrell expressed sorrow at the loss of brave firefighters, and recounted the heartbreaking story of the Abbotts of Charlestown, one of the most tragic family stories associated with the fire. Two brothers, Porter and Albert, were former Charlestown firefighters and responded to the scene to help. Porter went missing and his body was never recovered. Albert broke his back at the fire scene and died in the hospital a week later, whereupon the mother of the two men died, overcome with grief.

An angry Damrell told the commission that the city could have avoided the human toll and property losses if only officials had re-

Figure 7. Firefighters and businessmen pose in front of the smoldering ruins after the Great Fire was finally extinguished. (*Photo courtesy of the Boston Public Library, Print Department*)

sponded more quickly to his requests for updated hoses and hydrants. "The costs don't amount to anything," he said in response to a question. "Fifteen minutes of fire would destroy an amount equal to the cost of the hose for five years, so that it really doesn't amount to anything."

No one ever determined how the fire started in the basement of the building numbered 83 and 85 Summer Street. "There is no evidence whatever criminating any of the occupants of the building, nor is there anything to show that it caught from the furnace or the boiler, except that it began in that portion of the building," the official commission report concluded.

As much as Boston's Great Fire was at once a tale of bravery, destruction, unpreparedness, and political infighting, its aftermath was a story of the city's resilience, determination, and civic confidence. Indeed, it was Boston's response to the fire that is most telling. Even in the midst of a financial depression and bank panic that began in 1873 and lasted for nearly five years, Boston managed to rebuild its downtown and implement reforms to guard against another devastating fire. "The land is left, and the future, with its infinite possibilities," said the *Daily Advertiser* just days after the fire. "The burnt district will be rebuilt, the streets rectified, and buildings better adapted to resist the ravages of fire."

Boston wasted little time in fulfilling the newspaper's optimistic predictions. Workers quickly hauled away rubble, cleared debris, and began the monumental rebuilding process. Businesses set up temporary storefronts and factories across the city so that commerce could continue. One account noted: "Tenements were transformed into salerooms, every vacant inch of store room within a mile radius was made available, and a temporary colony of corrugated iron buildings sprang up like mushrooms…for the accommodation of the boot, shoe, leather, and iron trade[s]."

Despite the economic slowdown that struck many other businesses and major capital projects (for example, although the Back Bay landfill work continued, no lots were sold during the five-year depression of 1873–1878), the city's business community and municipal government came together to rebuild the downtown. Within a year, 450 new buildings had been erected at a construction cost exceeding $15 million. The city spent more than $5 million installing larger water pipes and new hydrants on Summer, Devonshire, Arch, Otis, and Washington streets; widening seventeen streets, including Summer, Washington, Devonshire, High, and Federal streets; and extending four more to provide easier access to firefighters and equipment; and clearing land around William Burt's new post office to form a large open space that would become known as Post Office Square in the heart of the city's financial district.

New buildings were constructed with roofs of stone, brick, or other fire-proof material, rather than the wood that fueled and intensified the 1872 fire as it raced across rooftops. Walls were made sturdier, and brick and iron replaced Quincy granite, which was considered "more easily destructible by fire than other materials," especially since memories were still fresh of the twenty-pound chunks of hot, glowing granite hurled through the air by the force of the fire's backdraft.

"In two years virtually no trace of the fire remained," author Stephanie Schorow wrote.

The City of Boston also passed a slew of fire-prevention regulations: elevators were forbidden in warehouses unless they were built with self-closing hatches to prevent fires from traveling at breakneck speed up the shafts; new standards were established for gas valves; and hand fire extinguishers became a fixture under new laws. By 1881, the city had installed a new keyless system of sounding fire alarms in the business district, which ended the requirement that a policeman had to be found before an alarm could be triggered; in the same year, all alarm boxes were painted red. In addition, the Great Fire spawned the reorganization of the Fire Department itself; under the leadership of a three-member committee it became wholly professional.

And in 1877 Boston created a new position of building inspector, a professional charged with the responsibility of, among other things, preventing fires before they started. Appointed to the position was former fire chief engineer John S. Damrell. He served for more than twenty-five years before retiring in 1903. He died two years later and his obituary read, in part: "He has been conceded to be a master of the extinguishment of fires and an expert on advanced ideas connected with that important service."

Damrell helped bring Boston into the modern age of firefighting, just as the Great Fire itself transformed the city. Boston's response to the monstrous blaze was to improve its firefighting infrastructure and operations, enact fire-prevention codes that would prevent such conflagrations in the future, and strengthen building codes and materials to make rebuilt structures virtually impervious to fire. In short, Boston was slowed by the Great Fire, but not defeated or even discouraged. Indeed, she used the fire as a means to continue her progress and, thanks to the reforms she implemented, even further enhanced her reputation.

As the *Boston Globe* pointed out a century after the fire: "In many respects, the Boston of 1872 was a transitional community, where people had developed modern technologies amid obsolete institutions, and the fire was responsible for change. It marked the end of Colonial Boston and the start of the present age."

CHAPTER 9

An End and a Beginning

His magnificent record is [Massachusetts's]. In his grand
personality are incarnated her schools, her religious liberties,
her practical morality, her intelligent knowledge of the
rights and duties of man.

> —*Rev. Samuel Johnson, eulogizing Senator Charles Sumner,*
> *before the Twenty-Eighth Congregational Society*
> *at the Parker Memorial Meetinghouse, March 1874*

MARCH 16, 1874. Henry Wilson, vice president of the United States,
stood stoically by the open grave in the dusky shadow of a large oak
tree. Next to him, heads bowed in prayer, stood Henry Wadsworth
Longfellow, Oliver Wendell Holmes, Ralph Waldo Emerson, and
John Greenleaf Whittier. All of them had served as pallbearers, accompanying the casket from the start of the extraordinary funeral
procession: from the State House, where the body had lain for thousands of mourners to view, to the brief prayer service at King's Chapel; and then for the trip down Cambridge Street to Beacon Street
to Charles Street, across the Charles River Bridge into Cambridge,
past the deceased's alma mater, Harvard College, and finally to Mount
Auburn Cemetery, where the cortege arrived as the late-winter sun
was setting. The pallbearers "reverently and by tender hands" placed
the casket by the side of the grave, while outside the cemetery gates,
thousands clustered to glimpse the burial and honor the late statesman who had helped change the nation's history during one of its
darkest periods, and had paid dearly for his efforts.

Charles Sumner was dead, and Boston and all of America were grieving the loss of the country's most passionate, vociferous, long-standing, unwavering, and inexhaustible antislavery champion. One publication summed up the senator's accomplishments, and thus, the impact of his death: "No man in this generation has done more to advance the cause of equal liberty for mankind…No death in the country, since that of Mr. Lincoln, has caused a deeper feeling of sorrow."

The heart attack that claimed Charles Sumner's life occurred during the early-morning hours of March 11 while the senator was at his Washington, D.C., home on Vermont Avenue and H Street, just across Lafayette Park from the White House. When word spread across the city that the sixty-three-year-old Sumner had been stricken, small groups of well-wishers—black and white alike—gathered quietly outside his house. With his close friends clustered at his bedside, Sumner's last phrases were "Tell Emerson I love and revere him," and "Don't let the civil rights bill fail." (Sumner was working on a post-Reconstruction bill to advance the cause of Southern blacks.) Among his deathbed visitors in Washington was the former slave Frederick Douglass, but the senator did not recognize him in the moments before his death. At 2:50 p.m., while his friend George T. Downing held his hand, Sumner gave a "convulsive movement" and grasped Downing's hand "so powerfully that he almost crushed it."

Sumner died a moment later.

Congress voted to set aside Friday, March 13, for funeral services in the Capitol. Douglass led a "great assemblage of colored men," who followed Sumner's hearse to the building, where thousands of mourners were waiting. His coffin was placed in the center of the great rotunda on the black catafalque where Lincoln's body had rested. "It was the first time in American history that a Senator's memory had been so honored," historian David Herbert Donald pointed out.

President Grant, senators and representatives, members of the Supreme Court, and a contingent of army officers led by General William T. Sherman, all gathered in the Senate chamber for services, while wives, friends, and other dignitaries packed the gallery. Every chair in the chamber was filled, save for Sumner's, which—as it had for three years after his caning—once again remained vacant, this time draped in black. At just before 12:30 p.m., pallbearers brought the coffin into the Senate chamber, and the entire assemblage watched in silence as it was carried to the front and placed before the main desk. "The nation in its three branches—legislative, executive, and judicial—stood close around the coffin, and the people from all quarters of the land looked down upon it," one Boston newspaper reported. Religious services lasted for about a half hour, and Sumner's friend, Senator Matt Carpenter of Wisconsin, then entrusted Sumner's remains to the sergeant at arms "to convey them to his home, there to commit them, earth to earth, ashes to ashes, dust to dust, in the soil of the Commonwealth of Massachusetts. Peace to his ashes."

Sumner's body was transported north by special train, nonstop to New York (much to the disappointment of crowds that had gathered in Wilmington, Delaware, and Philadelphia), where, arriving at midnight, it halted for the night. The next morning it continued through Connecticut, where one news account noted, "At New Haven and other cities, the whole population seemed to pour out to pay their last tribute to the dust of the great Statesman." And then the train crossed into Massachusetts, where, beginning in Springfield, throngs gathered at every station to watch it rumble eastward, while church bells tolled along the entire route. Meanwhile, in Boston, thousands had filled Faneuil Hall for a public prayer meeting, and mourners poured onto the tracks to greet the train when it reached the city in early evening. They then followed the coffin and procession up Beacon Hill to the State House, where Sumner's body was placed in Doric Hall "in sight of the memorials of Washington and the flags of Massachusetts regiments."

The next day, Sunday, March 15, with an enormous crowd waiting outside (some people fainted in the tightly packed lines), the doors to the State House were opened at 10:00 a.m. for mourners to pay their respects, and the resulting turnout stunned even Sumner's greatest supporters. Somberly, silently, two or three abreast, somewhere between forty thousand and fifty thousand people passed by Sumner's casket during Sunday and the early hours of Monday. The people of Massachusetts, many of whom disagreed with Sumner's inflexible tactics, antagonistic language, and uncompromising antislavery views twenty years earlier, today recognized the profundity of his contributions as they filed through the State House halls. "Under that roof," noted the *Boston Advertiser*, "was uttered the summons of the State to him to go forth in her name to withstand the great wrong."

On Monday, at around 2:30 p.m., church bells tolled once again, and since virtually all of Boston's businesses suspended operations, the downtown streets—most of which had been rebuilt after the Great Fire—were jammed with spectators and mourners. Police had to clear the roadway to allow the funeral procession to travel the short distance from the State House to King's Chapel for the Episcopal services, so chosen because it had once been the place of worship for Sumner's mother; the senator belonged to no church. From there, the procession wound its way toward Cambridge and Mount Auburn Cemetery, closely followed by dignitaries and, perhaps more notably, according to one reporter, "the representatives of the dusky race, for whom Charles Sumner battled and suffered, and in whose cause he laid down his life."

DECEMBER 8, 1875. If Charles Sumner's death marked the final chapter of Boston's heroic abolitionist movement, then an event a little more than one year later signified the beginning of another Boston movement—this one religious—that would last far longer and impact the city for the next century and beyond in political, economic, and cultural ways. After eight years of construction, the new Cathedral of the Holy Cross was dedicated on Washington Street in the South End, which the *Pilot* called "the greatest religious event for the Catholics of this generation in New England."

Coinciding with the Feast of the Immaculate Conception, the cathedral's dedication encapsulated the growing influence of Catholics in Yankee Boston, influence that would continue to grow for the next century and transform Boston into one of the most Catholic cities in America. Along with St. James (near South Station), St. Mary's in the dense North End, and St. Joseph's in the West End at the foot of Beacon Hill, the Holy Cross Cathedral was one of four anchor parishes in Boston. Moreover, the cathedral's opening dovetailed with the elevation earlier in May of Bishop John Williams to the rank of archbishop to lead the recently created Boston Archdiocese (once a diocese within the New York Province) and the Ecclesiastical Province of Boston, which included all of New England. The Boston Archdiocese alone numbered more than 300,000 Catholics, with nearly 30,000 children enrolled in parochial schools. In all, more than 860,000

Catholics resided in New England (which included Boston and the dioceses in Hartford, Portland, Providence, Burlington, Vermont, and Springfield), served by more than 400 priests; thirty years earlier, according to the *Pilot*, the New England region contained scarcely 68,000 Catholics. German and Irish immigrants—who would soon be joined by new arrivals from Italy—were changing the region's religious composition in profound ways.

Elsewhere in the country, anti-Catholic sentiments had subsided, but they had hardly disappeared. Just two months earlier, in a speech to an audience of veterans in Des Moines, Iowa, President Grant warned against what he saw as an increasingly aggressive Catholic Church. He also urged his fellow veterans not to permit a single dollar "to be appropriated to the support of any sectarian school." Such aid might destroy public schools, he said, "the promoter of intelligence which is to preserve us as a nation." Later in December, President Grant urged the passage of a constitutional amendment banning government aid to religious schools, and promoted taxation "on vast amounts of untaxed church property," according to historian John T. McGreevey. Republican newspapers and elected officials applauded Grant's initiatives. "The Catholics will rave," Senator Justin Morrill of Vermont declared, "but I suppose there is not one who has ever voted for free-men, free-schools, or the Republican party in war or peace."

But in Boston, the dedication of the cathedral was greeted with acclaim and celebration. Four thousand people filled the church and thousands more who could not fit inside remained on the sidewalk during the High Mass celebrated to mark the occasion.

Supported by annual fund-raisers, private contributions, and a series of "Cathedral Fairs" over the previous eight years, the $1.5 million structure was almost as large as Notre Dame in Paris, St. John Lateran in Rome, or St. Sophia in Constantinople, and larger than cathedrals in Dublin, Vienna, Strasbourg, and Venice. At forty-five thousand square feet, with the ability to seat thirty-five hundred and hold twice as many, and English Gothic features that included a lofty three-hundred-foot-high tower and a five-hundred-foot-long nave, the new structure was described as "magnificent" by the Boston *Advertiser*. As Rev. J. P. Bodfish asserted in his afternoon sermon, "We are assembled to complete the dedication to Almighty God of one of the finest cathedrals on this continent…the completion of the Cathedral of the Holy Cross is another victory in the history of the Catholic Church." Father Sherwood Healy added: "The new Cathedral of Boston is worthy of its name and its place, and will bear testimony forever to the faith and generosity of the community who erected it." The *Pilot* called the cathedral "the finest ecclesiastical structure yet finished in this country," and historian Robert Lord labeled it, "undoubtedly, one of the noblest religious edifices in America."

Perhaps the fact that best symbolized the city's religious evolution, however, was that some of the stones from the burned Ursuline Convent in Charlestown were reused in the construction of the new cathedral.

The convent had been destroyed by an anti-Catholic mob in 1834, only forty years earlier; but for Boston, a lifetime ago.

PART THREE

A City So Grand

1876–1900

It's a grand thing.

—*President William McKinley, after*
touring Boston's subway in 1899

CHAPTER 10

The Centennial,
the Sensational, and Beyond

Mr. Watson, come here—I want to see you.

—Alexander Graham Bell to his assistant, Thomas Watson,
in the world's first telephone transmission, 5 Exeter Place, Boston

Boston was a city of contradictions by the time it entered America's centennial celebration year of 1876.

Brimming with pride about their role in the country's founding, Bostonians looked forward to the July Fourth celebration—nationwide and at home—to mark the one-hundred-year anniversary of the signing of the Declaration of Independence and America's break with England. In the midst of its own municipal revolution a century later, Boston had also completely rebuilt its downtown section after the Great Fire four years earlier, and in the Back Bay, workers had reached present-day Gloucester Street in the massive landfill project, now nearly two decades old. Improved urban transportation enabled Bostonians to travel around their core city, and out to the newly annexed sections of Dorchester, Roxbury, and Charlestown.

On the other hand, Boston and the rest of the nation were three years into a five-year financial depression that had stifled wages and economic growth. Jobs were scarce and disposable income had dried up. The Back Bay filling project continued, but only a handful of lots had been sold in the previous two years. Factory workers and unskilled laborers, many of them immigrants, earned pennies a day performing piecework or backbreaking and exhausting physical tasks. Wages had dropped as much as 50 percent from just two years earlier. Boston newspapers were filled with classified ads from business owners looking to sell at reduced prices ("$500 buys stock and fixtures of a good cash provision store and fish market—actually worth the price!"). Merchants announced "astonishing sales" of dry goods, dresses, shawls, silks, jackets, and sweaters, seeking buyers to purchase goods for "less than half their real value."

Socially and culturally, too, Boston faced contradictions. By 1876, its population had grown to 341,000, a 26 percent increase since the end of the Civil War, with immigration and annexations fueling most of the growth. In good times, more people potentially meant more business activity, more access to labor, more consumer spending—but in the midst of an economic downturn a burgeoning population was a liability. Moreover, more than one-third of Boston's population was foreign-born, and 60 percent of those were Irish. Despite greater tolerance and improved relationships, Boston's Yankee elites were troubled by the continued rise in Irish numbers and power, and they became troubled further when Irishman Patrick Maguire emerged in 1876 as a powerful boss of the Democratic City Committee. A bright, ambitious back-room power broker—the *Boston Globe* referred to him as a "born leader"—Maguire would essentially run Boston for the next two decades, until his death in 1896. And while the Boston Police Department had made great strides since Barney McGinniskin was its sole Irish member in 1851 (there would be forty-five Irish-born police officers by 1871 and one hundred by 1880), nativists, Republicans, and the *Boston Herald* all expressed wariness and resentment at the increasing "Irish leanings" of the police force.

All of these issues were conversations in Boston during 1876. In addition, with anticipation heightening as the July Fourth centennial celebration drew closer, two occurrences during the early part of 1876 reflected a city whose population and influence would continue to grow even as America looked ahead to her second century.

The first involved the dedication of another church, St. Leonard, this time in Boston's North End. The ceremony signified the beginning of a demographic shift that would propel a new immigrant population—this one from Italy—into Boston's second-largest ethnic population within thirty-five years.

The second event, which took place across town just a few weeks after the St. Leonard dedication, not only dramatically bolstered Boston's national standing and prominence; it quite literally changed the world.

When the Boston Archdiocese dedicated the St. Leonard of Port Maurice Church building in February of 1876, three years after St. Leonard's was founded as the first Italian parish in New England, any student of demography may have wondered why; only a handful of Italians had made Boston their home. Built on the corner of Prince and Hanover streets in the North End on land the archdiocese had purchased for nine thousand dollars, the church would initially cater to a mere eight hundred Italian parishioners living in the North End, eleven hundred in Boston, and perhaps another two thousand residing on the North and South Shores and throughout the Merrimack Valley. Italians represented a tiny minority of Greater Boston's population and a far-flung one at that.

But things changed quickly.

The arrival of Boston's earliest Italians, mostly from northern Italy, signaled the beginning of an astonishing ethnic shift in the North End and Boston. After 1880, Jews, many of whom had fled pogroms in Russia, and southern Italians, escaping desperate impoverishment in their homeland, began to arrive by the thousands. Over the next quarter-century, most Irish residents had achieved enough upward mobility to leave the city's poorest neighborhood, choosing to move to areas such as South Boston, Charlestown, and Dorchester. Jews, who assimilated relatively quickly, also moved within a short time to neighborhoods such as Roxbury and Jamaica Plain. But Italians would call the North End home for years. By the turn of the century, Italians made up fifteen thousand of the North End's twenty-four thousand residents, and the North End was home to more than 85 percent of the total Italian population. By World War I, more than 95 percent of the forty thousand people who crowded into the North End were of Italian heritage.

For these Italians, the transition to America was traumatic, sometimes brutal, and often frightening. Like the Irish before them, the North End Italians suffered from congestion and overcrowding, substandard living conditions, and poverty. Southern Italian immigrants, who hailed from farming and fishing communities in Italy, were crowded into a neighborhood of dilapidated tenements as they struggled to make ends meet. The inhabitable portion of the North End is only about eighty acres, and by the first decade of the twentieth century, the enclave rivaled Calcutta in population density. City investigators found the tenements adjoined so closely that sufficient light and air could not enter outside rooms, except for those on the top floors; inside rooms were dark and musty. The Boston City Council would report in 1896 that "in the North End the tenement houses are today a serious menace to public health." One author who would comment on slums in Boston in 1898 described tenements along Fleet Street: "In none of the houses is there any thorough ventilation; air shafts were not thought of when the houses were built. Though the sun shines into some of the top floors, all the lower rooms are very dark." These conditions took their toll among Italians in the North End; they quickly became susceptible to tuberculosis, even though they were among the least likely to contract the disease in Europe. Other diseases and miseries also plagued Boston Italians. In 1898 and 1899, the North End would suffer the largest number of deaths in the city from pneumonia, meningitis, typhoid fever, and diphtheria, and the second-largest number of deaths from infant cholera and bronchitis. Not only would the North End lead the city of Boston in births in 1898 and 1899, it also would lead in the number of deaths of children under one year of age and between the ages of one and five. "This is no doubt largely the effects of extremely close tenement quarters upon people who belong out of doors in a sunny land," sociologist Robert Woods would write in *Charities* magazine in 1904.

Italians faced other hardships as well: grinding poverty, an inability to speak English, illiteracy, even in their own language. Moreover, southern Italians—darker skinned than their northern counterparts, more suspicious of government and authority, and more likely to travel back and forth between Italy and America as so-called birds of passage—faced intense discrimination in Boston and in most major cities in the United States.

Overt or subtle, it came from many quarters, even the Catholic Church. St. Leonard's pastor, Father Joachim Guerrini, whose responsibility was to care for the entire Italian community in the archdiocese, faced another challenge beyond ministering to a flock scattered for miles in and around Boston: his superiors insisted that he hear confessions only in English. "It appears that the archbishop hoped to encourage the Italian congregation gradually to make a transition to the English language by this introduction of bilingualism at Saint Leonard's Church," wrote historian William DeMarco.

And yet, despite the odds they faced and the problems that beset them, Italians made progress in Boston through strength of family, industriousness, and generosity—all hallmarks of their immigrant experience. By the late 1890s, the North End would become the center of Italian life in the Boston area. The narrow streets pulsed with vitality, as hacks, pushcarts, delivery trucks, and people competed for the right of way. Virtually no English was spoken in the neighborhood by the end of the first decade of the twentieth century. On newsstands, most newspapers and magazines were printed in Italian.

As the Irish had found jobs on the Back Bay landfill project, Italians would find work as laborers building roads, bridges, tunnels, sewer systems, and skyscrapers. Hundreds of Boston's southern Italians worked beneath the ground to build America's first subway at Park Street in the mid-1890s, and later, the elevated electric railroad that stretched from Charlestown to Forest Hills. Thousands more followed, bowing their backs and straining their arms to dig the ditches, cut the stone, lay the pipe, and hoist the steel that Boston required to accompany her expansion during the first decade of the twentieth century. Italians made remarkable gains: they saved relentlessly to realize the dream of home ownership and learned new skills to increase their earning power. Unskilled laborers became craftsmen, tradesmen, or entrepreneurs. Italians built businesses, families, and lives in America. And thousands of them called Boston home; only the Irish would exceed them in numbers as an ethnic group.

Still, in 1876, most native Bostonians had little inkling that this explosion of southern Italians would occur. When St. Leonard's Church in the North End was dedicated, almost all the Italians in Boston were from the North of Italy; they were more prosperous and better educated than their Southern countrymen who would follow. Although their language certainly made them different, their small numbers did not present nearly the problem that the Irish had thirty years earlier. That would change, of course, as southern Italians inundated the city after 1880; most nativists, then, recognizing the profound demographic change in Boston, would remain chagrined and concerned about the southern Italian issue for the remainder of the nineteenth century and well into the twentieth.

But in the months following the dedication of St. Leonard's, Bostonians focused on profound change of another sort taking place halfway across town—this one technological and almost unbelievable. A member of the Boston University faculty, on sabbatical to conduct research, had set up a small lab in an Exeter Place boardinghouse so he could work in secrecy. Now, in the third month of 1876, he had achieved the success he had dreamed about for years. He was ready to reveal his secret.

Boston, and the rest of America, was about to become acquainted, and even a little infatuated, with Alexander Graham Bell.

In many ways, twenty-nine-year-old Alexander Graham Bell had been preparing for March 10, 1876, since he was a child. He was born in Edinburgh, Scotland to extraordinary parents: a father who specialized in oration, elocution, and helping students with speech pathologies; and a deaf mother, who trained herself to be an accomplished pianist. The second of three sons—his two brothers, Melville and Edward, died young from tuberculosis within a span of four months—Alexander possessed enormous curiosity and began exploring new ideas early; by age fourteen, he had invented a machine to remove the husks from wheat. By sixteen, he was teaching music and elocution at a boys' boarding school. Blessed with a resonant voice as he matured, Alexander devised a unique system for communicating with his mother; unlike most people who spoke to Mrs. Bell through an ear tube, Alex placed his lips very close to her forehead and spoke in low, sonorous tones. He believed his mother could "hear" him through the vibrations his vocal tones would create.

In 1870, twenty-three-year-old Alexander, battling tuberculosis himself, emigrated to Ontario, Canada, with his parents, who were terrified that they would lose a third son to the disease if they remained in Scotland. In 1871 Bell moved to Boston to teach at the Boston School for Deaf Mutes, and a year later, opened his School of Vocal Physiology. He also met Boston attorney Gardiner Greene Hubbard, who would later become one of his key financial backers and his father-in-law. Bell loved Boston for its intellectual, scientific, and educational environment; he quickly became known as a voice and speech expert and his services were in great demand.

Later that same year, Boston University appointed Bell professor of vocal physiology and elocution at its School of Oratory, where one of his students, Mabel Hubbard, would one day become his wife.

While a member of the BU faculty, Bell conducted acoustics experiments and worked on plans for a "harmonic telegraph," which would allow the transmittal of multiple telegraph messages over a single wire using different sound-wave frequencies. Early in 1874, he met a young Boston electrical machinist named Thomas Watson—one account called the chance meeting "one of the most fortuitous in technological history"—and shared with Watson his dream of perfecting another machine that would allow the human voice to travel over wires. Intrigued, Watson agreed to work with Bell and the two forged a partnership to work on the transmitting and receiving device.

Initially, Bell had referred to his machine as an "advanced telegraphy instrument," but within a very short time he had come to call it by the household name it would soon be across America: the telephone.

It was another milestone day—June 2, 1875—that Bell decided his dream of transmitting human speech over a wire could become a reality.

On this late spring day, he and Watson were working on the harmonic telegraph. The two men were in different rooms, when Watson noticed that one reed was not making any sound at all; it had been too tightly wound to the pole of the electromagnet, meaning the battery current was not being interrupted when the reed vibrated and the sound of the current was not being sent to the next room, where Bell was listening. Watson plucked at the reed with his fingers and produced a twang, which Bell heard in the receiving room. Bell, trained in speech and music, rushed into the room. He believed the complex overtones and timbre of the twang to be similar to those in the human voice. Watson's efforts to free the reed had changed everything. Perhaps it wasn't just sounds, but *spoken words* that could be transmitted. As Watson recounted years later: "The twang of that reed I plucked on June 2, 1875, marked the birth of one of the greatest modern inventions, for when the electrically carried ghost of that twang reached Bell's ear, his teeming brain shaped the first electric speaking telephone the world had ever known. The sound of that twang has certainly been heard around the world and its vibration will never cease as long as man exists."

An excited Bell wrote to Gardiner Greene Hubbard in August of 1875: "I can see clearly that the magneto-electric current will not only permit the actual copying of spoken utterances, but of the simultaneous transmission of any number of musical notes (hence messages) without confusion." The twang that Bell heard convinced him that he and Watson were at "the most important point yet reached. I believe that it is the key to still greater things."

The pair threw themselves into their work for that summer and throughout the fall; Bell rented two rooms at 5 Exeter Street for increased privacy, even sleeping in one of the rooms for nights at a time. He became ill from exhaustion in the late fall and feared that his relentless work schedule was driving him away from his beloved Mabel. But the couple became engaged on November 25 after Bell visited her in Cambridge and pledged his devotion. "You seemed to me to be drifting away from me—so far away—and I almost despaired of ever reaching you," he wrote late in the evening of the same day. "I can scarcely believe that you really and truly love me—and that you will be my wife. I am afraid to go to sleep lest I should find it all a dream—so I shall lie awake and think of you. It will be my pride and delight, Mabel, to protect and to love you."

His personal affairs in order, Bell raced to perfect his telephone, and also drew up specifications to file with the U.S. Patent Office. On March 7, 1876—three days before he had achieved success with his new invention—he was granted one of the most famous patents in American history: No. 174,465 (hours later, the attorney for Elisha Gray, Bell's fiercest competitor, filed a caveat for a telephone). "I ... have invented certain new and useful Improvements in Telegraphy," Bell asserted in his patent application. "By these instruments two or more telegraphic signals or messages may be sent simultaneously over the same circuit without interfering with each other ... I desire to remark that there are many other uses to which these instruments may be put, such as the simultaneous transmission of musical notes ... and the telegraphic transmission of noises or sounds of any kind."

On March 10, in the Boston workshop, Watson heard the sound he and Bell had been waiting for.

—m—

What was so special, of course, was that the sound was a human *voice*—not a hum, not a vibration, but, as Bell wrote to his father, "articulate speech." The events of March 10, among the best-known pieces of Americana, actually began in the afternoon when Bell and Watson were testing Bell's transmitting and receiving machine. "Mr. Watson was stationed in one room with the Receiving Instrument. He pressed one ear closely against [it] and closed the other ear with his hand," Bell recorded in his notebook. "The Transmitting Instrument was placed in another room and the doors of both rooms were closed."

Either a scrap of folklore or a questionable detail intervenes in the story at this point—that Bell accidentally spilled acid on his clothing and thus required Watson's assistance. No mention of this appears in Bell's meticulously detailed notebook or Watson's logs, though Watson does recount the accident in his autobiography, written a half century later. Whether the "acid story" was true or merely a fanciful Watson embellishment, American schoolchildren grew up with it firmly lodged in their consciousness. What *did* occur, and what was recorded by both Bell and Watson, were Alexander's next words: "Mr. Watson, come here—I want to see you."

Watson raced into the other room and told the inventor, to Bell's "delight," that he had heard and understood the message. Bell asked Watson to repeat the words and Watson did so exactly. Bell and Watson then changed places and the assistant read a few paragraphs from a book. "It was certainly the case that articulate sounds proceeded" from the transmitter, Bell wrote, and while the effect was "loud" it was also "indistinct and muffled." Nonetheless, Bell declared, "If I had read beforehand the passage given by Mr. Watson, I should have recognized every word." Bell did hear quite clearly Watson's follow-up question: "Mr. Bell, do you understand what I say?"—though Bell wrote in his March 10 notebook entry that the question transmitted in staccato fashion, "Do—you—under—stand—what—I—say?" Bell and Watson tried other phrases and sentences—such as "How do you do?" and "God save the Queen"—and achieved "satisfactory results."

Joyful, Bell breathlessly recounted the historic moment in the letter he penned to his father that evening. "Dear Papa: Articulate speech was transmitted intelligibly this afternoon. I have constructed a new apparatus operated by the human voice." Bell's voice had traveled just ten yards along a wire from one room to another, but in his letter to his father he presciently recorded the momentousness of the occasion: "This is a great day with me. I feel that I have at last struck the solution of a great problem—and the day is coming when telegraph wires will be laid on to houses just like water or gas—and friends converse with each other without leaving home."

Watson recognized the import of the moment as well. Much later, he collected the wires that had carried the historic conversation and brought them to a bank safe-deposit box. He attached a signed note to the coiled wire that read: "This wire connected Room No. 13 with room No. 15 at 5 Exeter Place, and is the wire that was used in all the experiments by which the telephone was developed, from the fall of 1875 to the summer of 1877, at which time the telephone had been perfected for practical use. Taken down July 8th, 1877."

Bell and Watson toiled for several weeks, until finally, Bell felt confident enough to begin demonstrating his invention in scientific and academic circles. "The experiments at Harvard went off splendidly," he wrote to his parents on May 5. "Articulate sounds were heard by all who listened to the tube. Several professors distinguished vowel sounds." In the same letter, Bell reminded his parents that he was "hard at work" on a paper he would read in a few days before the American Academy of Arts and Sciences. "If successful, the reading of the paper will be one of the great events of my life," he wrote. "It will be one of the milestones by which I will measure time."

On May 10, Bell unveiled the telephone at the Academy of Arts and Sciences' meeting at the Boston Athenaeum. Distinguished members filled the hall—Bell later referred to them as a "dignified assembly of grey heads"—to hear the young scientist present what he called "Researches in Telephony." Bell had also prepared an experiment, stringing a wire from his office on Beacon Street to the Athenaeum. At the appropriate time in his presentation he telegraphed an assistant requesting some music. "While I was speaking, out burst the notes of 'Old Hundred' from an instrument upon the table—to the delight of all," he wrote to his parents. Later his assistant sent some "full rich chords" from what Bell described as a "telephonic organ" in his office. "Everything was most successful, and when I sat down I was somewhat surprised to be greeted by a hearty round of applause," Bell wrote, "which I am informed is such an unusual thing in the Academy." His experience at the academy, which he concluded was "a grand success," infused Bell with confidence and made him feel "borne up on a rising tide."

Two weeks later, on May 25, Bell repeated his experiment and presentation before a large gathering of MIT faculty before the school's Society of Arts. A brief *Boston Transcript* article noted that vowel sounds came through Bell's telephone intelligibly, while consonant sounds were all but "unrecognizable." Still, the report noted, "occasionally, however, a sentence would come out with startling distinctness." Bell's fiancée, Mabel Hubbard, wrote to her future mother-in-law two days later describing the MIT lecture: "Alec looked very nice indeed…and I was very proud of him. He was as usual quiet and self possessed and spoke very easily and distinctly. The lecture was a great success and his experiments were applauded several times."

Speaking at universities and before academic audiences was necessary to build credibility, but both Bell and his future father-in-law and major investor, Gardiner Greene Hubbard, realized the inventor needed a much wider, public venue to demonstrate his invention, attract greater interest and additional capital, and launch the telephone across America. The timing was perfect: Bell decided to showcase his telephone at the massive Centennial Exposition in Philadelphia, scheduled to run from May to November, 1876, with a goal (ultimately achieved) of attracting millions of Americans and people from around the world (nine million would eventually pay the fifty-cent admission price). Situated on three thousand acres in Fairmount Park, the Centennial Exposition would show off the nation's manufacturing and scientific achievements. "All across the country people made plans to attend," wrote researcher Robin Marrone. "Newlyweds [even] planned honeymoon trips to the exposition."

The normally reserved Bell, too, was duly impressed upon his arrival. "I really wish you could be here, May, to see the Exhibition," he wrote to Mabel on June 21, 1876. "It is wonderful! You can have no idea of it till you see it. It grows upon one. It is so prodigious and so wonderful that it absolutely staggers one to realize what the word 'Centennial Exhibition' means. Just think of having the products of all nations condensed into a few acres of buildings.…How I wish I could be with you now."

Bell conducted his Philadelphia experiment before about fifty people, including Scottish mathematician Sir William Thomson and Brazilian emperor Dom Pedro, and met with "glorious success," as he wrote to his parents a few days later. Pedro reportedly exclaimed, "My God, it talks…I have heard. I have heard," as Bell recited Hamlet's "To be or not to be" soliloquy from another building one hundred yards away. When Bell asked, "Do you understand what I say?" Sir William jumped up and shouted, "Yes—'Do you understand what I say?' Where is Mr. Bell? I must see Mr. Bell!"

Bell also took great delight that his archrival, Elisha Gray, was unsuccessful in trying to send two messages simultaneously, and that his instrument was far more costly than Bell's. "Mr. Gray accomplished the transmission of musical notes by very expensive apparatus—between $15 and $20 per note," Bell wrote to his mother and father. "I accomplished the same thing by means of instruments costing *two cents per note*." The two men did have a long conversation in Philadelphia, apparently resolved legal disputes, and "decided that it may be advantageous to both of us to unite our interests," Bell reported.

After the Centennial Exposition, Bell and his telephone were the talk of the international scientific community. During the summer of 1876, he conducted additional experiments in Ontario at his parents' residence, which the *Boston Daily Advertiser* described as "perfectly successful." He also traveled to Paris to demonstrate his invention to European scientists.

But his greatest success, what Bell referred to as "the proudest day of my life," occurred in Boston—or rather *between* Boston and Cambridge—on October 9, again in partnership with Thomas Watson. With Watson stationed in Cambridgeport and Bell in Boston, a distance of a little over two miles, and using a telegraph line owned by the Walworth Manufacturing Company, the two men carried on what newspaper reports later called "the first conversation ever carried on by word of mouth over a telegraph wire." The two men conversed "fluently and readily" for a stunning ninety minutes, Bell wrote to his parents, "with every word and every syllable being clearly understood at the other end of the line." Mabel wrote to her mother-in-law: "I have seldom seen [Alec] so pleased or excited about anything."

Newspapers in Boston and across the country carried accounts of the Bell-Watson conversation (the *Advertiser* printed the entire transcript of the memorable phone call) and recognized the gravitas of the moment. Samuel Morse's telegraph thirty years earlier had revolution-ized communication in such a way that mankind had never seen—allowing for the instant transmission of messages that, for thousands of years, had been carried by people riding horseback, walking, or traveling on boats. But while allowing instantaneous communication, the telegraph permitted only truncated, mostly emotionless messages that often left much to interpretation. Bell's telephone was an evolu-tionary advancement—humans could now speak to each other over long distances, and hear each other's intonations, inflections, and in-tensity. Telephone users could both express and infer the subtexts of insincerity and evasiveness, honesty and directness, anger and joy, in a way that was impossible with a written telegraph message.

After the conversation between Bell and Watson from Boston to Cambridge, a *Daily Advertiser* editorial wondered, "if the spoken word can thus be articulately transmitted so as to be audibly intel-ligent through two miles of wire, [might it] be transmitted through a hundred miles or more?"

The new invention buoyed Bell as well as the city of Boston.

In April of 1877, many of Boston's most prominent citizens—including Henry Wadsworth Longfellow and Oliver Wendell Holmes—signed a letter urging Bell to conduct a public demonstration, "con-fident that the general public of the city in which your researches have been made will be glad to witness a practical exhibition of your tele-phone." In May, E. T. Holmes opened the first telephone exchange at 342 Washington Street, Boston. Six subscribers were provided with daytime service only (a year later, Emma Nutt would become the first female telephone operator, hired after subscribers complained that male operators were too gruff). In July, Bell and Mabel were married and visited England for a year, and in early 1878 Bell demonstrated the telephone for Queen Victoria. The queen sought to purchase "two instruments with the wires attached," and Bell replied to her aide that he would offer the queen "a set of telephones to be made expressly for her Majesty's use." Later that same year, the first telephone directory in Boston was distributed, according to author Jim Vrabel. The single sheet of paper contained twenty-two names and no numbers; callers were required to signal the central office ("Hello, Central") and an-nounce the name of the party to whom they wished to speak. Bell,

Hubbard, and other investors also incorporated the New England Telephone and Telegraph Company in Boston in 1878, which later became the National Bell Telephone Company and then the American Bell Telephone Company.

For Bell and the telephone, of course, there was no looking back. He was granted American citizenship in 1882, and while not actively involved in the management of the company that bore his name, saw the formation of the American Telephone and Telegraph Company in 1885 to manage the expanding long-distance business of American Bell. In 1892 Bell participated in the formal opening of long-distance telephone service between New York and Chicago, as part of the Windy City's World's Fair celebration (Bell spoke into the phone in New York).

Bell and Watson would team up one final time on January 25, 1915, when the two participated in the first transcontinental telephone conversation. Bell, at AT&T headquarters in New York, repeated his first message from thirty-nine years earlier, "Mr. Watson, come here—I want to see you." Watson, stationed in San Francisco, heard Bell clearly and replied: "I should be very glad to, Dr. Bell, but we are now so far apart it would take me a week to come instead of a minute." The two men spoke over a wire stretching thirty-four hundred miles across the continent; part of an overall system that then included 9 million telephones connected by 21 million miles of wire.

Newspapers across the country celebrated the event. The telephone had once again captured the imagination of a country. Ziegfeld Follies, which performed vaudeville shows, commemorated the historic call with a song titled "Hello, Frisco!" which became the most popular song of 1915. Watson would later write: "I carried on the conversation with Dr. Bell, over this wire four thousand miles long, as easily as I had talked with him thirty-nine years before over the wire between Boston and Cambridge." (Another technological feat that same year brought New York, Boston, and the entire East Coast closer to San Francisco: the completion in February of the Panama Canal.)

Their coast-to-coast telephone exchange in 1915 was the last conversation between Bell and Watson. Bell died in August of 1922 at the age of seventy-six at his Nova Scotia home. His obituary in the *New York Times* called Bell's famous patent, No. 174,465, "the most valuable patent ever issued." The paper recapped Bell's historic 1876 breakthrough moment in his small Boston workshop and added: "The little instrument he patented less than fifty years ago, scorned then as a joke, was when he died the basis for 13,000,000 telephones used in every civilized country in the world."

On the day of Bell's burial, all telephone service in the United States was suspended for one minute in his honor.

One year after Alexander Graham Bell changed history in Boston, another historic event with Boston connections, if one less often heralded, occurred in Washington, D.C.

The former U.S. marshal in Boston, Charles Devens, the man who had remanded fugitive slave Thomas Sims back to slavery in 1851, became attorney general of the United States in the administration of President Rutherford B. Hayes. During the Civil War, Devens had aided Sims after the young man again escaped from slavery, crossed into Union lines, and returned to Boston a free man. After the war, Sims settled in Tennessee.

In 1877, Sims traveled to Washington and applied for a job in the attorney general's office. Perhaps to assuage his conscience from a quarter century earlier, perhaps for other reasons, Devens hired Sims as a messenger, a position he held for several years before being removed during the presidency of Chester Arthur.

Twenty-six years after Thomas Sims was captured in Boston and returned to his masters by federal troops, the onetime fugitive slave had become an employee in the United States Department of Justice.

SEPTEMBER 17, 1880. On a sun-splashed, humidity-free day—heavy rain the preceding several days had "laid the dust and freshened the atmosphere," according to one account—as many as 350,000 people clogged Boston's sidewalks, standing six to ten deep, and watched and cheered as the massive parade passed. More than 14,000 marchers, four hundred vehicles, thirty-five bands, and twenty-two drum corps stretched for four and a half miles and took more than three and a half hours to pass a given point. "For once it seemed as though all America had come to Boston," one reporter wrote later.

Four years earlier the nation had celebrated its centennial anniversary. Today, proud and parochial, Boston was enjoying a far more lavish celebration to commemorate the 250th anniversary of its founding in 1630 by John Winthrop, who arrived with the Massachusetts Bay Company's charter and later wrote of Boston: "Wee must Consider that wee shall be a Citty upon a Hill. The eies of all people are uppon Us."

Now, on the same September 17th date that marked Boston's founding, the signing of the U.S. Constitution in 1787, and Boston's Great Railroad Jubilee of 1851, tens of thousands of eyes focused on the bands and military companies that marched through city streets and the brightly decorated homes and businesses along the parade route. Celebrants awaited a second night parade, which was scheduled to include one thousand torchbearers and sixteen floats depicting the city's history, and culminate under the full moon with a concert performed by Patrick Gilmore's band. It was an era in which parades and pageants were expressions of municipal pride and progress, and Boston had much to celebrate on its 250th anniversary.

People began arriving early in the day, nearly 230,000 of them by train from outlying neighborhoods and towns, joining residents from the core city and visitors from around the country who had arrived in Boston during the past week. "Never before had the streets appeared more densely thronged," according to the City Council's report of the event. "In some places, notably on Hanover Street, it was a work of difficulty to open a space through the mass of spectators, sufficient for the passage of the procession." Nonetheless, despite the vast numbers, Bostonians were in a festive mood and "good order prevailed," one newspaper noted. Another report declared: "Business was generally suspended throughout the city, and there was evident determination on the part of every one to make the day a holiday, and give it up to pleasure."

The anniversary celebration had begun the previous evening with a reception at Faneuil Hall, at which Mayor Frederick Prince hosted distinguished guests and officials from other cities, and continued with the unveiling in Scollay Square of a bronze statue of John Winthrop, for which the city had appropriated five thousand dollars; the agenda resumed early the next morning with exercises at Old South Church, including a major address by Mayor Prince.

In the years sandwiching Boston's 250th anniversary in 1880, from the late 1870s to the mid-1880s, the city and her residents and civic leaders combined progress and preservation in visible strokes, embarking on projects and initiatives that thrust Boston into the national limelight again and again. None of these efforts rivaled Alexander Graham Bell's breakthrough in 1876, but many of them captured the maturity of a city that recognized its leadership role and its desire to benefit, and often profit, from it.

In late 1878 the Boston Park Commission engaged nationally renowned landscape architect Frederick Law Olmsted as an adviser to determine the best way for the city to create an urban park system, something Boston officials had been discussing since the 1850s. Olmsted had already planned New York City's Central Park, Brooklyn's Prospect Park, and Belle Isle Park in Detroit. For Boston, he proposed what would become known as the Emerald Necklace, a nine-mile, eleven-hundred-acre chain of public parks and green spaces that would rank among his greatest achievements. The necklace would stretch from the Boston Common to West Roxbury, and include the dredging and filling in of the Back Bay Fens—adjacent to the newly filled Back Bay neighborhood—which the Boston City engineer once referred to as "the foulest marsh and muddy flats to be found anywhere in Massachusetts, without a single attractive feature; a body of water so foul that even clams and eels cannot live in it, and that no one will go within a half mile of in summertime, unless of necessity, so great is the stench."

The cornerstone of Olmsted's Emerald Necklace, the crucial component of Boston's new park system, would be Franklin Park, which he would propose in 1886. Olmsted envisioned the park as a pastoral refuge from the stress of urban life, where Boston residents and other visitors could enjoy "the beauty of the fields, the meadow, the prairie, of the green pastures, and still waters. What we want to gain is tranquility and rest to the mind."

Construction on the park system began in 1879 with the Back Bay Fens and was completed in 1896. Much of Olmsted's vision of a tranquil Franklin Park was shattered by the large number of visitors who flocked there to play baseball and lawn tennis, or attend school and charity picnics; in 1885 park police calculated that the average Sunday attendance at the park was eleven thousand people, with nearly twenty thousand visitors attending one Sunday. Still, Franklin Park and the Emerald Necklace did provide a common ground for Bostonians to escape from the worst of the city's ills: excessive noise, pollution, and overcrowding.

While Olmsted was planning and designing Boston's future park system, city fathers worked feverishly between 1879 and early 1882 to preserve a visible and critical part of her past. On a sweltering July 11, 1882, the city officially rededicated the Old State House, which was nearly lost to neglect, indifference, greed, and municipal rivalry.

Built in 1713 to house the offices of the royal colony of Massachusetts, Boston's most venerable public building had narrowly escaped destruction in 1876 when its merchant leases expired and many businesspeople believed it was an obstruction to the extension of Devonshire Street. Since Boston had ceased using the building as a city hall in 1841, the structure had been converted to a trade and office building housing insurance and telegraph offices, stockbrokers, freight and passenger shipping lines, a tavern, and a restaurant. In the hands of successive tenants, the building rapidly deteriorated; a "hideous mansard roof disfigured its external lines," one city councilor noted, and signs that adorned its exterior, as well as telegraph wires and poles, "contributed to the shameful defacement" of the building.

Boston's Old State House had, between the early 1840s and the mid-1870s, "stood a bedraggled thing…a scandal to self-respecting Bostonians," according to contemporaneous newspaperman and author Edwin Bacon. Would this be the sad fate for a building so steeped in Boston history? Could residents not still hear the echoes of James Otis rousing the public against the Crown's Writs of Assistance in 1761 with a speech that, as John Adams said, "breathed into this Nation the breath of life?" Did they not remember that the Old State House walls were struck with bullets during the Boston Massacre of 1770? Or that the Declaration of Independence was first read in Boston from her balcony on July 18, 1776? Or that John Hancock was installed as the first state governor in 1780; or that from her balcony, George Washington watched a procession in his honor in October of 1789?

For several years, Bostonians debated about what to do with the Old State House—the city did renew the lease for five more years as the discussion continued—until, in 1879, the City of Chicago offered to purchase the building, dismantle it, and transplant and rebuild it there, with the promise that the building would be protected as a historical monument "that all America should revere." The brazen offer by Chicago seemed to snap Boston preservationists and officials from their lethargy. The City Council appropriated thirty-five thousand dollars to refurbish the building, and passed an order requesting the legislature to prevent the city government from "selling, removing, or altering the external appearance of the Old State House." Ward 12 common councilor William Whitmore and other preservationists formed the Boston Antiquarian Club to save and restore the building. The press began a concerted effort to push the Old State House's preservation, and prominent citizens lent their voices to the cause.

For most of 1881 and half of 1882, workers engaged in a huge refurbishing effort: an elaborate reconstruction of the lower floor and basement; removing the chimneys that were added in the nineteenth century, and installing steam heat; tearing off the French mansard roof and installing the old pitch roof; removing glass on the west end and a flight of stairs on the east end and replacing them with brick walls and proper doors and windows; and installing a circular stairway from the basement to the second floor. "The repairs to the tower were costly, but indispensable," the City Council committee report of June 29, 1882, pointed out. "The second story, containing the Memorial Halls, has cost considerable money, but there, every part of the finish had to be constructed afresh."

William Whitmore's stirring dedication address on July 11 embodied all of Boston's patriotic pride and virtues, and served as a reminder of how close the city came to losing one of its most historic buildings and a symbol of the nation's founding. The official City Council report on the dedication said the restoration of the Old State House "is an event of which every Bostonian may well be proud." The history of the building "is so indissolubly connected with the most stirring events in the annals of the city, and of the nation also, that it is a source of peculiar gratification to know that the ancient edifice has been saved from destruction."

In so doing, the council report declared, Bostonians had assured that the Old State House would be "handed down to future generations in a form substantially the same as it presented when, within its venerable walls, the child Independence was born."

Creating its urban Emerald Necklace and preserving one of the nation's most important structures were two of Boston's most ambitious projects in the late 1870s and 1880s, but the city's commercial innovations also continued to set the pace for the nation.

Two entrepreneurs who had spent their early careers selling coffee, teas, and spices joined forces in Boston and formed the first company that shipped ground coffee in sealed tins in 1878 (most consumers

Figure 8. Before Boston restored the historic Old State House and rededicated it in 1882, the building was home to numerous businesses, including insurance, telegraph, and law offices. (*Photo courtesy of the Boston Public Library, Print Department*)

still ground their own coffee). Caleb Chase and James Solomon Sanborn were successful from the outset, and by 1882, the firm of Chase & Sanborn was shipping one hundred thousand pounds of coffee a month. The company quickly built a worldwide reputation, and during the 1893 World's Fair in Chicago, Chase & Sanborn supplied the coffee for all the restaurants that served fairgoers. In 1892 one account labeled Boston's Chase & Sanborn "the largest importing and distributing tea and coffee house in the United States."

Another Boston entrepreneur, William Filene, opened his first department store at 10 Winter Street in 1881, and a decade later turned the business over to his two sons, Edward and Abraham Lincoln Filene (the latter was born three days after Lincoln's assassination). Filene's became one of the nation's most successful retail enterprises, known for its pioneering marketing techniques and employee benefits. Filene's established the first employee credit union in the United States and launched the "automatic markdown system," whereby slow-selling goods were reduced in price on an ongoing basis and relocated to the store's basement; Filene's Basement was eventually opened as a separate entity in 1912.

Chase, Sanborn, and the Filene family all contributed to Boston's growth as a mercantile metropolis and broadened her reputation for innovation across the country. But another businessman—a risk taker and big thinker in his own right—would do more to change Boston's face and propel her into the future than all the others. Henry H. Whitney made his first inroads in 1887 when he convinced the legislature to allow his West End Street Railway Company to emerge as a corporate consolidation of previously independent street railways. Whitney was now president of the largest public transportation company in the world, operating an enormous enterprise in Boston; West End owned 1,481 streetcars, operated 253 miles of track, stabled more than 7,700 horses, and carried more than 100 million passengers annually.

One year later, Whitney was ready to take another bold step. If he were successful, Boston's municipal transportation system would enter a new age. Whitney had read the news accounts of the technological achievements of a Connecticut-born Annapolis graduate who was being hailed as a genius.

In 1888, Henry Whitney boarded a train for Richmond, Virginia, to see if Frank Sprague could help him.

CHAPTER II

Breaking New Ground

That so conservative an American town should happen to be
the pioneer in adopting this is viewed as remarkable.

—*The* New York Times, *August 15, 1897, commenting on
Boston's impending opening of America's first subway*

Henry Whitney did not record his thoughts as his train rumbled
southward in late June of 1888, but it is hard to imagine that he did
not review the events that had brought him to that point.

A Brookline entrepreneur, real estate speculator, and steamship operator, Whitney had first formed a syndicate out of his relatively small
West End Street Railway and began to purchase stock in the other
five Boston-based horse-drawn street-railway operating companies.
He recognized an opportunity when he saw one. The city's expansion
and the desire for neighborhood-to-downtown travel had caused an
explosion in Boston's street-railway usage. The system served 13 million passengers in 1860, and by 1880, ridership exceeded 62 million;
now it approached 100 million passengers annually. Streetcar railways
not only transported passengers around Boston, but into the nearby
suburbs as well.

Growth, however, brought problems. Boston streets, already congested with streetcars in the downtown area, were just too narrow to
accommodate separate tracks for all the individual streetcar railway
companies, which required complicated lease arrangements for com-
petitors' use of each others' tracks. "All too often, rival drivers raced
for switches, stalled, and in general interfered with each other's prog-

ress," historian Sam B. Warner noted. In addition, some of the smaller railway companies were badly managed and undercapitalized, meaning they could not maintain their streetcars or tracks, care for their horses properly, or pay for quality employees in a highly competitive market.

Whitney and his colleagues had thwarted an attempt in 1880 by business rivals to erect an elevated-track structure that would transport steam-powered trains around the city, similar to a system New York had adopted. Proponents argued that it would alleviate congestion, reduce the time it took for trains to travel from one part of the city to another, and allow public transportation to continue to function when horse-drawn cars would otherwise be halted—during "snow blockades" and equine disease epidemics. But Whitney and his fellow streetcar operators successfully rebuffed the point, declaring that the syndicate seeking elevated-steam-railroad approval was doing so purely for profit and not for the public good, and in the process would harm railway entrepreneurs that both served Bostonians well and had spent years building their businesses.

Moreover, construction of an elevated steam-powered railroad would require land-takings and private property disruptions unlike anything the city had seen. Testifying before a legislative committee, Calvin Richards, president of the then-independent Metropolitan Railroad Company, argued also that elevated railways would "present to us all an ugly, unwieldy, monstrosity ... something that utterly destroys the architectural beauty of its surroundings, and banishes forever from them all that can delight the taste or please the eye." An elevated railroad might move people slightly faster, Richards said, but its very presence would represent a public nuisance.

The legislative committee agreed with the street-railway men, stating there was "neither public demand nor public exigency" for an elevated steam-powered railway system in Boston. New York was a different story, legislators pointed out. The city was much larger geographically and transported millions of additional passengers each day. Plus, the elevated steam-powered railway had only been operating there for about a year; perhaps New York's system was a necessity, but "the Legislature of Massachusetts may as well await the results of the New York experiment."

Indeed, the Massachusetts decision proved prescient. New York's elevated steam railways proved too costly to operate profitably on any but the most heavily traveled routes, and billowing smoke and steam blighted the streets on which they operated. Manhattan banned steam-powered "els" by 1883.

Though the threat of the steam-els was removed, Whitney still believed improvements had to be made to Boston's street-railway system. He envisioned a powerful, consolidated, efficiently managed monopoly that would provide low fares (he was an ardent proponent of the five-cent fare) and more frequent service to passengers throughout the city and dozens of surrounding suburban towns. Thus, after he had purchased large amounts of stock in the separate street-railway companies, Whitney offered an exchange of stock and bonds to combine all the companies into one. The promise of rapid expansion of service and the hope of reducing congestion and confusion in Boston's downtown streets helped persuade the legislature to approve the virtual monopoly.

Whitney was true to his word. In less than a year, consolidation did improve the overall transportation system: routes were planned more efficiently, additional routes were added, and Whitney reduced the fare to a nickel from the eight-cent fare prior to consolidation. Very quickly, too, a restless and visionary Whitney made an executive decision that he viewed as critical to his goal of keeping fares low, expanding service further and further from the city center, and thus increasing ridership by double-digit percentages each year.

In reality, Whitney's decision did much more: his simple choice changed everything about railway transportation in Boston and nationwide.

He decided it was time to stop using horses.

Relying on nearly eight thousand horses to power a major urban transportation system presented both practical and perception pitfalls, and Whitney was sensitive to both.

From a cost standpoint, horses equaled uncertainty at every juncture: buying them, feeding them, stabling them, caring for them, even cleaning up after them. The huge draft horses required to pull heavy streetcars filled with passengers were expensive, and the price of oats and hay were subject to sometimes wild market fluctuations, dropping dramatically one year, nearly doubling in price another. Stabling costs continued to rise—large-bred horses and a growing horse-railway system meant larger stables at a time when land costs were rising along the rail routes. Cheap wooden stables were no longer an option with the investment Whitney was making in his company; reducing the risk of fire and improving the living conditions and health of horses were paramount.

The economics of the manure resale business had changed, too. Expanding horse railroads in cities such as Boston and New York and new farming fertilizing techniques combined to drive prices down. Researchers Joel Tarr and Clay McShane estimated that Manhattan's horses produced more than seventeen tons of manure every day, and the Second Avenue Street Railway reported a decline in the daily value of manure produced per horse from $3.90 in 1870 to $1.10 in 1885, no small sum for a company that owned sixteen hundred horses. Also, urban residents concerned with foul odors were less willing to allow stable owners to "rot" or break down their manure in a pit or pile, which enhanced its value.

The nuisance factor was another issue. As Boston's downtown streets grew more and more congested—especially with most north-south traffic funneled onto Tremont and Washington streets—manure piles became a bigger problem; some horses were fitted with catch-pails, but the design of most trolleys and harnessing apparatus made the pails impractical. Historian William P. Marchione estimated that the average horse in Boston produced ten pounds of dung a day, "and much of it was left to dry and mix with the air." The smell and nuisance weren't the only problems; Marchione noted that many historians attributed the rise in the incidence of tuberculosis in nineteenth-century American cities to the "dried air-borne dung that residents were breathing."

The final cost variable that Whitney and other horse-railroad owners had to deal with was the overall health-risk to the animals. Bovine or equine diseases could prove disastrous. Overworked horses sometimes died in harness, and to prevent exhaustion, teams had to be switched out often, especially on long or hilly routes. After a devastating blizzard in New York in 1888, many horses were affected with a paralyzing disease known as azoturia, the result of being stabled too long without exercise. Authors Tarr and McShane reported that the American Society for the Prevention of Cruelty to Animals was forced to shoot one hundred ailing horses, and it took more than a week for the railroad to resume a normal schedule.

Whitney, like most successful businesspeople, preferred the predictability of fixed costs over the uncertainties—and potential for disastrous loss—presented by his horses.

Beyond the business reasons, Whitney was also well aware of the image problem of horse-drawn railroads. In Boston, horses were a throwback to a different era.

Boston prided itself on its cultural, scientific, educational, political, and commercial progress, all signs of its focus on the future. Alexander Graham Bell's telephone and Thomas Edison's success with the incandescent lightbulb at Menlo Park, New Jersey, had elevated the technological thinking and expectations of millions, in Boston and elsewhere. Edison had further excited Boston when he visited in 1886 to participate in opening ceremonies for Boston Edison, throwing the switch that sent the current to light the Bijou Theater on Washington Street. Boston's magnificent Back Bay landfill and neighborhood-development project, virtually complete, represented a modern crown jewel for the city. Emerson College was established in 1880, joining Boston College, Boston University, and the Massachusetts Institute of Technology within the city limits, all schools that had been founded since 1850, establishing Boston as an educational center. The Boston Symphony Orchestra, which debuted in 1881, had delighted Boston audiences and symbolized the refinement in taste most often associated with large European cities. And no fuss was made when W. W. Bryant was appointed deputy sealer of weights and measures, the first African American municipal official in Boston's history.

Could a city, or, rather, *should* a city, that had made so much progress continue to depend on beasts of burden for motive power in its all-important transportation system? No, Whitney believed. Harnessed and tame animals, once the hallmark of a civilized society, "now seemed atavistic in an age which was increasingly proud of its mechanization," noted authors Tarr and McShane. "Horse cars seemed old-fashioned for cities that prided themselves on their modernity."

To fully realize his goal of suburban expansion, Whitney needed a workable alternative to horses. He considered and ruled out steam. He considered a mechanical cable-car system similar to that of San Francisco's; in fact, engineers had arrived in Boston and were working on cable-car designs. But it was in the midst of their efforts that Whitney heard about Frank Sprague.

Whitney took his general manager with him to Richmond, a hard-nosed transportation veteran named Daniel F. Longstreet, who favored cable cars as the alternative to horses. If Whitney was skeptical about Sprague's initial success and its applicability to Boston, Longstreet simply doubted it altogether. The two Bostonians arrived in Virginia questioning Sprague's reputation and his achievement. Sprague had his work cut out for him—his credibility and his future depended on whether he could convince Whitney and Longstreet that his success in Richmond could be replicated across Boston's large-scale rail system.

Sprague did one better: under the most intense pressure, with Whitney and Longstreet just waiting for him to fail, he changed transportation history.

Less than two months before the arrival of the Bostonians, Frank Sprague had literally electrified Richmond when he demonstrated the country's first electric-powered trolley cars on the city's railway system.

Electricity traveled through an overhead line and down a long pole connected to the roof of the trolley. Richmond residents lined the streets on May 3, 1888, to witness history along twelve miles of track, and while there were mechanical problems ("Car after car would suddenly stop in the street and refuse to move under any conditions," Sprague recalled later. "New gears had a freak way of locking"), the undertaking was a success: the overhead trolleys worked.

Sprague had arrived in Richmond with a strong background in electrical engineering and science. After his graduation from the Naval Academy, he served on the battleship USS *Richmond* from 1878 to 1880 and then on the training ship *Minnesota*. In the Navy, he met Moses Farmer, who had been experimenting with electric traction, and later visited Thomas Edison at Menlo Park, where the two discussed electric lighting installation for ships, according to author Michael Robbins. In 1882 he obtained a three-month leave and traveled to London to visit the Electrical Exhibition at the Crystal Palace, and while in the city, frequently rode on the underground railway. Afterward, Sprague said he was sure the trains could be operated more efficiently with an overhead positive conductor and return through the running rails. He resigned from the Navy the next year, went to work for Edison, but parted from him in 1884 because the great inventor wanted Sprague to focus only on lighting issues.

He started the Sprague Electric Railway and Motor Company,

which reflected his true passion, where he produced a number of inventions of major significance, including a constant-speed, nonsparking motor with fixed brushes, the first motor to maintain constant revolutions per minute under different power loads. Thanks to an impressive showing at an electrical exhibition in Philadelphia and the endorsement of the Edison Electric Light Company, Sprague's company sold 250 motors in two years. Next, Sprague designed a method to regenerate, or return, power to the main supply systems of electric-motor-driven equipment, such as elevators and trains, for economy and braking. He also designed a number of other mechanical and electrical motors and related devices that could be applied to railway cars.

In 1887, seeking to bring several of these technologies together, he signed a contract, about which he later said, "no prudent businessman would ever have entered into," for the electrification of the Union Passenger Railway in Richmond. "We had little to show," he recalled. "But faith was strong and the contract was taken under terms, price, and guarantee, easily placing it ordinarily in the 'knave of fool' class."

Indeed, the scope and terms of the deal seemed almost impossible to achieve, even by today's standards. The $110,000 contract in Richmond called for Sprague, within ninety days, to retrofit forty cars, build a generating plant, and install distribution and overhead equipment to power twelve miles of track—as yet unlaid—over a route with grades as steep as 10 percent. Thirty cars needed to be able to operate at one time. The contract sum would be "payable on completion to the purchasers' complete satisfaction," author Michael Robbins noted. Sprague and two assistants toiled day and night and overcame "a confederacy of physical difficulties, adverse financial and operating conditions, and all the ills of a new and untried system," according to one newspaper account.

When the first electrified car made its way over Richmond streets, "it scared old ladies and frightened dogs, but the success of that undertaking marked the first definite stride in the development of electric railway transportation in America."

But would Sprague's success in Richmond be enough to convince Whitney and Longstreet that his electric trolleys would work in Boston?

In June of 1888, Richmond was a peaceful southern city, still rural in many areas; Boston was a congested and thriving metropolis, the sixth-largest city in the country, with a population approaching 450,000. Boston was colder, windier, its air saltier than Richmond's—would that affect electrification performance? And the biggest question of all, one that plagued Longstreet, especially: would Sprague's system allow a large number of cars to be started at once? Could the slim overhead wire safely handle the electrical load and transmit enough current to move many cars simultaneously when they were concentrated on a short section of track?

When the Boston businessmen expressed their concerns to Sprague, the inventor knew simple reassurances would not be enough. He was a scientist first, yes, but he was also a salesman who knew dramatic visual evidence was worth more than a thousand words. He arranged for a risky midnight demonstration that, if successful, could convince his Boston prospects to become customers.

While most of Richmond slept, Sprague summoned Whitney and Longstreet from their hotel rooms and directed their attention to twenty-two electric cars, lined up nose to tail, on a short section of street railway designed to power only four widely spaced cars. Upon a lantern signal from Sprague, each car started up in rapid succession and they started to move, one behind the other as soon as the one in front was just far enough ahead to give running clearance, until all twenty-two were moving down the track. "No motor melted, no fuses blew, and the system performed exactly as Sprague knew it would," wrote transportation historian Brian Cudahy.

Convinced, and exuberant, Whitney and Longstreet returned to Boston, and in July, West End Railway placed its first order with Sprague for electric power, line, and car equipment.

By January 1, 1889, just six months after Whitney and Longstreet visited Richmond, Bostonians were taking their first rides in electric trolleys. By 1894, most of the horse-drawn trolleys had disappeared. A few years later, on September 30, 1896, Boston became the first major city in the United States to electrify its entire system.

But electrification was far from a panacea for Boston's transportation congestion—quite the opposite. For, even as the horses disappeared, the downtown problems grew worse.

—⚏—

Electrification changed Boston's physical face and positioned it once again, as the Railroad Jubilee of 1851 had done, at the vanguard of one of the most sophisticated transportation advancements in the country's history.

Horses began disappearing from Boston's cityscape almost immediately, and other big cities followed suit. Most had phased out horses on their street-railway systems entirely by about 1894, but horses were still used to haul freight wagons through city streets, and the contrast in period photos is striking as the "old" and "new" forms of transportation often crossed each other. In Boston, the West End Railway reduced its horse population from 7,700 in 1889 to a mere 857 by 1895, and had boosted its electric trolleys from 47 to 1,714. Some city residents complained about the visual eyesore created by strings of overhead wires, but most people were delighted to remove horses from the streets. Electric trolleys were cleaner, more modern, and perhaps most importantly in a city whose geographic footprint had expanded so dramatically, faster—almost twice as fast as horse-drawn cars—from the outlying neighborhoods to downtown. This enabled residents who worked downtown to live farther away, where land and housing were less expensive; though eventually, as the network of electric trolley lines spread, land values increased away from the core city as well.

But the electric trolleys also succeeded in dramatically increasing ridership, which created the sharpest of double-edged swords: it bolstered West End's profits, which Whitney had predicted and hoped, but simultaneously worsened congestion in Boston's downtown area. Between 1889 and 1894, ridership increased on the West End Railway by more than 40 percent, to nearly 137 million passengers annually. Engineer Thomas Curtis Clarke, who wrote a two-part article in *Scribner's* magazine in 1892, reported that 327,000 people came into the city by streetcar every day. Boston mayor Nathan Matthews estimated in the early 1890s that at least 200,000 people a day used the electric trolley cars within the downtown area, which had sixteen miles of track laid out on forty-three different streets. Again, almost all the electric streetcars funneled onto Washington and Tremont streets, clogging the downtown, creating near-impassable density problems. Mayor Matthews reported that on Tremont Street, as many as 332 streetcars passed in one hour, which translated to a passing car every eleven seconds. A West End Street railway survey showed congestion to be even worse: in one month, 215 northbound and 191 southbound trains per hour passed the intersection at Tremont and Park streets. The *Boston Herald* quoted a former manager of the West End Street Railway as estimating that, on weekday mornings, if all the cars entering the downtown from the southern end during one hour were placed end to end, they would form a continuous column more than one mile long.

The electric trolley's greatest differentiator—speed—was completely undermined in the downtown congestion. One Boston official described Tremont Street at rush hour: "The cars on that line drag their slow length along the mournful processions, and at the hours of greatest traffic...it was not unusual for cars to take fifteen minutes to go half a mile, and sometimes they took even longer than that." Several riders commented that, instead of riding inside trolleys, it would be quicker to walk across the roofs of the nose-to-tail cars at rush hour to reach a destination on time. Choking congestion strangled movement and stifled commerce in downtown Boston, angering commuters and merchants alike. Bostonians also grew increasingly disenchanted, for both aesthetic and safety reasons, with the collection of overhead wires and poles required to operate the electric system.

Finally, conditions became so intolerable downtown that Mayor Matthews, weary of public complaints, convinced the legislature in 1891 to create a Rapid Transit Commission, whose charter was "to promote rapid transit for the City of Boston and its suburbs." In April of 1892, the commission issued a comprehensive report recommending the consolidation of railroad depots from nine to two terminals to reduce the downtown pressure, the widening of many Boston streets, the creation of a new north-south "alley" between Tremont and Washington streets (later defeated by voters), and the creation of electrified elevated lines that, unlike the steam-elevated proposals of the past, would operate without spreading smoke, soot, and dirt. The elevated would run from South Boston to Charlestown and from Roxbury to Cambridge, but would bypass the Tremont-Washington street downtown area, because officials feared ruining the cityscape and damaging the historical character of the city by blighting it with permanent steel trestles and overhead bridges.

Rather, for the immediate downtown, the commission proposed something far more innovative, something that no other American city could boast, a new technological breakthrough that had only been tried in the European cities of London, Budapest, and Glasgow (though Paris and New York were considering it, too)—for its time a breathtaking and controversial proposal.

The commission recommended diverting trolley traffic from the street or the proposed elevated by sending the cars underground beneath Tremont Street and a portion of the Boston Common. At first, some referred to this idea simply as "the underground trolley."

But within a few months, the bold, unprecedented plan was known by a new name: the Tremont Street Subway.

APRIL 19, 1895. Standing ankle-deep in dirt and debris, Dr. Samuel Green examined the human skull he held in his hands. He was not surprised that his suspicions had come to pass.

He had correctly predicted that workers digging the subway tunnel would find bones and tombs, remnants of an old graveyard that had been relocated to the apron of Boston Common when Boylston Street was widened back in 1836. Now, nearly sixty years later, and just weeks after the subway project began, the dead had been disturbed. The first human remains were discovered twenty-four hours earlier, when a medical student poking around the construction site had stepped on something hard that gave way with a loud snap. Believing he had broken a stick, the student had scratched away some dirt with his boot, reached down, and picked up the object, only to find it was a human thighbone. Moments later, other students found a skull, the disjointed parts of two arms and hands, and crumbling bits of bone scattered in the area.

Things had deteriorated from there. Workers unearthed additional bones and began piling them carelessly against a retaining fence adjacent to Boylston Street at the southwest entrance to the Common. Passersby watching the construction had blanched at the sight and began spreading word of the grisly discovery. In the evening, vandals had entered an unguarded open tomb, removed human remains, and paraded around the Common, led by one grinning youth holding aloft a skull as the others followed. Neighbors finally contacted police, who put a stop to the demonstration.

The Boston Transit Commission quickly contacted Dr. Green, a former mayor and now librarian of the Massachusetts Historical Society, who had anticipated this in his report to the commission months earlier. Green's job was to take control of properly and respectfully disposing of the remains, both for practical reasons and to quell a public relations nightmare. The morning papers had pounced on the "desecration of the Old Boston Graveyard" and huffed that the commission and the subway contractor would let nothing stand in the way of the subway project. "They have sacrificed the Common, which is the playground of Boston, and now it seems that the dead are not to be allowed to rest quietly in their graves," the *Daily Advertiser* blanched. "The subway must be passed through the Boston Common, even if sacrilegious hands are to be laid on the dust of Boston's historic dead."

Upon his arrival, Green moved at once to ensure the proper care of the remains, ordering them placed in special boxes he had delivered for their disposition. As excavation progressed over the next several days, Green and work crews discovered that buried tombs extended from one end of the Common to the other along Boylston Street. Some of the tombs had decayed or had been destroyed, while others were in good condition. "Nearly all contained coffins which for the most part were so decayed that they could not be handled," he reported, "and the enclosed bones were much decomposed." The tombs themselves were partially filled with earth, bones, stones, and other matter, and then covered over with granite slabs. "So confused were the contents that it was impossible to find out the number of original interments," Green said.

Nonetheless, Green and the workers persevered, treating the human remains with reverence and attempting to literally piece together skeletons to estimate the number of souls that would require reinterment. "The subway contractors have been touched with a sense of decency," the *Daily Advertiser* reported just a few days after Green's arrival. "The contractors have been convinced that they cannot play with the sacred things of the city. When any parts of the human skeleton are discovered, as is continually happening, the workmen have orders to pick them up carefully" and place them in "boxes specially constructed for this purpose."

It took nearly seven months, but by November 1895, Green had estimated that portions of 910 bodies had been dug up and would need to be reinterred. On November 14 and 15, workers performed the task in an adjoining burial ground on the Common, carefully burying nearly seventy-five small boxes, each containing a miscellaneous assortment of bones. The boxes, about one foot by six inches in size, each bearing the date "1895," were buried in a lot twenty-three by thirteen feet, which was marked by a single slate tablet bearing these words: "Here Were Reinterred the Remains of Persons Found Under the Boylston Street Mall During the Digging of the Subway. 1895." Green commended the crews and the contracting firm of Jones & Meehan: "Through them the work has been carried out in a manner respectful to the memory of the dead, and satisfactory to the feelings of the living," he reported.

Not everyone agreed. Many Bostonians viewed the reburial of the bodies as symptomatic of the controversy surrounding the subway in the first place. Of the burial of bones, the *Daily Advertiser* reported: "Everything was done in business-like fashion, orderly perhaps, but roughly, and with utter absence of any feeling.... This dreary day was perhaps most appropriate for the last scene in the drama of desecration."

Those astute enough to read between the lines realized that the newspaper was expressing its feelings—and those of many Bostonians who opposed traveling underground—on the entire subway project.

America's first subway was never a foregone conclusion.

It called for the use of untested technology, promised to be costly and disruptive, presented enormous risk and dangers during construction, and carried with it the psychological and ghoulish stigma of asking people to travel beneath the earth's surface. Many Bostonians feared the notion; they associated the underground regions with death and tombs, as the habitat of snakes, rats, and insects, all of which made the idea of subway travel distasteful and even frightening. "Underground still remained uncharted territory," said author Charles Bahne. "It was the realm of Lucifer himself, inhabited by lost souls, moldering corpses, strange forms of animal life, and noxious vapors." Further, land-taking, business interruptions, increased congestion during construction, encroachments on the sacred Boston Common—all of these arguments also factored into strong and organized opposition during the subway debate.

That opposition intensified after the legislature created, subject to approval of the Boston City Council, a three-person Board of Subway Commissioners to be appointed by the mayor, whose mandate was to report on the feasibility of building a subway under Tremont Street to alleviate congestion; further legislation and a vote of Boston citizens would be needed to bring about final approval. Mayor Matthews, who supported the subway, appointed the first commissioners on January 1, 1894.

Even early assurances on the part of the commission that the Common would not be permanently defiled by either subway construction, or, as some had feared, by laying aboveground tracks across its broad expanse, failed to deter opposition. Some of the Common would be torn up during construction, and although plans called for its land to be restored upon completion of the project, some trees would be lost forever. "Who supposes for an instant that if a block of buildings, instead of the people's breathing space, stood on the west side of Tremont St., any such scheme would be devised?" asked a letter-writer to the *Daily Advertiser.* "Is there no hope for our beautiful historic Boston?"

By March 1894, Tremont Street businessmen organized the Merchants Anti-Subway League to stall passage of a subway bill. While the group certainly mentioned the aesthetic threats to historic Boston Common, it made no pretense that its major opposition to the subway was for commercial reasons. President W. G. Harris urged members to fight against "the great disadvantage and damage to business men which will necessarily follow so extensive a tearing up of the street." Other opponents cited a loss of business during heavy construction, the inability of fire apparatus to respond rapidly while negotiating "surface street disturbance," and the inconvenience and potential dangers merchants would face with the disruption of sewers, water pipes, catch basins, and electric wire conduits.

A subway would also pose a threat to public health, the Anti-Subway League argued, both during construction, when wind would carry dirt and dust across the downtown area, and afterward, when underground molds, mildew, and other germs would infect subway riders with respiratory ailments. Further, rodents and reptiles, whose nests would be destroyed during construction and disappear entirely once the subway began operating, would be driven to the surface, carrying diseases and presenting a nuisance factor that Bostonians would not tolerate.

In April, the league formally submitted a petition to the Massachusetts legislature, signed by twelve thousand merchants and residents, opposing "any subway in any portion of the City of Boston." Members called for restraint and further study of other options such as widening Tremont Street to allow easier flow of electric surface trolleys, reconsidering a north-south "alley" between Tremont and

Washington streets, running trolley traffic southbound only on Tremont and northbound only on Washington, and constructing an elevated railway in the heart of downtown that would avoid unsavory and unhealthy underground travel.

But opponents were too late. On the other side, momentum for the subway was barreling forward with a locomotive's force. And much of Boston, which just now was marveling at the final touches being applied to the new Back Bay neighborhood, argued that the city had an opportunity to attack and overcome another monumental problem with a boldness that America had never before seen.

Anti-Subway League protests notwithstanding, Boston had not come this far by exercising timidity and restraint.

While opponents roared loudly, the fact was that Boston's political establishment, most of its press, and many of its influential citizens supported a subway.

Testifying during commission hearings, Herbert L. Harding, secretary of the city's Citizens Association, summarized the feelings of many Bostonians when he said a subway would "restore the surface of Tremont Street to its proper and normal use for pedestrians and other than street cars." Lamont Burnham, a rare downtown merchant who favored the subway, argued that his business relied heavily on the on-time arrival of delivery teams within the downtown area, and testified that a subway would alleviate the congestion that interfered with the horse-drawn vehicles. The *Boston Herald* editors were convinced that the "great service" of a subway "will lie in the speedy means for passing through the congested district…a passage whose tediousness constitutes one of the greatest annoyances to which the people of Boston are now subject." The *Advertiser*'s editorial page predicted that the subway would reduce Tremont Street "blockades" by three-quarters, and the *Boston Globe*—though not overly enthusiastic in its support—wrote in late 1893, "If that subway was only in operation today, what a multitude might journey in peace and comparative comfort who now must take to the streets if they wish to get anywhere in less than 60 minutes by the clock."

Others argued that a massive subway project would create jobs in the city, an important consideration with the arrival of thousands of new immigrants from Italy and eastern Europe, coupled with the economic downturn the nation was entering in the early 1890s.

For his part, the influential Mayor Matthews told the commissioners that the time of transit "will be reduced from two-thirds to one-half of the present time" once a subway opened. In addition, Matthews argued, the subway would truly show its value during inclement weather, when travelers would no longer be subjected to delays caused by "the presence of snow and ice and by the slipping of the cars upon rails in wet weather."

Commissioners agreed with proponents and recommended to the legislature approval of the subway bill. On July 2, 1894, favorably predisposed Massachusetts lawmakers approved landmark legislation that created a public entity, the Boston Transit Commission, which would oversee the subway's operation, and the incorporation of a new private company, the Boston Elevated Railway Company, that would be responsible for building and operating the elevated railway that would link to the subway entrances north and south of the downtown area. The state would eventually lease for twenty years the operation of the soon-to-be completed subway to Henry Whitney's West End Railway; West End also continued to operate the outlying trolley lines. A new group of investors formed the Boston Elevated Railway Company.

The law also required a citizen referendum, and the legislature wasted little time; Boston voters went to the polls just three weeks later. On July 25, 1894, in a rather tepid turnout, residents approved the subway and the elevated plan by a vote of 15,492 to 14,214. Mayor Matthews estimated that morning rainfall may have kept more than ten thousand voters from the polls, but predicted that the outcome would not have changed.

The relatively small 1,278 margin notwithstanding, Matthews proclaimed the vote a ringing endorsement of both the subway and the elevated electric-powered railway. "The verdict should be accepted as a final and as a reasonably satisfactory conclusion to the rapid transit agitation," Matthews said after the vote.

A series of court challenges followed the Boston vote, but all were unsuccessful. Now, nothing stood in the city's way.

America's first subway project, at an estimated cost of $5 million, would proceed.

On March 29, 1895, "with lowering skies, dark scudding clouds overhead, soft sticky mud underfoot, and sharp scurries of snow driving before the increasing wind," according to one newspaper account, Boston and Massachusetts broke ground on America's first subway project.

In a ceremony carried out with "due solemnity" at the Boylston Street mall of the Public Garden, across from Park Square, city and state officials gathered amid a crowd of laborers, "piles of tool chests and general air of bustle," which signaled to passersby "that something of unusual importance was about to take place." Several hundred onlookers gathered to watch, but maintained a respectful distance, helped by "a dozen white-gloved officers of the law [who] kept the plank walk cleared for the passage of the dignitaries."

At just after 9:00 a.m., Massachusetts governor Frederick T. Greenhalge grasped a bright new shovel, turned to Boston Transit Commission Chairman George G. Crocker, and said: "I hand this shovel to you.... You will take it and begin the great work which will bring relief and comfort to the municipality of Boston."

Crocker speared the sod, and at 9:10 a.m., removed the first shovelful of earth on yet another civil undertaking that would signal Boston's leadership across America.

Aboveground and beneath it, for the next two and a half years, the subway's construction transformed Boston's downtown core into a writhing mass of steel and sinew, machinery and motion, noise and nerves, dirt and determination, concrete and confidence.

From early morning to dark, hundreds of laborers, surveyors, welders, engineers, railroad men, carpenters, teamsters, electricians, painters, stonecutters, masons, and steelworkers scurried around the area, along and beneath Boylston, Tremont, and Park streets, on the edges of the Public Garden and the Boston Common. They hauled tons of dirt from underground; measured lengths, widths, and heights precisely, since the subway would be wedged into an extremely confined area; constructed conveyor belts fifteen feet above street level that carried tools and equipment and excess fill to waiting railroad cars for transport and disposal; relocated underground electrical wires, sewer and gas pipes, and storm drains; and erected and reinforced steel bracings to support the subway walls and ceilings. They eventually laid underground track seventeen feet beneath the earth's surface; hammered together subway platforms a foot higher than the track, where passengers would await their trolleys; built aboveground circulation towers and fans that freshened air in the subway tunnels during construction and would do so for riders once service began; installed electrical conduits that would power current down the trolley poles to move the cars; placed and tested hydraulic pumps to remove rainwater that found its way down the inclines from the surface tracks to the mouth of the subway; and built the elaborate concrete structures that served as the entrances to the Park Street, Boylston Street, Scollay Square, and Haymarket Square stations, as well as the smaller "stair coverings" that protected secondary entrances and exits from inclement weather.

All of this work took place while surface trolleys continued to operate on Tremont and Boylston streets, turning Boston's downtown into a nightmarish tangle of tools, tracks, trolleys, workers, pedestrians, and spectators. Construction teams erected solid wooden fencing to wall off the excavation work on the edge of Boston Common and the Public Garden, but curious Bostonians gathered by the hundreds on some days, squinting through the occasional tiny breaks in the fencing to catch a glimpse of the historic work. Others simply viewed the construction from windows high above street level in multistory office buildings and retail establishments. As it had in the Back Bay some four decades earlier, Boston had embarked on a massive and ambitious project with the Tremont Street subway.

Indeed, in some ways this was the Back Bay project in reverse. Whereas contractors had hauled in tons of dirt from distant places to fill the Back Bay, the subway required workers to *remove* tons of dirt, clay, rock, and gravel from the subway construction area. Workers filled small carts that traveled on the conveyers and dropped their fill through trapdoors into waiting railcars. Some fill was used along Boston's wharves and in the South Cove area; most was transported at night from the city to suburban projects that required landfill.

Plans called for subway construction to move rapidly and be completed in stages; in all, more than twelve hundred men would work—days, nights, and Sundays—on eleven separately contracted sections. But these would be opened in two major phases: the first from the Public Garden entrance (near Arlington and Boylston streets across from Park Square) to Boylston and Tremont Street to Park Street; and a second from Park Street to North Station, through Scollay, Adams, and Haymarket squares. Major subway stations would be built

Figure 9. During construction of America's first subway between 1895–97, above-ground electric-trolley traffic was disrupted along Tremont Street. This photo shows the area near Park and Tremont streets. Note the volume of electric-trolley traffic; congestion on Tremont and Washington streets was one of the arguments subway proponents put forth to justify the underground rail project. (*Photo courtesy of the Boston Public Library, Print Department*)

at Boylston and Tremont; Park and Tremont; Scollay Square, Adams Square, and Haymarket Square. In all, the Transit Commission reported that the subway, upon completion, would be 1.8 miles long, contain 5 miles of track (there were four tracks between Boylston Street and Park Street stations), and require 150,000 barrels of cement.

Engineers, builders, and laborers took on the subway project with enthusiastic fervor, borne from the knowledge that their efforts could change history. A daunting task, engineers combined the deep underground "tube" style of construction pioneered in London with a newer open-excavation method that Paris was considering. Boston did not want to dig as deep as tube construction required, fearing the project would take far too long and would present dangers to the structural soundness of nearby buildings. On the other hand, the open-excavation method would disrupt traffic on Tremont and Boylston streets, something city fathers and merchants abhorred. In fact, state law required that "all streets under or near which a subway is constructed shall be open for traffic between eight o'clock in the forenoon and six o'clock in the afternoon."

Thus, Boston project engineers pioneered a new so-called cut-and-cover technique, in which workers supported the walls of freshly dug trenches with temporary wooden braces. Once the trenches reached the appropriate depth, laborers added the walls and floors, made of concrete and steel beams and reinforced with waterproof grout. Finally, masons and steelworkers constructed the roof of the tunnel by building brick arches between steel support beams. The upper surface was then finished with a layer of concrete and soil.

The new approach was a resounding success. "The surface was kept bridged over in such a manner that the traffic in the streets suffered little or no interruption," reported chief engineer Howard Carson to the Boston Transit Commission. "Most of [the work was] done so that only a small proportion of those travelling on the surface knew that the work of subway building was going on underneath." Indeed, Carson added: "The method was such that the street-railway tracks were not disturbed at all, and the whole surface of the street was left in the day-time wholly free for its normal traffic."

After its successful implementation in Boston, the cut-and-cover system would become standard practice in nearly all American subway construction.

—◊—

Work progressed steadily, almost relentlessly, with just a few problems. The discovery of the graves along the Common was unsettling, and during construction, some residents complained that "subway filth" was "poisoning trees" in the Public Garden. "Wherever the earth dredged up from the subway cribs has been spread over the ground, the trees have sickened," the *Daily Advertiser* reported in the summer of 1895. "Some of them have died. Why should this foul, poisonous sod be laid out in the city's parks to perfume the neighborhood and spread disease germs over the surrounding regions?" Later, when a water main ruptured and coated his office with mud, the pastor of Park Street Church called the subway an "infernal hole" and an "unChristian outrage." He bellowed from the pulpit: "Who is the boss in charge of the work? Is it the Devil?"

The linkage between traveling underground and the nether regions was a constant theme, even during construction. The discovery of bones and the minister's comments added to this fear, and it did not help that the huge subway stations at the major stops were tomb-like in appearance. "They somewhat resemble the plainer type of mausoleums that are seen in the cemeteries of Paris," the *New York Sun* reported. "All they lack...is a carved name on the front and a few death's heads or griffins in granite to make them look a little more grim and gruesome." (Even a few days after the subway opened, the *Boston Post* ran a story headlined, "Hideous Germs Lurk in Underground Air," with an illustration of a frightening "subway microbe" on its front page.)

Nonetheless, these were relatively minor protests, and as the subway project progressed, opponents were viewed almost with the bemusement reserved for gadflies who stood in the way of progress that was clearly beneficial to the greater good. Like any massive construction project, the subway work created normal disruptions and experienced the occasional setback, but considering the task, a generally jubilant Boston was proving once again that she could tackle the most complex undertakings with unparalleled success.

Then, a mere six months before the scheduled opening of the historic Tremont Street subway's Boylston to Park Street section, disaster struck.

MARCH 4, 1897. Paul Hackett never knew what hit him.

At 11:45 a.m., the twenty-six-year-old conductor of Mt. Auburn line electric street-trolley No. 461 stood on the platform of his car as it swung into the crowded intersection of Boylston and Tremont streets. A second electric trolley, a now-rare horsecar trolley, two private horse-drawn carriages, and dozens of pedestrians either traveled in or approached the same busy cross-streets. On one corner, subway laborers toiled inside the fenced-in area on Boston Common; on another, Hackett could see patrons seated in the lobby of the Hotel Pelham.

Suddenly, a massive explosion ripped through Trolley 461. Hackett, married and a father of three, was blown from the platform and landed on the street twenty feet away—bloodied, legs broken, skull gashed, clothing torn to pieces. Unable to move but still conscious, Hackett was surrounded by a sea of wreckage and carnage. Trolley 461 was a tangled, burning hulk, its passengers trapped in and under the debris, many moaning and screaming for help. The other two trolleys and the carriages were badly damaged. Dead and critically injured passengers and passersby, as well as mortally wounded horses, lay in the street. As flying glass and debris rained down on Hackett, he noticed that as far as he could see, window glass in every surrounding building had shattered. Perhaps most frightening, flames shot up from beneath the street, as if from hell itself, but actually, Hackett realized quickly (and expressed later), more likely from the subway construction that was going on under the intersection.

Within minutes, pedestrians rushed to the aid of the trolley passengers struggling to free themselves and escape, and fire department vehicles, ambulances, and police arrived on the scene. Shouts of "Over here!" and "Please help us!" mixed with the roar of the fire. Hundreds of onlookers gathered and watched as firefighters poured water on the eight-foot flames that leapt from a hole in the street from some subterranean source.

But the water did nothing to quell the fury and intensity of the fire. One report later said, "For a moment, it looked as if the whole subway at that section was aflame."

Firefighters quickly determined the problem. *Gas!* The subway work must have ruptured or cracked an underground gas line, and no amount of water could douse a gas-fed fire. They would have to staunch the supply by turning off the gas main.

Meanwhile, Hackett, bruised from head to foot and wracked with pain, was lifted onto a stretcher by rescuers, the cries of the injured haunting him as he slipped into semiconsciousness.

—ᨓ—

Figure 10. On March 4, 1897, just six months before the Tremont Street subway was completed, a massive explosion ripped through an aboveground trolley at the crowded Boylston-Tremont street intersection. Ten people were killed and more than fifty were badly injured in the blast, which was attributed to a gas leak ignited by a spark. (*Photo courtesy of the Boston Public Library, Print Department*)

Over the next few days, authorities pieced together the cause of the explosion and its tragic consequences. Between the ceiling of the Tremont Street subway and temporary planking on the streets that allowed access to the ceiling from above, was a four-foot space into which gas had been leaking, apparently for a week or more. "The odor of gas was almost overpowering in the vicinity for a long time prior to the explosion," commented the *Standard*, an insurance publication.

Inspectors found two cracks in a six-inch gas main and one in an eight-inch main, apparently damaged accidentally by subway workers. Gas and air filled the gap between subway ceiling and street, reaching explosive proportions and creating a volatile and catastrophic combination. When Paul Hackett's Trolley 461 strained around the curved track from Boylston onto Tremont, a small spark—caused either by the friction of the trolley's wheels, a short in the electric road under the tracks, or jumping from the trolley itself—ignited the highly flammable mixture and produced a tremendous explosion, one that created a cannon-like roar that was heard as far away as Roxbury. "We feel fairly confident that the massing of the gas beneath the flooring must have been going on for some time," the city's wire inspector reported. "This amount of gas was only waiting for something to ignite it." The *Daily Advertiser* called the blast "the most terrible explosion in [Boston's] history."

The human toll was devastating, although as the *Standard* noted, "Occurring as it did at a busy time of day, it is surprising that more people were not killed outright." As it was, ten people died, some painfully over a period of days, and more than fifty were badly injured, Paul Hackett among them. "He has suffered terribly but has been taken off the danger list," reported the *Daily Advertiser* the day after the explosion, noting in subsequent stories that Hackett would be hospitalized for a month. Fifty-year-old Mary Stone fractured her left thigh, her right kneecap, and her right ankle, and received scalp contusions. Others fared much worse. William Maybour, twenty-eight, a waiter on his way to work, suffered a fractured skull and fractured jaw, and was asked by doctors in the emergency room if he remembered being injured in the explosion. "What explosion?" he asked in wonder. Maybour died from his injuries two days later. The body of Tufts College professor W. A. Start was found "frightfully mangled; both legs were shattered, the clothing blown off." Matilda Bates was burned to death in her horse-drawn carriage, while her sister, Georgianna, who suffered severe burns, "miraculously escaped death," according to one account.

While the press and public speculated on liability issues (Boston Gas, the West End Street Railway, and the city all paid out some damages, but not for several years), city officials had to deal with another vexing problem: they needed to reassure the future subway-riding public that they would be safe in underground trains. For this, they issued statements and called on friendly reporters to reinforce the message. "While the accident was due indirectly to construction work in connection to the subway, it does not give the slightest cause for any apprehension as to the safety of the subway for use by the public," the *Advertiser* declared the day after the explosion. The subway's chief engineer, Howard Carson, declared that he saw no "danger spots" underground in the subway area. Other officials noted that no damage occurred *inside* the subway, meaning the explosive force did not penetrate the brick ceiling.

These messages were clear: while the gas explosion wreaked death and destruction in the heart of downtown Boston, and would long be associated with the Tremont Street subway, the subway itself did not cause the disaster.

Future underground travelers had nothing to fear.

Thus, as the city cleared the wreckage from what would forever be known as the "subway gas explosion," work continued apace underground. Workers, management, and public officials achieved one milestone date after another through the spring and summer of 1897: on May 13, just two months after the gas explosion, the first construction car entered the subway, transporting supplies from one station to the other; on July 3, state and railway officials traveled on an inspection tour from the Public Garden portal to Park Street and back; on August 13, the Boston Transit Commission instructed West End Street Railway that it wanted the first section of the subway open to the public on September 1.

And on August 15, the *New York Times* proclaimed with a headline story: "Boston's Subway Finished," noting in its lead paragraph: "Boston will be the first city of the country to have in operation through its centre the European transit system." The paper made no attempt to hide its astonishment: "That so conservative an American town should happen to be the pioneer in adopting this is viewed as remarkable." Despite initial protests on the part of "Boston's staid citizens," the "better informed and more progressive" viewpoint prevailed, the *Times* opined. The subway would "aid in solving [Boston's] seemingly insurmountable transit perplexities, and give the Hub a footing among cities that take pride in the present rather than tearfully commemorate the past."

Finally, on August 30 and 31, just two days before the commission's deadline, West End operated several test cars in the subway, primarily to familiarize motormen and conductors with the intricate twists and turns of the underground route, acclimate them to traveling beneath the streets, and instruct them on allaying fears that claustrophobic or timid passengers might express during their first few times in the tunnels.

All went according to plan. The preparation, construction, and

Figure 11. A gleaming Park Street underground station just before the Tremont Street subway's grand opening in September of 1897. (*Photo courtesy of the Boston Public Library, Print Department*)

testing were finished. The steel rails shone and the iron spikes that fastened the wooden ties glinted, the crushed-stone ballast trackbed sparkled beneath the ties, and the underground stations and the subway walls gleamed white; overhead, the jet-black high-voltage cable snaked snugly along a wooden track that guided the conducting rod that would transmit power to the trolley.

Bostonians went to sleep on the night of August 31, 1897, ready, once again, to see their city make history.

The impending subway opening truly captured the imagination of Bostonians during the late summer of 1897, but during the few years prior to the project's completion, the eyes of the nation and the world focused on the city for many other reasons as well.

It wasn't just for the city's intellectual leadership, or, as Oscar Wilde said at the Boston Music Hall in 1892, because Boston is "the

only city to influence thought in Europe…in Boston are the elements
of a great civilized city; a permanent intellectual tradition." Nor was
it merely for Boston's moral virtuousness proclaimed in a May 1894
lecture titled, "Boston—The City of God," by the Reverend Charles
Ames at the Old South Meeting House. Ames urged the congregation to continue the Boston tradition of pressing "steadily in the better
direction, without rest…putting good in the place of ill, right in the
place of wrong, blessing in the place of cursing, beauty in the place of
ugliness."

High-minded pronouncements were one thing (and by the final
decade of the nineteenth century, Boston luminaries often professed
with certainty both the city's superiority and its influence beyond its
borders), but it was practical achievements during these years that
continued to bolster Boston's reputation.

By the end of 1894, the massive Back Bay landfill and neighborhood-development project was complete with the filling of the Fens
area, marking one of nineteenth-century America's engineering, real
estate, city planning, and financial success stories. With the opening
of the new Boston Public Library in Copley Square in 1895, Boston
had created perhaps the country's most prestigious and fashionable
city neighborhood and redefined social and cultural life in an urban
setting.

And in a city that prided itself on both commercial and literary
breakthroughs, Boston Cooking School graduate (and later principal) Fannie Farmer provided both in 1896, when *The Boston Cooking
School Cook Book* was published, providing for the first time recipes
with precise ingredient measurements—including local favorites
such as fish chowder, Indian pudding, and baked beans. Aimed at
ordinary housewives rather than professional cooks, Farmer's book
stressed the science of nutrition and introduced measurements such
as teaspoon, tablespoon, and cup, terms that quickly became staples
of American recipes. "I certainly feel that the time is not distant when
a knowledge of the principles of diet will be an essential part of one's
education," she wrote in the preface. "Then mankind will eat to live,
will be able to do better mental and physical work, and disease will
be less frequent."

Initially skeptical of the sales potential of Farmer's unconventional
book, publisher Little, Brown required the author to pay for publication of the first edition. Its assessment of the market for the text

Figure 12. Workers lay the cornerstone for the new Boston Public Library on Boylston Street in Copley Square (its present location). The magnificent building's opening in 1895 added to the prestige of Boston's newly finished Back Bay neighborhood. *(Photo courtesy of the Boston Public Library, Print Department)*

was perhaps one of the great miscalculations in publishing history: Farmer's book launched a new and successful publishing genre; during the early twentieth century cookbooks found their way into most American homes. "It is my wish that [the cookbook] may not only be looked upon as a compilation of tried and tested recipes, but that it may awaken an interest through its condensed scientific knowledge which will lead to deeper thought and broader study of what to eat," Farmer wrote. In later editions, her book became known as the *Fannie Farmer Cookbook*, which has never been out of print. (The Fanny Farmer Candy Company was established in 1919, author Jim Vrabel noted, but only after agreeing to change the spelling of Farmer's first name.)

Other 1896 events kept Boston in the national and international spotlight.

In April, South Boston's James Brendan Connolly won the first event in the modern Olympics in Athens, Greece—and the first Olympic event in fifteen centuries. A twenty-seven-year-old Harvard freshman forced to drop out of school to compete, he won the hop, step, and jump (later known as the triple jump), and finished second in the high jump and third in the long jump in the Games of the First Olympiad. "The thought came to me that our National Hymn was for my winning my event," he recalled later. "To myself I said, 'You're the first Olympic victor in fifteen hundred years.'" Later, South Boston held an enormous parade for Connolly.

In the fall, the Boston City Council sponsored memorial services for former slave and abolitionist Frederick Douglass, who died in February 1895 from heart failure at his home in Washington, D.C. Dignitaries from around the country attended. Civil rights activist and judge Albion W. Tourgee opened his eulogy with these words: "This life we commemorate tonight was, in some respects, among the most remarkable the world has ever known." Later, in his own personal reminiscence, African American abolitionist and orator Charles Lenox Remond focused on Douglass's Boston connection: "It was upon this free soil of Massachusetts that Frederick Douglass, the panting fugitive, first felt secure from the bay of the bloodhounds of slavery."

Elsewhere, Boston continued its leadership in the medical field, with the dedication of the New England Deaconess Hospital in February 1896, an opening that added to the list of prestigious medical institutions launched in Boston during this period—the Tufts School of Medicine and the New England Baptist Hospital in 1893; and the Boston Floating Hospital in 1894 (the establishment of the Joslin Diabetes Clinic in 1898 would complete this remarkable medical decade).

But of even greater medical significance was the work that occurred between March and October of 1896 at Massachusetts General Hospital. There, a photographer and apothecary named Walter Dodd produced the first X-ray image in the United States.

His achievement would change the way physicians diagnosed patients and prepared for surgery, but would also come at a terrible personal cost.

Walter Dodd's rapid ascendancy in American radiology and X-ray technology use in hospitals was remarkable in its own right, but was even more noteworthy considering his initial connection to science and research.

For five years, he served as a janitor at a Harvard University chemical laboratory.

"He was by far the best janitor we had," noted Professor C. L. Jackson of Dodd's years at Harvard, from 1887 to 1892, "the only disadvantage being that he was much too good for the place that we knew we must lose him soon."

As janitor, Dodd cleaned, swept up, and—as fate would have it, the most important component of his job, for both his career and the benefit of millions of future hospital patients—prepared materials for student experiments. He became fascinated with chemistry, and sought and received permission to conduct the experiments himself; soon faculty members were taking notice of the talented janitor. "While he was in our laboratory, [he] attended regularly the lectures given in general chemistry and performed all the experiments required of our students," Professor W. B. Hill pointed out. "His experimental work was unusually good and he also passed with credit the two written examinations of the course." Hill's conclusion? "I think that he profited more from the instruction...than most of our matriculated students."

Dodd's good friend and biographer, John Macy, sketched Dodd's new career path. In April 1892 he was appointed assistant apothecary at Mass General and continued his studies in chemistry. Two years later he passed the state examination and became a registered pharmacist, and in 1894, was named chief apothecary, whose job description called for dispensing supplies, filling prescriptions, and one unrelated task: official photographer for the hospital.

Striving for excellence as always, Dodd quickly became an expert photographer, and over the next year, continued to learn more about chemistry and medicine within the halls of Mass General.

In late 1895, when word came from Germany that Wilhelm C. Roentgen had discovered X-rays, Walter Dodd was ready in Boston.

The discovery of the X-ray, or the roentgen ray, was one of the four great moments in the history of surgery, Macy asserts. The first was the use of ether as an anesthetic, which occurred at Mass General in 1846. The next was the discovery of bacteria and the science of bacteriology founded by Louis Pasteur; that was followed by the related work of Joseph Lister and others in the area of infection control and prevention.

Roentgen did not know what the invisible rays were when he accidentally discovered that they were produced by a current of electricity passing through a vacuum tube; hence he called them "X" or unknown. What he did know was that the rays penetrated substances opaque to ordinary light, such as fat and muscle, and cast on a photographic plate (or a fluorescent screen) the shadows of substances of greater density than fat and muscle, such as bone and metal.

Dodd received word of Roentgen's discovery with his characteristic enthusiasm. Working late into the nights at Mass General with an assistant, Joseph Godsoe, he began applying his photographic and medical knowledge and experimenting with vacuum tubes to produce and refine X-rays that could be applied to surgical techniques. As John Macy explained, Dodd's "great contribution was made not in the physical laboratory, but...in the diagnostic interpretation of what this wonderful new light revealed in the bodies of the wounded and the sick."

In October of 1896, as workers built the Tremont Street subway about a mile away, Mass General celebrated the fiftieth anniversary of the use of ether. As part of the display, Walter Dodd's first X-ray plates were among the exhibits that generated the most excitement throughout the medical community. The hospital continued to invest in X-ray technology, and Dodd worked even more feverishly, often late at night in a closed, dark room where the temperature sometimes reached 110 degrees Farenheit (Macy noted that this required the men to put ice in the developing fluid to prevent the film from leaving the glass). With Godsoe's help—though Dodd often worked alone—Dodd soon produced a radiograph of the adult thorax, "one of the earliest satisfactory plates of the chest ever taken," noted Dr. G. W. Holmes.

But amid the euphoria about X-rays, an unsuspecting Dodd was silently being poisoned.

His continued exposure to the invisible ultraviolet light rays, something scientists knew nothing about at the time, took a ghastly toll on the Boston scientist. He began suffering almost immediately, and in November of 1896, was treated for severe dermatitis—whose symptoms resembled an acute sunburn. By the following April, he was put on the danger list at the hospital. "It was as though his hands and face had been scalded, and the pain...was beyond description," Macy wrote more than twenty years later. "At that time, it was not known that the familiar sunburn and arctic burn are caused by ultra-violet light rays." Indeed, with each experiment, with each late night, an unsuspecting Dodd did irreparable damage to his tissues and internal organs. "A limited exposure to the X-ray is as harmless as a walk in the sunlight," Macy said. "It is the repeated, continuous bombardment of the ray that is calamitous. Dodd and other pioneers *lived* in the X-ray."

In the ensuing few years, Dodd underwent more than a dozen operations, including extensive skin grafting, amputations of his fingers (operators would test and adjust their tubes by throwing the shadow of their hands on the fluoroscope, exposing them repeatedly to the dangerous rays), and removal of cancerous growths and lesions— some from his face and others from his exposed neck and upper chest. "Sometimes neither surgeon nor patient could judge in advance just how extensive an operation might prove to be necessary," Macy said. "Dodd went to the operating table without knowing how much of his hands would be left when he awoke from ether."

By the autumn of 1915, Dodd had been subjected to more than fifty surgeries, yet through it all he had earned a medical degree and, suffering though he was, continued his grueling work schedule. "To dwell too much on Dodd's suffering would be a violation of his spirit," Macy wrote. "The memory of his reticence and uncomplaining fortitude all but imposes silence." Only for a short period did Dodd contemplate suicide, "during a time of intense suffering," Macy recalled. "He sometimes loitered when he crossed the street, praying that a truck might run him down."

In June of 1915, a weakened Dodd traveled to France as a roentgenologist with the first Harvard Medical Unit, part of the British Expeditionary Force in World War I. He had just undergone a severe operation and used the voyage overseas as convalescence time. When he arrived at the hospital camp in France, he made it clear to his commanding officer, fellow doctors, and troops that "no concession should be made to him on account of his infirmities." He provided X-ray support for wounded soldiers and later received a citation from the British government. Buoyed by his overseas experience, his general condition seemed better than it had been for years when he returned to Boston in October. "He was full of plans, preparing to buy a house on Marlborough Street," Macy recounted.

But in the spring of 1916, Dodd's cancer triggered a series of severe infections; he lost weight and suffered with a continuous fever throughout the summer. By autumn, he had developed a persistent cough and grown weaker as the metastatic cancer reached his lungs. Despite his illness—perhaps in defiance of it—he bought the Back Bay house, and was in the midst of equipping his office when his end came.

Walter Dodd, the "roentgen saint" as he was sometimes called, died on December 18, 1916. In his will, he left one hundred dollars to his beloved Massachusetts General Hospital X-ray department, "with the hope that others who can afford more will give according to their means."

In the centennial history of Mass General, published in 1921, roentgenologist George W. Holmes noted that Dodd's friends "generously subscribed" to his wishes, establishing the Dr. Walter J. Dodd Memorial Fund.

SEPTEMBER 1, 1897. Pink dawn faintly streaked the eastern sky as the first excited Boston commuters arrived at the Allston car sheds at 5:00 a.m. Motorman James Reed, impressive-looking in his new uniform despite an admitted lack of sleep in anticipation of this momentous day, prepared trolley car No. 1752 for its 6:00 a.m. departure. Conductors Gilman T. Trufant and D. R. Murray collected fares, registering 119 riders for a car with seats for only 45 passengers, and were surprised to see that a full one-third of the passengers were women. In Allston, and throughout Boston, residents and merchants bristled with excitement. After five years of planning, including nearly two and a half years of construction, the dream of underground-trolley travel—a subway—was about to become reality.

At about twenty minutes to six, the doors to the car-shed opened and No. 1752 began its historic journey, with loud cheers from passengers and shouts of encouragement from the hundreds who had gathered at the Allston Depot. Newspaper reporters and photographers jammed the front row of the car. Chief Inspector Fred Stearns shouted cautions to passengers seated in the open car and crowded onto the running boards—"each of which was two deep with humanity, while both fenders were loaded down until there was not enough room for a fly to cling," according to one report—to watch out for posts, trees, and branches lining the surface streets, and by all means, not to extend their hands as the trolley entered the subway.

Bostonians turned out by the thousands to witness the event. Boylston Street was "black with humanity," one newspaper reported, with spectators cheering the No. 1752 trolley as it approached the Public Garden entrance to the subway. The incline to the great tunnel was lined with hundreds of people wedged tightly against the walls that flanked the tracks. Passengers aboard the car, "packed in like sardines," began "yelling like a jungle of wild animals … to the verge of apoplexy" as the car dipped down the incline to begin its underground run to Park Street. "First Car Off the Earth!" the *Boston Globe* would proclaim with its extra edition later that day, unfazed by the fact that many cars already had "left the earth" in London, Glasgow, and Budapest. "Out of the sunlight of the morning and into the white light of the subway rolled the first passenger car at 6:01 a.m."

Three minutes after entering the tunnel, the Allston trolley discharged its exuberant passengers at Park Street station, where nearly three hundred people greeted its arrival. The *Boston Globe* recorded the moment: "Hats were whirled, hurrahs ripped out, and a crowd of swarthy Italians yelled: 'Bravo, bravo, bravissimo!'" The inaugural car was followed by a second trolley, and then a third, and then dozens more in rapid succession. "All were loaded to their fullest capacity with a gleeful, jolly, novelty-seeking crowd and everyone got the novelty," the *Boston Traveler* reported. Within minutes, the subway had become part and parcel of Boston's commuting experience. "By 6:30 a.m., the novelty of entering the subway was [already] showing signs of age," the *Globe* sighed.

During the first day, an estimated 150,000 to 200,000 people paid the five-cent fare to ride the subway, from the 6:00 a.m. opening until the midnight close. "Nearly everything went as smoothly as the proverbial clockwork," the *Globe* reported, "and the opinion heard on all sides was that, as far as it goes, the subway is an unqualified success." In fact, ticket agents handled the "great crush of business" without any trouble. One reporter called the Park Street station "pleasant, well-ventilated, well-lighted and good to look at." Another enamored writer focused on "that spacious archway with its solid masonry, its white walls gleaming brightly under its frequent jets of electric lights; its suggestions of largeness, of dignity."

Aesthetics aside, the *Globe* articulated the subway's most practical benefit—the lack of congestion of Tremont Street now that the surface trolleys had disappeared, literally overnight. On this day, the paper informed its readers, riders enjoyed "the ease and speed with which hitherto snaillike electrics [trolleys] now glide through the underground passage."

At the end of the first day, author Brian Cudahy wrote, Bostonians could reflect on yet another landmark achievement: "Boston had done it—had planned, financed, built, and on this day, opened the first subway in the New World."

It is hard to overstate the success of America's first subway. Bostonians simply flocked to it in droves; as many as 50 million passengers the first year, according to the Boston Transit Commission, more than double the number of passengers entering and leaving Boston by steam-railroad trains. And the subway accomplished exactly what it was intended to do. It dramatically reduced the choking street traffic in the downtown area and it allowed trolley cars to reach their destinations more quickly.

The Boston Transit Commission estimated that about 200 trolley cars per hour had traveled not more than two miles per hour each way on the surface of Tremont Street, resulting in "congestion and blockades" whenever this volume occurred. Conversely, the subway handled 282 underground trolleys per hour traveling between seven and eight miles an hour, including station stops. Put another way, it took subway trolleys three to four minutes to travel underground from the Public Garden entrance to Park Street, "instead of an uncertain time on the surface varying from 10 to 20 minutes." *Harper's Weekly* analyzed the new subway's impact this way: "The effect was like when a barrier is removed from the channel of a clogged up river."

The subway progress occurred rapidly after the initial opening, and one year later, in September of 1898, the entire line was finished, enabling riders to travel underground from the Public Garden to Haymarket Station. By the end of November, 1898, the Tremont Street surface-streetcar tracks, once the cause of so much gridlock, were removed. Better still, the Boston Transit Commission reported, the subway construction costs were less than predicted: the initial estimate was $5 million, but total costs came in at less than $4.2 million.

Boston's shift to underground rail travel pleased passengers, merchants, city officials, taxpayers, and even President William McKinley, who toured the tunnels on a visit to Boston in February of 1899 and proclaimed of the subway: "It's a grand thing."

—〰—

Grand, indeed, but Boston was just getting started on its labyrinthian network of municipal rail transportation.

Just a few months before the subway opened, state lawmakers approved a bill that called for construction of a rapid-transit tunnel between East Boston and Boston, a measure considered forward thinking and dangerous at the same time. "[It] has made many of those involved in the project uneasy and not without reason," the *Globe* reported. "The building of underwater tunnels is carried out by men who must excavate thousands of cubic yards of earth by hand in the most dangerous of conditions...Those digging at the face of the tunnel are often victims of flooding or collapse."

Nonetheless, work eventually began at the turn of the century, with laborers digging round the clock from both sides of the harbor, moving slowly toward a central meeting point, "using picks and shovels...chipping their way through earth, seashells, and stone," according to author Joe McKendry. On July 4, 1903, the two sides met below Boston Harbor, completing the underwater route between East Boston and Boston. In the months that followed, crews installed concrete sidewalls, steel supports, tracks, electric wires, and ventilation pipes, and the tunnel opened to trolley traffic on December 30, 1904. The East Boston tunnel reduced the time it took to cross the harbor from more than twenty minutes by ferry to about seven minutes by electric trolley. At the tunnel opening ceremony, John Bates, previously Massachusetts Speaker of the House who had sponsored the construction bill and later governor of Massachusetts, was lauded as "the man who had found East Boston an island and left it a continent."

While crews labored beneath Boston Harbor, others toiled above Boston's streets. On March 30, 1899, the Boston Elevated Railway Company (BERY) began construction of its sprawling elevated-railway system, more than seven miles of track that would carry electrified trolley cars through parts of Charlestown, downtown, and Roxbury (essentially, the precursor of today's Orange Line). It included a new bridge between Charlestown and Boston, a special reserved lane in the Tremont Street tunnel for passing—but not stopping —downtown, and a connecting loop that ran along Atlantic Avenue.

On June 10, 1901, the main line el opened, with more than two hundred thousand paid fares. The first southbound train left Sullivan Square at 5:30 a.m. and arrived at Dudley Station in Roxbury exactly twenty-three minutes later.

The el also connected to the Tremont Street subway, creating an efficient system of public transportation that, as the twentieth century dawned, networked the entire metropolis of Boston, eventually linked the suburbs, and capped fifty years of aggressive expansion in Boston's urban railway system.

From horsecar railroads to the electrified subway, from the steel-girded el to the East Boston tunnel, Boston closed out the second half of the nineteenth century as it had begun it with the Great Railroad Jubilee of 1851: as the standard-bearer for the nation in urban transportation.

Whereas the jubilee portended unbridled hope for Boston's future, the opening of America's first subway was the capstone of her achievements by the late nineteenth century. Necessitated by Boston's meteoric growth in population, commerce, and wealth, the subway was also made possible by all of these—plus her technological advancements and the willingness of men like Henry Whitney to take risks. Industrialization, immigration, and transportation together had fired the economic engine of nineteenth-century Boston. Merchant capital and a new abundance of workers helped the city grow, and grow prosperous, as never before. Expensive homes were built in the South End and Back Bay, and lavish estates graced Roxbury and Jamaica Plain. By the time the subway was built, Boston had undertaken an unprecedented number of municipal projects: streets were widened, marshes filled, hills leveled, parks built, and miles of waterworks constructed.

Yet the subway represented even more than this. The project symbolized, as the Back Bay landfill project had already done, Boston's willingness to tackle any challenge. Her leadership position in so many endeavors had fueled her with the confidence to take on the subway regardless of its difficulty and because it had never before been done in the United States.

Historian Sam Warner explained this municipal confidence: "This whole fifty-year era brought with it a special kind of life," he said of the years 1850 to 1900. "Its dynamism and prosperity...generated a kind of enthusiasm for...productivity which gave contemporary enterprise a romantic quality."

And Boston wasn't quite done yet.

Boston newspapers were full of stories about progress across the city and the state during 1898 and 1899.

They informed readers of the opening of the Joslin Diabetes Clinic and the founding of yet another university: Northeastern. A new literary organization, the Boston Authors' Club, met for the first time and was presided over by Julia Ward Howe, and Thomas Wentworth Higginson sent a "friendly letter" wishing the group well. Boston's manufacturing sector continued to be among the country's most profitable, and Massachusetts maintained its overall preeminence as one of the nation's major industrial states, boasting more than eleven thousand factories. The port of Boston was the second busiest in the country and the leading port in the value of its fish trade. Job opportunities in Boston, the subway's construction among them, continued to fuel immigration and population growth; 560,000 people lived in the city by the end of the nineteenth century, nearly 25 percent more than a decade earlier.

With progress came pitfalls, too. New immigrants, Italians and Jews mostly, still huddled in crowded tenements in the North End. Working-class wages had not kept pace with inflation, and during 1899, manufacturing wages "were not proportionally any greater than the cost of living," the *Daily Advertiser* said. In addition, the paper noted, a new safety hazard had appeared on Boston's streets, which the paper referred to as "the new juggernaut"—most people knew it better as the automobile. "As the number of such vehicles in use on our streets increases, [serious automobile accidents] will inevitably be multiplied unless some means are taken to prevent them."

Still, as the final year of the 1800s opened, with the subway running and the el ready for construction, the vast majority of Boston's attention was focused on yet another symbol of the city's national and worldwide leadership; it did involve transportation, but it had nothing to do with automobiles.

Once again, and to no one's surprise, the symbol related to railroads.

The subway had impressed the world; now, with the end of the century nearing, Boston had one final mark to make.

The construction of Boston's new South Union Terminal—it would soon be known simply as South Station—was initially overshadowed by the excitement surrounding the Tremont Street subway; though as the new structure rose majestically near the Fort Point Channel during mid-1897 and early 1898, it is hard to imagine South Station's imposing classical revival–style architecture being overshadowed by anything.

The total terminal property covered twenty-five acres, with the enormous main structure spanning thirteen acres, and supported by twenty-five thousand piles driven deep through the landfill that was once water. More than fifteen million bricks, fifteen thousand tons of steel, and twenty thousand barrels of cement were used in the terminal's construction. One newspaper said that twenty-four prominent Boston buildings—including the Old South Meeting House, Faneuil Hall, the public library, and City Hall—could fit within the new terminal building. The main station rose more than 135 feet from the street, stretched 850 feet in length, and covered 725 feet at its widest point. By far, the new terminal, intended to serve railroads entering Boston from the south, would be the largest railroad station in the world when it opened for business, in both size and service; indeed, the *Boston Advertiser* emphasized, "larger in service rendered than any other two such structures in existence."

As with so much in the late nineteenth century, South Station's origin had its genesis as a result of Boston's growth and progress.

Already the railroad hub for the Northeast by the mid 1880s, Boston was served by a collection of smaller stations, one on the South Cove property where the new terminal would sit, and four others in the South End. Executives from five major railroads—the Boston & Albany, the New England, the Boston & Providence, the Old Colony, and the New York, New Haven, & Hartford—recognized that some sort of consolidation was needed. They formed the Boston Terminal Company and drew up plans for a new South Station, to be funded primarily with public bonds—about $9 million for the land and $14 million for construction. In addition, the City of Boston contributed about $2 million to relocate roads and utilities. Much of the land came from razing buildings owned by the New York and New England railroads and adding a seawall to the Fort Point Channel and filling in the land behind it, mostly with dirt from the subway's construction.

When South Station was dedicated on December 30, 1898, hundreds of invited guests and public officials swarmed through the cavernous building after the formal ceremonies, thoroughly impressed with what they saw, essentially a small city inside the terminal: the waiting room, the ticket offices, the wooden benches, the open-beam ceiling, the elevated colonnade, the large clock in the façade; and the ancillary conveniences within the terminal such as the barber shop, restaurant, and bootblack station. "The beauty and completeness of every detail appealed alike to the experienced railroad official familiar with other famous stations and to the general public," read one account.

But it was South Station's capacity for rail service that was most impressive. With twenty-eight tracks, the terminal could fit more than 340 sixty-five-foot passenger cars and another 60 forty-foot cars on its main floor—a total seating capacity of more than twenty-eight thousand passengers—all under a single roof. Once it opened on January 1, 1899, the station had the capacity of handling one train per minute, in and out, each day, for a total of more than twenty-eight hundred trains daily.

"This will hereafter rank as one of the great public buildings of this city," Mayor Josiah Quincy said at the dedication, "a source of pride to its citizens, an object of admiration to strangers." The new South Station, Quincy said, "will raise to a distinctly higher level the impression which Boston will hereafter make upon the traveler who visits our city."

And there were millions and millions of travelers.

For the next two decades, South Station would be not just the biggest, but the busiest, railroad station in the world. By 1904, it was actually handling about three thousand trains each day, and by 1920, it serviced more than 30 million passengers each year. It reached its peak travel year in 1945, as returning World War II veterans swelled South Station's passenger load to more than 45 million travelers.

Again, Boston had guessed right—the passenger thirst for rail travel justified a new, consolidated, modern station. And again, she made her mark in a resounding way, closing the second half of the nineteenth century with twin magnificent rail projects, South Station and the Tremont Street subway, one designed to move passengers to and from Boston, and one to move them through the great city.

It was, Mayor Quincy had told the audience at South Station's dedication, the character and will of Boston and her leading citizens that made the ambitious and complex project a reality, "the very finest example of a great passenger terminal found anywhere in the world."

The mayor concluded his remarks with a sentiment that was intended to describe the success of South Station, but could also have referred to the reasons for Boston's growth, advancement, and unparalleled success in so many endeavors over the preceding half century:

> Narrow-minded men would not have been able to comprehend the problem, timid men would not have dared to assume the necessary responsibilities. Weak men would not have been strong enough to carry them, corrupt men would have abused their trust. It is because those connected with this enterprise, in so many different capacities, were types of New England character, of her enterprise and courage, of her solid strength and rugged honesty, that this station stands completed here today.

EPILOGUE

The century ends today, and if any one still thinks it ended
a year ago, he isn't saying much about it now.

— *The* Boston Globe, *December 31, 1900*

DECEMBER 31, 1900. As the hour approached midnight, an awe-struck Reverend Edward Everett Hale stood on the State House balcony, surveying the thousands of Bostonians thronged before him, filling Beacon and Park streets, blanketing the Common and the Public Garden and Tremont and Boylston streets beyond, spilling onto the side streets off Beacon and those that connected Tremont and Washington. People stood "too closely crowded to move" as far as the eye could see, those nearest the State House illuminated by the five hundred electric lights that covered the great dome, the rest of the crowd streaked by the lights of carriages lining both sides of the streets. Hale would one day describe the crowd watching him on this New Year's Eve as "a perfect sea of upturned faces," and the entire event a "magnificent" spectacle.

Boston was ready to usher in the new century.

There were some claims throughout 1899, especially by members of the Twentieth Century Club, that 1900 would actually mark the beginning of a new century, but most of official Boston disagreed. City fathers pointed out that January 1, 1901, would be the first day of the twentieth century in the same way that January 1, 101, began the second century, that without a year "0" the first one hundred years—or first century—of the Christian calendar ended on December 31, 100, not December 31, 99. In addition, the city turned to more recent history to note that Boston welcomed in the eighteenth century with a large celebration on January 1, 1701. In case there was still any dispute about when the nineteenth century ended, the *Boston Globe* reported earlier on this day: "The century ends today, and if any one still thinks it ended a year ago, he isn't saying much about it now."

Thus, tonight, on the balcony with Hale, was the governor of Massachusetts, numerous other dignitaries, musicians, and nearly three hundred chorus members selected from the Handel and Hayden Society and the Cecilia Society. Four trumpets had sounded at exactly fifteen minutes before twelve and played taps, followed by applause, and then thousands of spectators had joined the chorus in singing, "Be Thou, O God, Exalted High."

Now, the crowd was hushed as Hale stepped to the railing, and in a clear, strong voice—without a megaphone—began reading verses from the Nineteenth Psalm. "People were still as death," he wrote later. "The balcony and people made a good sounding-board. My voice was all right and I read very slowly. I have since seen people who were nearly as far as Winter Street who heard me."

When Hale finished at 11:57 p.m., the great crowd remained silent, the entire city seemed stilled "with a hush, absolute and very solemn," until, soon, the King's Chapel bells struck the first note of midnight. In the several seconds between each stroke, the trumpeters on the State House balcony answered the bells. Finally, after the twelfth stroke, Hale recited the Lord's Prayer and was joined by the multitudes below; when he finished, he added, "God bless our city, our State, and our country."

Then, finally, the trumpets blasted, the crowd roared, and, "the shrieks of distant whistles from the harbor" echoed across the cityscape.

With great fanfare, the twentieth century had begun.

As the crowd of nearly forty thousand departed downtown Boston after the "new century" celebration, what thoughts did they harbor? What of their dreams and aspirations, their recollections and reminiscences? Those that involved families, friends, and loved ones were likely top of mind, but did these revelers think about the changes their city had undergone in the last fifty years?

Did elderly crowd members proudly recall Boston's leadership role in the now-distant abolitionist movement after the shameful Thomas Sims episode jolted the city to its core? Did they tell their grandchildren about the Great Railroad Jubilee of 1851, or Boston's audacious vision for the Back Bay that seemed so unattainable even as the first train-carloads of dirt were poured into the muddy bog? Did Irish attendees share their experiences of disembarking from the dreadful famine ships and crowding into the hovels and rickety tenements of the North End, or perhaps relate their war stories about donning Union blue and fighting to save a nation they barely knew?

Those a generation younger had memories to share, too. They remembered when Boston consisted of a peninsula attached to the mainland with a small neck, before the big city annexed the independent towns of Roxbury, West Roxbury, Dorchester, and Charlestown. They remembered the excitement that rippled through Boston when President Ulysses S. Grant opened the 1869 Peace Jubilee, as well as the despair that gripped the city during the Great Fire of 1872 and the buoyancy and sense of accomplishment that accompanied the rebuilding. And, yes, they remembered life *before* telephones, before Alexander Graham Bell had shocked the world in the same year Boston celebrated the centennial.

What about the youngest of those meandering their way home through Boston's bustling streets in the wee hours of January 1, 1901? Fresh in their minds, perhaps, was Henry Whitney's bold decision to abandon horses and electrify Boston's trolley system, which, in turn, led to the drama and engineering marvel known as America's first subway. Fresh, too, perhaps, was the science-fiction-like news that continued to flow from Massachusetts General Hospital about the breakthrough medical promise of Walter Dodd's X-rays.

Whatever their age, whatever their frame of reference, whatever their memories, if the thousands of Bostonians returning home on New Year's morning 1901 pondered their city's current state of affairs, even for a moment, most would have shaken their heads in wonderment. Boston's overall vision and boldness and confidence, coupled with its leadership in technology and transportation, in education and medicine, in engineering and industry, in the arts and the sciences, in political and social influence—all of this had expanded and transformed the Boston Town of fifty years earlier into a powerful metropolis at the dawn of the twentieth century.

In so many ways, in almost *every* way, Boston had surpassed Emerson's lofty vision, which he shared with an audience in 1861: "Boston commands attention as the town which was appointed in the destiny of nations to lead the civilization of North America."

By the end of the nineteenth century, Boston had become much more.

She was now a city that led the world, a city for the ages.

ACKNOWLEDGMENTS

This is my fourth book and, for the fourth time, I have been blessed with the assistance of many people who have helped make my work easier and better.

First, there were the staff members at several libraries. They are too numerous to cite individually, so my collective and sincere thanks go to the librarians, assistants, and other workers at the Boston Public Library, the Massachusetts Historical Society, the Houghton Library at Harvard, the Healey Library at the University of Massachusetts–Boston, the Mugar Memorial Library at Boston University, the State Library of Massachusetts (located in the State House), and the New England Historic Genealogical Society's library. I would like to single out two people: Lynn Matis, chief librarian and archivist at the Massachusetts State Transportation Library, was enormously helpful in assisting with images and with the fragile Boston Transit Commission annual reports that provided so much rich information about the Tremont Street subway; and Aaron Schmidt of the Boston Public Library's Print Department/Photo Division assisted greatly in finding and providing the photos used in this book.

I also want to take this opportunity to convey my profound gratitude to you and the rest of my readers—the people who buy, borrow, and read my books, attend my presentations, and write, call, or e-mail with thoughts and suggestions. I've been extremely fortunate that my books have caught on with book clubs and historical societies, professional groups and schools, history lovers and those who thought they would never again read history after high school. I am grateful to all of you. Keep the letters and e-mails coming, and I will always strive to be worthy of your support.

As always, I'm thankful for the contribution of so many friends and family members whose interest and enthusiasm help keep me going. Their unwavering encouragement is irreplaceable, and has made me a better author. Space makes it impractical to list everyone here, but there are two people I want to single out.

My friend Paula Hoyt once again lent her superb editing instincts and proofreading skills to the manuscript, and once again, hit a home-run. I have found that Paula's gentle suggestions (which usually start with something like, "Do you think you should consider . . . ?") are nearly always right. She also employs her considerable writing and communications strengths on the design and management of my Web site; visitors there have offered dozens of well-deserved compliments on her work. What a bonus for me that someone so talented is also a great friend.

The same is true for my dear and longtime friend Ellen Keefe, who has contributed so much to all of my books—editing, proofreading, research, general advice, and unmatched word-of-mouth marketing! She has done it all this time around, too, and added to her repertoire by providing an even greater level of vital assistance with the research. Ellen spent many hours digging for (and finding) critical primary documents, particularly at the State Transportation and State House libraries. Her immense contributions, important as they are, pale in comparison to the love and support she has given the Puleos over the years, and the wonderful qualities she brings to our enduring friendship.

I owe a debt of gratitude to Amy Caldwell, my editor at Beacon Press, for her skill, enthusiasm, and guidance, but even more so for the faith and confidence she has shown in me from the beginning—something I shall never forget. It's hard to believe that this is our third book together, but working with Amy and the entire professional team at Beacon has made each experience a pleasure.

Speaking of pleasures, I still pinch myself at my great fortune in winding up with a truly marvelous agent, Joy Tutela. With the publication of this book, our fourth, Joy and I have been a team for more than nine years. Wisdom, patience, tenacity, and loyalty are just a few of her endearing qualities. Joy is always up-front with me, and always has my back—attributes of a superb agent, yes, but also, of a steadfast friend. I am grateful beyond words for all Joy is and all she has done on my behalf.

On a sad note, as I entered the homestretch writing this book, I lost my father suddenly to a catastrophic stroke. It was a shock to our family—Anthony Puleo was the healthiest and most vibrant eighty-three-year-old we knew—and we miss him terribly every day. Next to my wife, Kate, dad was my best friend and he got the biggest kick out of talking about "his son, the author." His pride, encouragement, example, and love were great constants in my life, and I carry them in my heart always. My mom, Rose Puleo, has demonstrated remarkable strength and courage since losing her best friend of nearly fifty-six years, and still continues to provide those same constants. For all they've done and continue to do, I will never be able to thank my parents enough.

Finally, my deepest thanks goes to the one person in the world who loves me at my best, at my worst, and at every place in between—my "First Lady," Kate, to whom this book is dedicated. As in everything else, we are partners in book writing. She is a skilled editor and a sage adviser ("Kate, what do you think of this sentence?"). She embraces good ideas when she hears them, and thoughtfully urges me to reconsider the others. On a grander scale, we are celebrating our thirtieth wedding anniversary in the year of this book's publication, and during that time, we have stood side-by-side, sometimes celebrating big events and sometimes simply helping each other through a tough day. Kate is, and always has been, my best friend and my inspiration; she is, and always has been, the person who fills me with joy. Because of her, work is simpler and life is immeasurably sweeter. Her love makes anything—and everything—possible. I am a lucky man.

BIBLIOGRAPHIC ESSAY

I used a vast and rich array of primary and secondary sources to produce the narrative, develop the major real-life characters, and structure the broad sweep of this book, with a goal of conveying, as fully and as accurately as possible, the story of Boston's remarkable emergence between 1850 and 1900.

I was helped by the fact that many key players in this story were also prolific writers—Alexander Graham Bell, Frederick Douglass, William Lloyd Garrison, and Thomas Wentworth Higginson to name a few—and Boston and Massachusetts government bodies produced voluminous reports on some of the major events discussed in this book. Official government documents often laid out the debate and always chronicled the progress of the critical activities in Boston's growth and emergence, including the Sims affair, the Railroad Jubilee, the Back Bay project, the acquisition of Roxbury and Dorchester, and of course, the Tremont Street subway.

In my previous books, I provided a list of primary sources and a brief description of how I used them, and grouped secondary sources according to topical categories. I continue this approach here, based upon many favorable comments readers have shared with me, and, for easier reference, I've also divided the sources according to the three main chronological sections that form this book.

These sources, many of which are listed in the text, provide the foundation and the heart of the book. All the book's quotes are drawn from a document of some kind: a diary entry, a letter, a government report, a newspaper or journal article, a book. I have taken no poetic license. I also formed any conclusions based on the source material. I limited speculation or conjecture to those matters for which no documentation exists, but where my knowledge of the character or the event places me on solid footing (for example, my pondering of Henry Whitney's state of mind as he rode the train to Richmond to meet with Frank Sprague). In any case, I make these few instances clear to readers.

Otherwise, everything you've read is drawn from a deep and revealing collection of primary sources, and a broad cross-section of secondary work.

Finally, I relied on hundreds of articles from several nineteenth-century newspapers as good secondary sources for all sections of the book. Rather than refer to them separately in the topical areas that follow, I list them here since I used them throughout to capture the feel of the time period. They include the *Boston Daily Advertiser*, the *Boston Daily Atlas*, the *Boston Investigator*, the *Emancipator & Republican*, the *Congregationalist*, the *Liberator*, the *Boston Courier*, the *Boston Journal*, the *Boston Weekly Transcript*, the *Boston Post*, the *Boston Sunday Evening Gazette*, the *Lowell Daily Citizen*, the *Baltimore Sun*, the *Pennsylvania Freeman*, the *Trenton Gazette*, the *Brattleboro* (Vermont) *Weekly Eagle*, the *New Hampshire Sentinel*, the *New York Times*, the *Daily National Intelligencer*, and—upon its founding in 1872—the *Boston Globe*. Most of these are available by way of the New England Historic Genealogical Society's (NEHGS) wonderful online collection of nineteenth-century newspapers (www.newenglandancestors .com). Others are available at the Boston Public Library's Microtext Department in Copley Square.

PART ONE: A CITY SO BOLD, 1850–1859

Chapter 1: Abolitionists and the Fugitive Slave Law

Primary Sources

Thomas Wentworth Higginson writes at length about the Thomas Sims affair in his correspondence and journal entries contained in the Higginson Letters and Journals at the Houghton Library at Harvard, and offers a detailed account of the incident (as well as the Anthony Burns affair) in an essay titled "The Fugitive Slave Epoch," printed in his book, *Cheerful Yesterdays* (Boston: Houghton, Mifflin and Company, 1898). Higginson also writes about the Fugitive Slave Law, the Sims case, and the Anthony Burns affair in a collection of his writings, edited by Howard N. Meyer, titled *The Magnificent Activist: The Writings of Thomas Wentworth Higginson, 1823–1911* (New York: Da Capo Press, 2000).

The ship captain Austin Bearse, who tried to procure a vessel as part of the plot to free Sims, wrote of his efforts in *Reminiscences of Fugitive-Slave Law Days in Boston* (Boston: Warren Richardson, 1880).

In addition, see *Massachusetts Senate Document No. 89*, April 9, 1851, for an in-the-moment account of Sims's capture and confinement just days after his arrest.

William Lloyd Garrison's extensive papers and his *Liberator* file are available in the Boston Public Library's main location in Copley Square. The *Liberator* is also available by way of the NEHGS's online collection of nineteenth-century newspapers (www.newenglandancestors.org), which I accessed frequently.

Charles Sumner writes on May 4, 1851, to John Greenleaf Whittier about the "Sims outrage," and to Ralph Waldo Emerson three days later, in *The Selected Letters of Charles Sumner, Volume One; 1830–1859*, edited by Beverly Wilson Palmer (Boston: Northeastern University Press, 1990). Emerson delivered a May 3, 1851, speech titled "Address to the Citizens of Concord—on the Fugitive Slave Law," in which he castigated Boston citizens for permitting the arrest of Sims. The speech is reprinted in *The Complete Works of Ralph Waldo Emerson*, Volume 2, edited by Edward Waldo Emerson (Cambridge, MA: Riverside Press, 1904), as well as in other Emerson collections. Harvard librarian John Langdon Sibley also comments on Sims and Burns in his diary (also known as Sibley's Private Journal) from 1846–1882, available at http://hul.harvard.edu/hvarc/reshelf/sibley.htm (accesssed numerous times).

In addition to several of the above-named sources, for the abolitionist movement in general, I made use of the Frederick Douglass Papers, many of which are online from the Library of Congress at http://lcweb2.loc.gov/ammem/doughtm/doughome.html (accessed numerous times), and the words of Douglass himself in his three autobiographies: *The Narrative of the Life of Frederick Douglass, an American Slave* (1849), *My Bondage and My Freedom* (1855), and *The Life and Times of Frederick Douglass* (1881). Also instructive was Henry David Thoreau's "Slavery in Massachusetts," a piece the writer created from his journal entries, which is available online at http://thoreau.eserver.org/slavery.html (accessed February 22, 2008).

In addition, to get a feel for race issues of the time, see the Massachusetts House of Representatives Report from March of 1851, available at www.primaryresearch.org/bh/show.php?dir=1851house100&file=3 (accessed April 30, 2008).

And, for a source that straddles the line between "primary" and "secondary," see the powerful 1872 work *The Underground Railroad: A Record of Facts, Authentic Narratives, Letters, etc. Narrating the Hardships, Hair-Breadth Escapes and Death Struggles of the Slaves in Their Efforts for Freedom, as Related by Themselves and Others Witnessed by the Author: Together with Sketches of Some of the Largest Stockholders, and Most Liberal Aiders and Advisors of the Road*, by William Still, available through Quinnipiac College at www.quinnipiac.edu/other/abl/etext/ugrr/ugrr.html (accessed numerous times).

In addition, numerous writings, speeches, and illustrations of notable abolitionists and other antislavery champions are available at the Library of Congress's "The African-American Mosaic," at www.loc.gov/exhibits/african/afam

006.html and at the Massachusetts Historical Society's "Images of the Anti-slavery Movement in Massachusetts" at www.masshist.org/database/essay2 .cfm?queryID=70. I accessed both sites frequently during my research and writing.

The Fugitive Slave Law requires a separate section all by itself.

For Daniel Webster's famous March 7, 1850, speech, and several responses, including John C. Calhoun's, see the appendix to the *Congressional Globe* (the precursor to the Congressional Record), beginning on page 269. Also, the powerful and fascinating debate in the Senate over California's admission to the Union and the Compromise of 1850 can be found on the *Congressional Globe* beginning on page 476. The *Congressional Globe* is available at http://lcweb2.loc .gov/ammem/amlaw/lwcg.html (accessed frequently).

I referred to two handbills that helped crystallize the debate. The first, published in May of 1850 by Gideon and Co. in Washington, D.C., was titled *Letter from Citizens of Newburyport, Mass., to Mr. Webster in Relation to his Speech Delivered in the Senate of the United States on the 7th of March, 1850 and Mr. Webster's Reply*. The second, published in August of 1850 also by Gideon and Co., was entitled *Correspondence Between Mr. Webster and His New Hampshire Neighbors*, in which Webster takes the opportunity to further explain his support for the Fugitive Slave Law.

For a comprehensive look at the depth of opposition to the Fugitive Slave Law in Boston, I found helpful the nineteen-page Massachusetts Senate Report No. 51 (March 24, 1851), titled *Joint Special Committee on So Much of the Governor's Address as Relates to Slavery and on Petitions Praying to the Legislators to Instruct Their Senators and to Request Representatives in Congress to Endeavor to Procure a Repeal of the Fugitive Slave Law*.

In addition, I made use of Beverly High School 2004 graduate Alison Woitunski's primary-research digital project, *Boston's Reaction to the Fugitive Slave Law Through Voluntary Associations, Particularly the Boston Vigilance Committee*. This collection contains numerous primary sources including Henry Ingersoll Bowditch's "Instructing on Repelling Slave Hunters," and is available at www .primaryresearch.org/bh/research/woitunski/index.php.

Charles Sumner's caning is recounted in the *Congressional Globe's* account of House hearings (June 2, 1856), which includes extensive Sumner testimony, beginning on page 1348. Extensive primary-source material on the Sumner caning is available as part of Cornell University's Samuel J. May Anti-Slavery Collection, which I accessed often at http://dlxs.library.cornell.edu/m/mayantislavery. In addition, see *The Sumner Outrage: A Full Report of the Speeches at the Meeting of Citizens in Cambridge in Reference to the Assault on Senator Sumner in the Senate Chamber at Washington*, which was prepared by a committee of abolitionists and printed in Cambridge by John Ford in June of 1856.

Secondary Sources

Books

I consulted five excellent biographies recounting the lives of giants in the abolitionist movement: David Herbert Donald's *Charles Sumner and the Coming of the Civil War* (Chicago: University of Chicago Press, 1960); Tilden G. Edelstein's *Strange Enthusiasm: A Life of Thomas Wentworth Higginson* (New York: Atheneum, 1970); Henry Mayer's comprehensive *All on Fire: William Lloyd Garrison and the Abolition of Slavery* (New York: St. Martin's Griffin, 1998); William S. McFeeley's *Frederick Douglass* (New York: W. W. Norton, 1991); and David S. Reynolds's well-researched *John Brown: Abolitionist* (New York: Alfred A. Knopf, 2005). Mary Thacher Higginson, the abolitionist's second wife, recounts her husband's antislavery work in *Thomas Wentworth Higginson: The Story of His Life* (Boston: Houghton Mifflin, 1914).

Other important books related to the Boston movement include Gary Collison's *Shadrach Minkins: From Fugitive Slave to Citizen* (Cambridge, MA: Harvard University Press, 1997); Albert J. Von Frank's *The Trials of Anthony Burns: Freedom and Slavery in Emerson's Boston* (Cambridge, MA: Harvard University Press, 1998); and *Courage and Conscience: Black & White Abolitionists in Boston*, edited by Donald M. Jacobs (Bloomington: Indiana University Press for the Boston Athenaeum, 1993).

For information about the Fugitive Slave Law, slavery tensions in general, and the mid-1850s sectional strife between North and South, I consulted Bruce and William Catton's *Two Roads to Sumter* (New York: McGraw-Hill, 1963); Louis Filler's *The Crusade against Slavery, 1830–1860* (New York: Harper Torchbooks, 1960); William W. Freehling's *The Road to Disunion: Volume II, Secessionists Triumphant, 1854–1861* (New York: Oxford, 2007); Allan Nevins's two-volume classic work on the run-up to the Civil War: *Ordeal of the Union: Fruits of Manifest Destiny, 1847–1852* and *Ordeal of the Union: A House Dividing, 1852–1857* (both New York: Charles Scribner's Sons, 1947); Wendy Hamand Venet's *Neither Ballots Nor Bullets: Women Abolitionists and the Civil War* (Charlottesville: University Press of Virginia, 1991); Eric H. Walther's *The Shattering of the Union: America in the 1850s* (Wilmington, DE: Scholarly Resources, 2004); and the less-than-flattering account of Northern abolitionism and Southern proslavery extremists by Arnold Whitridge, *No Compromise! The Story of the Fanatics Who Paved the Way to the Civil War* (New York: Farrar, Straus and Cudahy, 1960).

The two best books I've found on the Gold Rush that eventually led to statehood for California and the Compromise of 1850 are H. W. Brands's *The Age of Gold: The California Gold Rush and the New American Dream* (New York: Doubleday, 2002) and Paula Mitchell Marks's *Precious Dust: The American Gold Rush Era, 1848–1900* (New York: William Morrow, 1994).

Articles, Essays, and Periodicals

Periodical literature on the Fugitive Slave Law, the abolitionists, and slavery is voluminous. I made use of the following:

"Boston and the Fugitive Slave Law." *Bulletin of the Business Historical Society* (Harvard College) 4. no. 3 (May 1930), 1–7.

Brooks, Elaine. "Massachusetts Anti-Slavery Society." *Journal of Negro History* 30, no. 3 (July 1945), 311–30.

Collison, Gary. "This Flagitious Offense: Daniel Webster and the Shadrach Rescue Cases." *New England Quarterly* 68, no. 4 (December 1995), 609–25.

Fellman, Michael. "Theodore Parker and the Abolitionist Role in the 1850s." *Journal of American History* 61, no. 3 (December 1974), 666–84.

Horton, Lois E., and James Oliver. "Power and Social Responsibility: Entrepreneurs in the Black Community in Antebellum Boston." In *Boston Histories: Essays in Honor of Thomas H. O'Connor,* edited by James M. O'Toole and David Quigley (Boston: Northeastern University Press, 2004), 37–51 .

Hunt, Rockwell D. "How California Came to Be Admitted." *San Francisco Chronicle,* September 9, 1900.

Johnson, Linck C. "Liberty Is Never Cheap: Emerson, the Fugitive Slave Law, and the Antislavery Lecture Series at the Broadway Tabernacle." *New England Quarterly* 76 (December 2003), 550–92.

Kaplan, Sidney. "The *Moby Dick* in the Service of the Underground Railroad." *Phylon* 12, no. 2 (2nd Quarter, 1951), 173–76.

Landon, Fred. "The Negro Migration to Canada After the Passing of the Fugitive Slave Act." *Journal of Negro History* 5, no. 1 (January 1920), 22–36.

Le Beau, Bryan F. "She Told the Story, and the Whole World Wept." Reviews of Thomas F. Gossett's *Uncle Tom's Cabin and American Culture* and Moira Davison Reynolds's *Uncle Tom's Cabin and Mid-Nineteenth Century United States, Pen and Conscience. American Quarterly* 38, no. 4 (Autumn 1966), 66–674.

Lee, Deborah A. "Leonard Andrew Grimes." In *The Essence of A People II: African Americans Who Made Their World Anew in Loudoun County, Virginia, and Beyond,* edited by Kendra Y. Hamilton (Leesburg, VA: Black History Committee of the Friends of the Thomas Balch Library, 2002).

Levy, Leonard W. "Sims' Case: The Fugitive Slave Law in Boston in 1851." *Journal of Negro History* 35, no. 1 (January 1950), 39–74.

Maginnes, David R. "The Case of the Court House Rioters in the Rendition of Slave Anthony Burns, 1854." *Journal of Negro History* 56, no. 1 (January 1971), 31–42.

Pease, Jane H., and William H. Pease. "Confrontation and Abolitionism in the 1850s." *Journal of American History* 58, no. 4 (March 1972), 923–37.

Schwartz, Harold. "Fugitive Slave Days in Boston." *New England Quarterly* 27 (June 1954), 191–212.

Shewmaker, Kenneth E. "Daniel Webster and the Politics of Foreign Policy, 1850–1852." *Journal of American History* 63, no. 2 (September 1976), 303–15.

Sibert, Wilbur H. "The Underground Railroad in Massachusetts." *New England Quarterly* 9, no. 3 (September 1936), 447–67.

"The Trial and Rendition of Anthony Burns." In *Some Events of Boston and Its Neighbors* (Boston: State Street Trust Company, 1917), 50–53.

Wiegand, Steve. "A Zigzag Path Led to Statehood: Congress Had Doubts in 1850, but Compromise was Struck." *Sacramento Bee*, January 18, 1998.

Chapter 2: The Great Railroad Jubilee

Primary Sources

For the authoritative account of this event, see the lengthy (285 pages) official City Council report (written by an editor who remained anonymous) titled *The Railroad Jubilee: An Account of the Celebration Commemorative of the Opening of Railroad Communication Between Boston and Canada, September 17th, 18th, and 19th, 1851*, which was published by official city printer J. H. Eastburn in 1852. In addition, for a good analysis of Boston's railroad and civic might around the time of the jubilee, see the September 17, 1851, report titled *A Tabular Representation of the Present Condition of Boston in Relation to Railroad Facilities, Foreign Commerce, Population, Wealth, Manufactures, etc.; with a Few Statements relative to the Commerce of the Canadas*, prepared under the direction of a Sub-Committee of the Joint Special Committee on the Railroad Celebration. For President Millard Fillmore's description of his role in the Railroad Jubilee, see Frank H. Severance, ed., *Publications of the Buffalo Historical Society, Volume X, Millard Fillmore Papers, Volume One* (Buffalo, NY: Buffalo Historical Society, 1907).

For a comprehensive and illuminating report on Boston's leadership in the railroad industry, and the railroads' success, see *Abstract of the Returns of the Railroad Corporations of the State of Massachusetts for 1856*, prepared, according to law, by the Massachusetts Secretary of State in 1857.

Secondary Sources

Books

Little has been written in book form on the jubilee, save for the occasional sentence or two mentioned in overall histories of Boston (some of those histories are listed throughout this essay). For a comprehensive treatment of Fillmore and the Whigs, see Michael F. Holt's *The Rise and Fall of the American Whig Party: Jacksonian Politics and the Onset of the Civil War* (New York: Oxford, 1999).

Articles, Essays, and Periodicals

Virtually all the Boston newspapers I cited above covered the Great Railroad Jubilee extensively. In addition, for a thoughtful and shrewd analysis of the jubilee as a way to advance the Whig political agenda, see Michael J. Connolly, "The Correction of Our Political Philosophy: New England Whigs and the 1851 Boston Railroad Jubilee," *New England Quarterly* 79, no. 2 (June 2006), 202–26.

For in-depth looks at Boston's commuter rail services (steam and horse-drawn) and the growth of its industry that the jubilee, in part, celebrated, see Charles J. Kennedy, "Commuter Services in the Boston Area, 1835–1860," *Business History Review* 36, no. 2 (Summer 1962), 153–70; and David Ward, "The Industrial Revolution and the Emergence of Boston's Central Business District," *Economic Geography* 42, no. 2 (April 1966), 152–71.

Chapter 3: The Irrepressible Irish

Primary Sources

For a compelling look at the state government's concerns about Irish immigration and the increase in "foreign paupers" in Boston, see the untitled *Massachusetts Senate Report No. 46* (February 1848). See also the related *Concerning Alien Passengers and Paupers* legislation passed in June 1846, which created a "Superintendent of Alien Passengers" with broad powers to board immigrant ships arriving in Boston, prevent ships from docking, and collect a two-dollar fee for each passenger who disembarked.

For insight into Irish living conditions and attitudes of "official Boston" toward the Irish, see the *1850 Report of the Sanitary Commission of Massachusetts*, written by teacher and statistician Lemuel Shattuck and others. The Shattuck report is widely considered well ahead of its time in dealing with health, drainage, paving, and sewage issues, but portions of it serve as an anti-Irish manifesto. For a complete recount of Charles Dickens's 1842 visit to Boston, see the *Report of the Dinner Given to Charles Dickens in Boston on February 1, 1842* by Thomas Gill and William English of the *Morning Post*, and printed into handbill form shortly afterward by William Crosby and Company of Boston.

Three important sources detail the voyage of the USS *Jamestown* from Boston to Ireland to deliver supplies to famine-stricken residents. Those dealing with commissioning the *Jamestown* for merchant use include the *Annual Report of the Secretary of the Navy, Navy Department, December 6, 1847* (Washington, D.C., 1847), 8–9; and George Minot, ed., *The Statutes at Large and Treaties of the United States of America from December 1, 1845 to March 3, 1851, Arranged in Chronological Order; With References to the Matter of Each Act and to the Subsequent Acts on the Same Subject*, Vol. 9 (Boston: Little & Brown, 1851). In addition,

Captain Robert Forbes recaps his mission of mercy in a volume titled *The Voyage of the Jamestown on her Errand of Mercy* (Boston: Eastburn's Press, 1847).

Henry David Thoreau recounts the story of the brig *St. John* in his collection of essays entitled *Cape Cod* (Boston: Ticknor and Fields, 1864). His essay, "The Shipwreck," is must reading to fully appreciate the heartbreak of this disaster. In addition, I have noted the secondary sources below that make wide use of primary sources related to the famine and the coffin ships.

Secondary Sources

Books

The classic academic and statistical study of immigration in Boston is Oscar Handlin's *Boston's Immigrants* (Cambridge, MA: Belknap Press of Harvard University Press, 1959), which deals extensively with the Irish. For a comprehensive look at the Irish's political ascendancy in Boston, see Thomas H. O'Connor's *The Boston Irish: A Political History* (Boston: Northeastern University Press, 1995). For an excellent summary of the Irish struggles and accomplishments in the United States, see Carl Wittke's *The Irish in America* (Baton Rouge: Louisiana State University Press, 1956).

A summary of Barney McGinniskin's appointment to the Boston Police force, the increase in Irish police officers during this period, and Marshall Francis Tukey's leadership can be found in Roger Lane's *Policing the City: Boston, 1822–1885* (New York: Atheneum, 1975).

For details on the famine that drove thousands of Irish from their homeland, as well as the ordeal they suffered during their travels to America, see Edward Laxton's *The Famine Ships: The Irish Exodus to America* (New York: Henry Holt, 1996) and John Percival's *The Great Famine: Ireland's Potato Famine, 1845–51* (New York: Viewer Books, 1995). Cecil Woodham-Smith's classic *The Great Hunger: Ireland 1845–1849* (New York: Old Town Books, 1962) is rich in primary sources, such as British government documents. For a well-drawn contemporaneous account of the Irish experience, see John Francis Maguire's *The Irish in America* (New York: D. J. Sadlier & Co., 1868).

Articles, Essays, and Periodicals

The following aided my understanding of the Irish experience in Boston.

Kennedy, Lawrence W. "The Irish Question and Boston Politics." In *Boston's Histories: Essays in Honor of Thomas H. O'Connor,* edited by James M. O'Toole and David Quigley (Boston: Northeastern University Press, 2004), 124–42.

Lojek, Helen. "Thoreau's Bog People." *New England Quarterly* 67, no. 2 (June 1994), 279–97.

O'Toole, James M. "Portrait of a Parish: Race, Ethnicity, and Class in Boston's Cathedral of the Holy Cross, 1865–1880." In *Boston's Histories: Essays in Honor of Thomas H. O'Connor*, edited by James M. O'Toole and David Quigley (Boston: Northeastern University Press, 2004), 92–111.

Rawson, Michael. "The Nature of Water: Reform and the Antebellum Crusade for Municipal Water in Boston." *Environmental History* 9, no. 3 (July 2004), 411–35.

Streiff, Meg. "Boston's Settlement Housing: Social Reform in an Industrial City." PhD diss., Louisiana State University and Agricultural and Mechanical College, August 2005.

In addition, it is important to note here that the Boston newspapers I citied earlier provided extensive coverage on all aspects of the Irish issue, including the Barney McGinniskin matter, the famine ships, Irish poverty, housing and crime, and Bostonians' attitudes toward the Irish as their numbers continued to increase.

Chapter 4: Filling the Back Bay

Primary Sources

I relied on numerous official reports to narrate the story of the massive and innovative Back Bay landfill and neighborhood-development project. Among the most extensive was the forty-three-page *Massachusetts Senate Document No. 45* (March 1852), which was a report of the commissioners appointed under the 1850 Resolves concerning Boston Harbor and Back Bay, recommending that the Back Bay be filled.

Other key documents that pertained to the Back Bay project included *Massachusetts Senate Document No. 16* (January 1856); *Massachusetts Senate Document No. 55* (February 1856); *Massachusetts Senate Document No. 99* (March 1856); *Massachusetts Senate Document No. 173* (April 1856); the massive *Fifth Annual Report of the Commissioners of the Back Bay combined with a Report of a Senate Committee appointed in relation to Lands in the Back Bay with Accompanying Documents* (Boston: William White, Printer to the State, 1857); the *Seventh Annual Report of the Commissioners of the Back Bay* (January 1859); and the *Eighth Annual Report of the Commissioners of the Back Bay* (January 1860).

See also Dr. Jesse Chickering's "A Comparative View of the Population in Boston in 1850," *Boston City Document No. 60* (1851); and George Adams's "Population of Boston," in *Boston City Document No. 42* (1851).

Secondary Sources

Books

The best single-volume work on the Back Bay landfill project is William A. Newman and Wilfred E. Holton's *Boston's Back Bay: The Story of America's Greatest Nineteenth-Century Landfill Project* (Boston: Northeastern University Press, 2006).

Other books I consulted for this topic included Jane Holtz Kay's *Lost Boston* (Amherst: University of Massachusetts Press, 1980, 1999, 2006); Barbara W. Moore and Gail Weesner's *Back Bay: A Living Portrait* (Boston: Century Hills Press, 1995); Anthony Mitchell Sammarco's *Boston's Back Bay* (Dover, NH: Arcadia Publishing, 1997); Nancy Seasholes's *Gaining Ground: A History of Landmaking in Boston* (Cambridge, MA: MIT Press, 2003); Walter Muir Whitehill's in-depth study, *Boston: A Topographical History* (Cambridge, MA: Belknap Press of Harvard University Press, 1963); and a more contemporaneous treatment, Justin Winsor's *The Memorial History of Boston*, vol. 4 (Boston: Ticknor and Company, 1880).

Articles, Essays, and Periodicals

Hundreds of articles were written in Boston newspapers throughout the life of the Back Bay project. I consulted and drew from many of these, particularly the wide coverage given by the *Boston Daily Advertiser*. The following journal articles were also helpful: Bainbridge Bunting, "The Plan of the Back Bay Area in Boston," *Journal of the Society of Architectural Historians* 13, no. 2 (May 1954), 19–24; and George Wrenn, "A Return to Solid and Classical Principles— Arthur D. Gilman, 1859," *Journal of the Society for Architectural Historians* 20, no. 4 (December 1961), 191–93.

Chapter 5: The Gallows Glorious

Most of the sources for the chapter on John Brown's death have already been cited; for example, Garrison's *Liberator*, Higginson's writings, numerous Boston newspaper accounts, and David Reynolds's biography on John Brown.

For two additional sources, see *The Letters of Henry Wadsworth Longfellow, Volumes 3 and 4, 1844–1865* (Cambridge, MA: Harvard University Press, January 1972) and a revealing biography from Longfellow's younger brother, Samuel Longfellow, entitled *Life of Henry Wadsworth Longfellow, With Extracts from His Journals and Correspondence, Vol. II* (Boston: Ticknor and Company, 1886).

Additional Sources

Francis, William, and Russell Jones. "A Letter from Dr. William Francis Channing to Louis Kossuth," *New England Quarterly* 39, no. 1 (March 1966), 88–93.

Schorow, Stephanie. *Boston on Fire: A History of Fires and Firefighting in Boston* (Beverly, MA: Commonwealth Editions, 2003).

Shaw, David W. *Flying Cloud: The True Story of America's Most Famous Clipper Ship and the Woman Who Guided Her* (New York: Perennial, 2000).

Whitehill, Walter Muir. *Boston Public Library: A Centennial History* (Cambridge, MA: Harvard University Press, 1956).

PART TWO: A CITY TRANSFORMED, 1860–1875

Chapter 6: No Turning Back

Primary Sources

Longfellow recounts his trip to the Old North Church steeple, his inspiration for "Paul Revere's Ride," in his journal and other writings. See both sources listed in their entirety above, *The Letters of Henry Wadsworth Longfellow, Volumes 3 and 4, 1844–1865*, and Samuel Longfellow's *Life of Henry Wadsworth Longfellow, With Extracts from His Journals and Correspondence, Vol. II.*

For a firsthand account of the famous midnight ride, see Paul Revere's 1798 letter to Jeremy Belknap, founder and then corresponding secretary of the Massachusetts Historical Society. The original manuscript and transcription of the letter can be found at www.masshist.org/cabinet/april2002/april2002.htm (accessed May 23, 2008). In addition, the society owns two versions of a deposition describing the ride, which Revere provided late in 1775, when the Massachusetts Provincial Congress required them from eyewitnesses of the battles of Lexington and Concord.

Charles Sumner's fiery June 1860 speech, "The Barbarism of Slavery," is published in many places, but for Sumner's own thoughts about the speech, see *The Barbarism of Slavery: Speech of Hon. Charles Sumner on the Bill for the Admission of Kansas as a Free State in the United States Senate, June 4, 1860* (New York: Young Men's Republican Union, 1863), which contains a dedication from Sumner. Sumner also refers to the speech in a letter to Abraham Lincoln in Beverly Wilson Palmer, ed., *The Selected Letters of Charles Sumner, Volume Two, 1859–1874* (Boston: Northeastern University Press, 1990).

For Lincoln's feelings during this period, see *Abraham Lincoln: Speeches and Writings 1859–1860: Speeches, Letters, and Miscellaneous Writings, Presidential Messages, and Proclamations* (New York: Library of America, 1989).

Secondary Sources

Books

For the best treatment of the widespread impact of Longfellow's "Paul Revere's Ride," and its contribution to the Union cause, see David Hackett Fischer's *Paul*

Revere's Ride (New York: Oxford, 1994). For more on Longfellow, see Charles C. Calhoun's *Longfellow: A Rediscovered Life* (Boston: Beacon Press, 2004). Also, see Bonnie L. Lukes's *Henry Wadsworth Longfellow: America's Beloved Poet* (Greensboro, NC: Morgan Reynolds Publishing, 1998).

In the first section of this essay, I listed numerous books that dealt with the run-up to the Civil War during the 1850s. A few others helped to set the scene in the days immediately prior to the war: Charles B. Dew's *Apostles of Disunion: Southern Secession Commissioners and the Causes of the Civil War* (Charlottesville: University of Virginia Press, 2001); Maury Klein's *Days of Defiance: Sumter, Secession, and the Coming of the Civil War* (New York: Knopf, 1997); and Nelson D. Lankford's *Cry Havoc! The Crooked Road to Civil War, 1861* (New York: Penguin, 2007).

Articles, Essays, and Periodicals

Austin, James C. "J.T. Fields and the Revision of Longfellow's Poems: Unpublished Correspondence." *New England Quarterly* 24, no. 2 (June 1951), 239–50.

Britton, Diane F. "Public History and Public Memory." *Public Historian* 19, no. 3 (Summer 1997), 11–23.

Gioia, Dana. "On 'Paul Revere's Ride' by Henry Wadsworth Longfellow." www.danagioia.net/essays/elongfellow.htm (accessed May 23, 2008).

Chapter 7: War

Primary Sources

Much of the story of the Massachusetts Sixth Regiment's ordeal in Baltimore en route to Washington, D.C., can be found in the 1880 United States War Department's Record and Pension Office's account of the Civil War, entitled *The War of the Rebellion: A Compilation of the Official Records of the Union and Confederate Armies*, Series 1, Volume 2.

Thomas Wentworth Higginson writes extensively about his leadership of the all-black South Carolina regiment in his *Army Life in a Black Regiment and Other Writings*, first published in Boston by Osgood & Co. in 1870; however, I also referred to the 1997 Penguin edition that included an introduction and explanatory notes by R. D. Madison. In addition, an extremely valuable collection for my purposes was Christopher Looby, ed., *The Complete Civil War Journal and Selected Letters of Thomas Wentworth Higginson* (Chicago: University of Chicago Press, 2000). This volume contains several of Higginson's letters to his mother while he was stationed in South Carolina.

For another descriptive war account from a prominent Bostonian, I referred to Mark De Wolfe Howe, ed., *Touched with Fire: Civil War Letters and Diary of Oliver Wendell Holmes, Jr.* (New York: Fordham University Press, 2000).

Secondary Sources

Books

Literally hundreds, perhaps thousands, of books have been written on the Civil War, and I make no claims that the ones I reference here are indispensable to others; they were to me, however, and I believe several of these books are required reading to gain a full understanding of America's deadliest conflict.

For a one-volume account of Thomas Wentworth Higginson's command of the First South Carolina black regiment, see Stephen V. Ash's *Firebrand of Liberty: The Story of Two Black Regiments That Changed the Course of the Civil War* (New York: W. W. Norton, 2008). For a good account of the panic that seized Washington, D.C., after the attack on Fort Sumter, and thus the importance of the Massachusetts Sixth's arrival, see David Detzer's *Dissonance: The Turbulent Days Between Fort Sumter and Bull Run* (New York: Harcourt, 2006). For Charles Sumner's continued influence during the Civil War and Reconstruction, and for an account of his funeral, see the second volume of David Donald's biography, *Charles Sumner and the Rights of Man* (New York: Alfred A. Knopf, 1970). Readers seeking a full understanding of the sixteenth president's role in the Civil War should consult Donald's masterful biography, *Lincoln* (New York: Simon & Schuster, 1995).

For a look at the City of Boston's expenses to quell the 1863 draft riots, see Charles Phillips Huse's *The Financial History of Boston from May 1, 1822 to January 31, 1909* (Cambridge, MA: Harvard University Press, 1916). For insight into Massachusetts governor John Andrew, see Howard Mumford Jones and Bessie Zaban Jones, *The Many Voices of Boston: A Historical Anthology 1630–1975* (Boston: Atlantic Monthly Press, 1975) and examine two essays: James Freeman Clarke's "A Great War Governor," first written in 1878, and Peleg W. Chandler's "Governor Andrews' Religion," first written in 1880. The Fifty-fourth Massachusetts's heroism is detailed in numerous publications and newspapers, but for a particularly dramatic (albeit short) account of the assault on Fort Wagner, see "Colonel Robert G. Shaw Leads His Negro Regiment to the War," in *Some Interesting Boston Events* (Boston: State Street Trust Company, 1916).

It is hard to imagine learning about the Civil War without reading James M. McPherson's one-volume history *Battle Cry of Freedom: The Civil War Era* (New York: Oxford, 1988). Similarly, for Boston's role in the conflict, the standard-bearer is Thomas H. O'Connor's *Civil War Boston: Home Front & Battlefield* (Boston: Northeastern University Press, 1997). And, for a riveting account of one of the war's—and the country's—most important months, see Jay Winik's *April 1865: The Month That Saved America* (New York: Harper Collins, 2001).

The dramatic wait on New Year's Day 1863 for news of the Emancipation Proclamation's signing is recounted in several of the works listed above, and in the previously mentioned Mayer's *All on Fire* and McFeeley's *Frederick Douglass.*

Articles, Essays, and Periodicals

Boston newspapers ran scores of stories on the attack of the Sixth Massachusetts in Baltimore; the Emancipation Proclamation drama on January 1, 1863; Governor Andrew's dispatching of troops; and virtually every other aspect of the war. See also:

Bruce, Susannah Ural. "Remember Your Country and Keep Up Its Credit: Irish Volunteers and the Union Army, 1861–1865." *Journal of Military History* 69, no. 2 (April 2005), 331–59.

Jewett, Philip L. "Clara Barton: Soldier's Friend." *Spirituality Today* 40, no. 3 (Autumn 1988), 237–48.

"Oliver Wendell Holmes, Jr., Captain and Brevet Colonel, U.S. Army; Associate Justice, U.S. Supreme Court." Arlington National Cemetery Web site, www.arlingtoncemetery.net/owholmes.htm (accessed July 18, 2008).

Chapter 8: Peace, Expansion, Perseverance

Primary Sources

Several primary sources on the founding of MIT are available on the MIT Archives Web site at http://libraries.mit.edu/archives (accessed numerous times). See *Objects and Plan of an Institute of Technology Including a Society of Arts, A Museum of Arts, and a School of Industrial Science Proposed to be Established in Boston, Prepared by Direction of the Committee of Associated Institutions of Science and Arts and Addressed to Manufacturers, Merchants, Mechanics, Agriculturists, and Other Friends of Enlightened Industry in the Commonwealth* (Boston: John Wilson and Son, 1861); *An Account on the Proceedings Preliminary to the Organization of the Massachusetts Institute of Technology with a List of the Members Thus Far Associated and An Appendix Containing Petitions and Resolutions in Aid of the Objects of the Committee of Associated Institutions of Science and Art* (Boston: John Wilson and Son, 1861); Dr. M. D. Ross's *Estimate of The Financial Effect of the Proposed Back Bay Lands,* prepared for the Committee of Associated Institutions of Science and Art (Boston: John Wilson, 1861); *Acts and Resolves of the General Court Relating to the Massachusetts Institute of Technology, Acts of 1861, Chapter 183;* and a *Letter from Massachusetts Governor John A. Andrew to William Barton Rogers,* March 9, 1861.

For the formation of Boston University, see *Acts of 1869, Ch. 322,* "An Act to Incorporate the Trustees of Boston University," on the BU Web site at http://web.bu.edu/handbook/goverance/charters/1869.html (accessed March 26, 2008).

Numerous government documents detail the annexations of Roxbury and Dorchester. See *City Document No. 23, Report of the Commissioners on the Annexation of Roxbury*, in Board of Alderman, February 18, 1867; *City Document No. 57, Resolutions Concerning the Annexation of Roxbury*, in Common Council, May 16, 1867; *City Document No. 73, Reports in Relation to the Annexation of Roxbury to Boston and The Act of the Legislature to Unite Said Cities* (Boston: Alfred Mudge & Son, City Printers, 1867); *City Document No. 104, Report on the Division of Wards in Roxbury*, in Board of Aldermen, November 7, 1867; Massachusetts General Laws Chap. 349, *An Act to Unite the City of Boston and the Town of Dorchester*, 646–52; plus see various references in the *Massachusetts Journal of the House 1869*, 279, 285, 345, 359, 363, 364, 366, 367, 370, 392, 394, 395, 400, 410, 422, 430, 447, 480, 487, 492, 500, 504, 513, 515, 518, 521, 529; and the *Massachusetts Journal of the Senate 1869*, 398, 406, 409, 450, 459.

Mark Twain makes reference to the 1869 Boston Peace Jubilee in a July 1869 letter to the San Francisco *Alta California*, published by the Mark Twain project at www.marktwainproject.org (accessed April 3, 2008).

For the authoritative account of the Great Fire of 1872, see the official, meticulous, and lengthy *Report of the Commissioners Appointed to Investigate the Cause and Management of The Great Fire in Boston* (Boston: Rockwell and Churchill, City Printers, 1873). Virtually every secondary account (contemporaneous or modern) of the fire refers to this report.

Secondary Sources

Books

For near-contemporaneous accounts of the annexations, see Edwin M. Bacon, ed., *Boston Illustrated: Containing Full Descriptions of The City and its Immediate Suburbs, its Public Buildings and Institutions, Business Edifices, Parks and Avenues, Statues, Harbor and Islands, etc. With Numerous Historical Allusions* (Boston: Houghton Mifflin and Company, 1891 edition, but previously published in 1872, 1875, 1878, and 1883), and Justin Winsor's previously mentioned *The Memorial History of Boston, Volume 4*. Winsor also writes about Boston's Great Fire of 1872.

The Great Fire is detailed in Arthur Wellington Brayley's *A Complete History of the Boston Fire Department Including the Fire-Alarm Service and the Protective Department From 1630 to 1888, Arranged in Three Parts* (Boston: John P. Dale & Co., 1889). For more on the fire, see also Larry Pletcher's *Massachusetts Disasters: True Stories of Tragedy and Survival* (Guilford, CT: Morris Book Publishing, 2006) and Stephanie Schorow's previously mentioned *Boston on Fire*. Finally, for captivating stories and pictures, see the *Boston Globe*'s one-hundred-year retrospective titled *The Great Boston Fire 1872: A Disaster With a Villain; Old-Style Politics*, edited by John Harris and published as a full-length magazine on November 12, 1972, and since bound in hardcover.

For a general recounting of Boston events during this period, see Thomas O'Connor's *The Hub: Boston Past and Present* (Boston: Northeastern University Press, 2001).

Articles, Essays, and Periodicals

For details of Charles Dickens's reading performances, see "Dickens Onstage: Up Into the Clouds Together" on the New York Public Library Web site at www.nypl.org/research.

For more on the annexation of Dorchester, see Peter F. Stevens, "Dorchester's Ultimate Turf War," December 7, 2000, at the *Dorchester Reporter* Web site at www.dotnews.com/annex (accessed February 14, 2008).

For a fine account of the founding and precedents of Children's Hospital in Boston, see Abelardo A. Retureta et al., "The Children's Hospital, Boston," *International Pediatrics* 13, no. 4 (December 1998), available at www.int-pediatrics.org/Volume%2013/vol_13,2.htm.

For accounts of Boston's Peace Jubilee of 1869, see Rufus Jarman, "A Big Boom in Boston," *American Heritage Magazine* 20, no. 6 (October 1969), available at www.americanheritage.com/articles/magazine/ah/1969. For an account written just a few decades after the big event, see Sarah B. Lawrence, "The Great Peace Jubilee," *New England Magazine* 32 (April 1905), 161–72. In addition, for information on Patrick S. Gilmore, see the Songwriters Hall of Fame Web site at www.songwritershalloffame.org (accessed June 9, 2008).

For more on the Great Fire, I consulted John Ottoson, "The Great Boston Fire, 1872," *Fire Journal* (November 1972), 7–10; and a collection of primary and contemporaneous secondary documents at a Web site called Damrell's Fire, at www.damrellsfire.com (accessed frequently).

For general information about Boston's growth during this period, see Richard A. Meckel, "Immigration, Mortality, and Population Growth in Boston, 1840–1880," *Journal of Interdisciplinary History* 15, no. 3 (Winter 1985), 393–417.

Chapter 9: An End and a Beginning

Primary Sources

Sources on Senator Charles Sumner's funeral included Rev. Samuel Johnson's *A Memorial of Charles Sumner: A Discourse Delivered at the Parker Memorial Meeting House to the Twenty-Eighth Congregational Society of Boston on Sunday March 15, 1874* (Boston: A. Williams & Co., 1874) and a paid-subscription-only account of the senator's life and death by C. Edwards Lester entitled *Life and Public Services of Charles Sumner* (New York: United States Publishing Company, 1874).

For a statistical and demographic report on the Boston Archdiocese around the time the Cathedral of the Holy Cross opened, see Rev. John M'Clintock and James Strong's *Cyclopaedia of Biblical, Theological, and Ecclesiastical Literature* (New York: Harper Brothers, 1889).

Secondary Sources

Books

For details on Charles Sumner's funeral, see David Donald's previously mentioned *Charles Sumner and the Rights of Man*. For a more contemporaneous account, see Edward L. Pierce's *Memoirs and Letters of Charles Sumner, Volume IV, Period 1860 to Death* (London: Sampson, Low, Marston and Company, 1893).

I consulted numerous books on the history of the Boston Archdiocese during this period, including Robert H. Lord and others' *History of the Archdiocese of Boston in the Various Stages of its Development, 1604 to 1943*, vols. 2 and 3 (Boston: Pilot Publishing Company, 1945); John T. McGreevy's *Catholicism and American Freedom* (New York: Norton and Company, 2003); Thomas H. O'Connor's *Boston Catholics: A History of the Church and Its People* (Boston: Northeastern University Press, 1998); and James M. O'Toole's *Militant and Triumphant: William Henry O'Connell and the Catholic Church in Boston, 1859–1944* (Notre Dame, IN: University of Notre Dame Press, 1992).

Articles, Essays, and Periodicals

See the previously cited James M. O'Toole, "Portrait of a Parish: Race, Ethnicity, and Class in Boston's Cathedral of the Holy Cross, 1865–1880," in *Boston's Histories: Essays in Honor of Thomas H. O'Connor.*

In addition, Boston newspapers devoted extensive coverage to Charles Sumner's funeral.

PART THREE: A CITY SO GRAND, 1876–1900

Chapter 10: The Centennial, the Sensational, and Beyond

Primary Sources

The Library of Congress has made a vast number of Alexander Graham Bell's papers available as part of *The Alexander Graham Bell Family Papers at the Library of Congress, 1862–1939*. These include Bell's famous notebook pages, letters to his parents, Mabel, and others, and can be accessed at http://lcweb2.loc

.gov/ammem/bellhtml/bellhome.html (accessed frequently). I made wide use of these in piecing together Bell's work with Thomas Watson. In addition, see *The Proceedings of the American Academy of Arts and Sciences, Vol. XII, Papers Read Before the Academy*, which contains Bell's "Researches in Telephony" that he read on May 10, 1876, at the Boston Athenaeum.

For a detailed account of Boston's 250th anniversary celebration, see the City Council report, *Celebration of the Two-Hundred and Fiftieth Anniversary of the Settlement of Boston, September 17, 1880* (Boston: Printed by Order of the City Council, October 12, 1880).

Similarly, for an in-depth account of Boston's battle to save the Old State House, see the City Council report, *Re-Dedication of the Old State House Boston* (Boston: Printed by Order of the City Council, 1893).

Secondary Sources

Books

For the story of Italian immigration to Boston and the formation of St. Leonard's Church, see my own *The Boston Italians: A Story of Pride, Perseverance, and Paesani, from the Years of the Great Immigration to the Present Day* (Boston: Beacon Press, 2007). See also the previously cited Robert H. Lord et al., *History of the Archdiocese of Boston in the Various Stages of its Development, 1604 to 1943*.

As readers would expect, many authors have tackled one of America's household names, Alexander Graham Bell. I consulted Robert V. Bruce's *Bell: Alexander Bell and the Conquest of Solitude* (Ithaca, NY: Cornell University Press, 1990) and Charlotte Gray's *Reluctant Genius: Alexander Graham Bell and the Passion for Invention* (New York: Arcade Publishing, 2006). For a well-researched biography of Thomas Watson, see Ted Clarke's *Thomas A. Watson: Does That Name Ring a Bell?* (Denver, CO: Outskirts Press, 2008). For a recent book that challenges Bell's reputation, see Seth Shulman's *The Telephone Gambit: Chasing Alexander Graham Bell's Secret* (New York: W. W. Norton, 2008). For a good, short, contemporaneous book on the transcontinental telephone call between Bell and Watson, see *The Story of a Great Achievement: Telephone Communication from Coast to Coast*, published on behalf of the American Telephone & Telegraph Company (New York: Bartlett-Orr Press, 1915).

Solid biographical summaries of Horace Chase and James Solomon Sanborn can be found in the contemporaneous Richard Herndon's *Boston Of Today: A Glance at its History and Characteristics, With Biographical Sketches and Portraits of Many of Its Professional and Business Men* (Boston: Post Publishing Company, 1892); and the near-contemporaneous Richard William Cutter, ed., *Genealogical and Personal Memoirs Relating to the Families of the State of Massachusetts* (New York: Lewis Historical Publishing Company, 1910).

Edward M. Bacon colorfully recounts the efforts to save the Old State House in his *Rambles Around Old Boston* (Boston: Little Brown, and Company, 1914).

Articles, Essays, and Periodicals

Banks, Alan S. "Frederick Law Olmstead's Emerald Necklace: Gardens in the Machine." Available at the National Park Service's Frederick Law Olmstead National Historic Site, 99 Warren St., Brookline, Massachusetts.

Bendroth, Margaret. "Rum, Romanism, and Evangelism: Protestants and Catholics in Late Nineteenth-Century Boston." *Church History* 68, no. 3 (September 1999), 627–47.

Bluestone, Daniel M. "Review: Olmstead's Boston and Other Park Places." *Reviews in American History* 11, no. 4 (December 1983), 531–36.

Bushee, Frederick. "The Growth of the Population of Boston." *Publications of the American Statistical Association* 6, no. 46 (June 1899), 239–74.

Fitzgerald, Brian. "Alexander Graham Bell: The BU Years," in the *BU Bridge* 5, no. 5 (September 14, 2001), available at www.bu.edu/bridge/archive/2001/09–14/bell.html (accessed September 8, 2008).

Galvin, John T. "Patrick J. Maguire: Boston's Last Democratic Boss." *New England Quarterly* 55, no. 3 (September 1982), 392–415.

Marrone, Robin. "The Centennial Exposition of 1876: Perceptions of Progress." Honors thesis, History Department, Temple University, March 15, 2007 (33 pages), available at www.temple.edu/history/honors/archive/documents/MARRONEHONORSTHESIS2007.pdf.

Peterson, Jon A. "The Impact of Sanitary Reform upon American Urban Planning, 1840–1890." *Journal of Social History* 13, no. 1 (Autumn 1979), 83–103.

Schneider, John C. "Homeless Men and Housing Policy in Urban America, 1850–1920." *Urban Studies* 26 (1989), 90–99.

Shulman, Seth. "A Game of Telephone." *MIT's Technology Review* (October/November 2008). Available at www.technologyreview.com/article/21504 (accessed September 8, 2008).

Von Hoffman, Alexander. "Of Greater Lasting Consequence: Frederick Law Olmstead and the Fate of Franklin Park, Boston." *Journal of the Society of Architectural Historians* 4, no. 4 (December 1988), 339–50.

Chapter 11: Breaking New Ground

Primary Sources

Primary sources covering the Tremont Street subway are voluminous. I relied on several early reports to frame the debate about steam-powered elevated railways, including *Elevated Railways Report Submitted to the Senate of Massachusetts by the Honorable Nathan M. Hawkes, Committee on Street Railways* (Boston: Rand, Aberg & Co., Printers to the Commonwealth, 1879); *Elevated Railroads: Closing Argument Before the Legislative Committee on Street Railways by Calvin A. Richards, Esq., President of the Metropolitan Railroad Co., for the Street Railroad Companies, Friday, March 12, 1880* (Boston: Alfred Mudge & Son, Printers, 1880); *Shall the Metropolis of New England Have an Elevated Railroad? Opening Arguments in Favor Before the Legislative Committee on Street Railways by Charles E. Powers, February 10, 1880* (Boston: Alfred Mudge & Son, Printers, 1880); and *Shall the Metropolis of New England Have an Elevated Railroad? Argument in its Favor Before the Legislative Committee on Street Railways by Linus M. Child, March 13, 1880* (Boston: Alfred Mudge & Son, Printers, 1880).

For the subway story itself, I relied on the *First Annual Report of the Boston Transit Commission for the Year Ending August 1895* (with appendix) (Boston: Rockwell and Churchill, City Printers, 1895); and the subsequent *Boston Transit Commission Second Annual Report, August 15, 1896; Boston Transit Commission Fourth Annual Report, August 15, 1898*; and *Boston Transit Commission Fifth Annual Report, August 15, 1899* (all Boston: Rockwell and Churchill, City Printers).

In addition, for a good summary of the Boston el, see *The Washington Street Subway: Comments on the Financial Condition of the Boston Elevated Railway Co., Submitted by Louis D. Brandeis on Behalf of the Boston Associated Board of Trade to the Committee on Metropolitan Affairs of the Massachusetts Legislature, April 26, 1902.*

Frank Sprague's patents for his "Electric-Railway Trolley" (Patent No. 465,806, December 22, 1891) and his "Electric Motor and Regulating Device Therefor" are available on the United States Patent and Trademark Office Web site.

An account of the memorial services for Frederick Douglass was published by the City Council in a document entitled *A Memorial of Frederick Douglass, from the City of Boston* (Boston: Ward and Churchill, 1896).

James B. Connolly, the first Olympic champion of the modern games from South Boston, wrote an autobiography titled *Sea-Borne: Thirty Years Avoyaging* (New York: Doubleday, Doran and Company, 1944), in which he recounts his 1896 achievement.

Secondary Sources

Books

For the Boston subway and related portions of this section, I consulted the following: Charles W. Cheape's *Moving the Masses: Urban Public Transit in New York, Boston, and Philadelphia* (Cambridge, MA: Harvard University Press,

1980); Bradley H. Clarke and O. R. Cummings's *Tremont Street Subway: A Century of Public Service* (Boston: Boston Street Railway Association, Inc., 1997); Brian J. Cudahy's *A Century of Subways: Celebrating 100 Years of New York's Underground Railways* (New York: Fordham University Press, 2003), and Cudahy's *Change at Park Street Under: The Story of Boston's Subways* (Brattleboro, VT: Stephen Greene Press, 1972); and Joe McKendry's *Beneath the Streets of Boston: Building America's First Subway* (Boston: David R. Godine, 2005).

In addition, for background on the street railways and horse railways, I also relied on A. E. Pinanski's *The Street Railway System of Metropolitan Boston* (New York: McGraw Publishing Company, 1908); and Sam Warner's *Streetcar Suburbs: The Process of Growth in Boston, 1870–1900* (Cambridge, MA: Harvard University Press and the MIT Press, 1962).

I gathered much of the information about Walter Dodd's breakthroughs and tragic demise from his friend John Macy's sympathetic—yet relatively objective—biography *Walter James Dodd: A Biographical Sketch* (Boston: Houghton Mifflin Company, 1918).

Articles, Essays, and Periodicals

Albert, Michael R., Kristen G. Ostheimer, and Joel G. Berman. "The Last Smallpox Epidemic in Boston and the Vaccination Controversy, 1901–1903." *New England Journal of Medicine* 344, no. 5 (February 1, 2001), 375–79.

Allen, Walter S. "Street Railway Franchises in Massachusetts." *Annals of the American Academy of Political and Social Science* 27, Municipal Ownership and Municipal Franchises (January 1906), 91–110.

Brown, Percy. "American Martyrs to Radiology." *American Journal of Roentgenology* 165 (July 1995), 181–84.

Cheape, Charles W. "The Evolution of Urban Public Transit, 1880–1912: A Study of Boston, New York, and Philadelphia." *Journal of Economic History* 36, no. 1, The Tasks of Economic History (March 1976), 259–62.

Eisinger, Peter K. "Ethnic Political Transition in Boston, 1884–1933: Some Lessons for Contemporary Cities." *Political Science Quarterly* 93, no. 2 (Summer 1978), 217–39.

French, Alexander, and William Fowler. "The Renovation of Boston's South Station," *Term Project, 1.011—Project Evaluation,* Massachusetts Institute of Technology (May 9, 2003).

Goodman, Philip C. "The X-Ray Enters the Hospital." *American Journal of Roentgenology* 165 (November 1995), 1046–50.

Jutte, Evelyn. "Frank J. Sprague." Available at the Web site of the Museum for the Preservation of Elevating History, www.theelevatormuseum.org/e/e-1.htm (accessed February 27, 2009).

Marchione, William P. "Boston's First Electric Streetcar Line: Allston-Brighton 1888." Boston Allston Historical Society. Available at www.bahistory.org/history/streetcar.html (accessed August 4, 2008).

McShane, Clay, and Joel Tarr. "The Decline of the Urban Horse in American Cities." *Journal of Transport History* 24, no. 2 (September 2003), 177–98.

Robbins, Michael. "The Early Years of Electric Traction." *Journal of Transport History* 21, no. 1 (March 2000), 92–101.

Semsel, Craig R. "More Than an Ocean Apart: The Street Railways of Cleveland and Birmingham [England], 1880–1911." *Journal of Transport History* 22, no. 2 (March 2001), 47–61.

Silverman, Robert A. "Nathan Matthews: Politics of Reform in Boston, 1890–1910." *New England Quarterly* 50, no. 4 (December 1977), 626–43.

Tunis, Allyn. "Father of the Trolley: Frank J. Sprague Made Richmond Cradle of Electric Transportation Just 48 Years Ago Next Month." *Richmond Times-Dispatch*, December 29, 1935. Available at www.richmondthenandnow.com/newspaper-articles/streetcars.html (accessed August 4, 2008).

Weinstein, Asha Elizabeth. "The Congestion Evil: Perceptions of Traffic Congestion in Boston in the 1890s and the 1920s." PhD diss., University of California, Berkeley (Fall 2002).

Wolpert, Samuel W. "Neuroradiology in Boston: Historical Beginnings." *American Journal of Neuroradiology* 16 (May 1995), 1093–98.

Epilogue

Primary Sources

Edward Everett Hale recounts the events of New Year's Eve 1900 in his *Memories of a Hundred Years, Two Volumes in One* (New York: MacMillan Company, 1904).

Secondary Sources

Books

I found helpful Edward E. Hale Jr.'s biography about his father entitled *The Life and Letters of Edward Everett Hale* (Boston: Little Brown and Company, 1917), which describes the New Year's Eve 1900 event.

In addition, numerous Boston newspapers carried stories about Boston's celebration as the city entered the twentieth century.

A Few Final References…

I made use of a number of general books that helped me understand this time period. They include the previously cited *The Hub* by Thomas O'Connor and Justin Winsor's *The Memorial History of Boston*. In addition, I am grateful for the following works: Robert J. Allison's *A Short History of Boston* (Beverly, MA: Commonwealth Editions, 2004); Richard D. Brown and Jack Tager's *Massachusetts: A Concise History* (Amherst: University of Massachusetts Press, 2000); Julia Boulton Clinger's *It Happened in Boston* (Guilford, CT: Twodot Press, 2007); Paul Kendrick and Stephen Kendrick's *Sarah's Long Walk: The Free Blacks of Boston and How Their Struggle for Equality Changed America* (Boston: Beacon Press, 2004); and Timothy Orwig's stunning *Historic Photos of Boston* (Nashville, TN: Turner Publishing Company, 2007).

For a fictional account of the time period, it is worth reading William Dean Howells's classic *The Rise of Silas Lapham*, first serialized in *Century* magazine in 1884 and published in one volume in 1885. I used the Barnes & Noble Books edition published in 2007.

Lastly, I found Jim Vrabel's *When in Boston: A Time Line & Almanac* (Boston: Northeastern University Press, 2004) invaluable in checking—and double-checking—chronological events. Vrabel organizes Boston's nearly four-hundred-year history into a continuous timeline (the only work I'm aware of that does so), and was an irreplaceable companion during the writing of this book.